◆

Peter Parker and the Opening of China

Harvard Studies in American–East Asian Relations   3

The Harvard Studies in American–East Asian Relations are sponsored and edited by the Committee on American–Far Eastern Policy Studies of the Department of History at Harvard University.

Dr. Peter Parker, oil by Lamqua; gift of Dr. Parker to the University about 1840. *Courtesy of Yale University Art Gallery.*

◆

Peter Parker
and the Opening of China

Edward V. Gulick

Harvard University Press
Cambridge, Massachusetts
1973

◆

For Five Great Teachers

Carol Hulbert
Emory Basford
Jimmy Leyburn
Harry Rudin
Phil Greene

◆

Preface

Missionaries are traditionally canonized or insulted. Depending upon the writer, one finds them to be participants in a course which is "the noblest on earth" * or "sacred and silly gentlemen" † full of rasping piety. Given the probability that their impact either as a group or as individuals was often very significant, one finds it startling that little work has been done by professional historians on the many nineteenth-century missionaries from England, Europe, and the United States who had extraordinary careers in Asia, Africa, and the Pacific Islands. Thus a biography which utilizes part of the rich materials now available can make a useful contribution.

This book deals with Dr. Peter Parker, a nineteenth-century pioneer in the contact between West and East, a hard-line religious expansionist, a daring and gifted surgeon of wide clinical experience, and a cosmopolitan mission figure well known to our great-grandfathers but now almost entirely forgotten.

Through the timeliness of Dr. Parker's work and the persuasiveness of his example, more than through the contribution of any other physician anywhere, there evolved approval for and acceptance of the new profession of medical missionary, the creation of

*ABC, *First Ten Annual Reports of the American Board of Commissioners for Foreign Missions*, Report of 1820, p. 318.

†Sydney Smith, *Edinburgh Revue*, 14:40–41 (April 1809).

which was the most significant contribution to foreign missions in the Christian Church's greatest century of expansion. The timeliness rather than the "first-ness" of his career was especially important. As an inventor of the new profession of medical missionary, he had been preceded by Dr. John Scudder in Ceylon and possibly by some Catholic father who yet remains unresearched, but Peter Parker was clearly the first Protestant medical missionary to go to China, and the key figure out of whose sustained work China's mission hospitals, lay clinics, and medical schools chiefly derived. The Manchu government, unlike British India, did not itself develop an elaborate medical system; thus, the mission contribution in China was not only markedly helpful but unusually influential.

The present study, in its earliest incarnation, derived from the general circumstances of family background; from the specific opportunity of investing two years as a young English teacher at the Yali Union Middle School in Central China; and from exposure there to Dr. Phillips Foster Greene, medical missionary at the Hsiang Ya Hospital, Changsha. Years passed before I undertook exploratory work on Dr. Parker during a year at Harvard as a Fellow in East Asian Studies (1959–60), which had been made possible by special leave and financial assistance from Wellesley College. Encouragement from Professors John King Fairbank of Harvard and the late Kenneth Scott Latourette of Yale enabled me to move beyond the tentativeness of exploration to the bondage of the book itself.

The biographer of Peter Parker is faced with the special problem of touching on such diverse nineteenth-century topics as New England, Amherst and Yale Colleges, Macao, Canton, Singapore, Hong Kong, Japan, Washington, D.C., and London; Western medicine, Chinese medicine, evangelism, mission boards, and medical missions; American, British, French and Chinese diplomacy. The jumble of contexts for Parker's career is one of its fascinating aspects, but it creates manifold difficulties. My treatment aims to be adequately self-explanatory so that a reader who may be familiar with American history and unfamiliar with China, or vice versa, will not be driven wild by unrelenting obscurities.

Writing a biography in the field of mission history is, moreover, rather different from putting together a new book on some repetitively studied figure like Lincoln, Gladstone, or Bismarck. On such men the already existing mass of research articles and books means that the writer can devote much of his time to subtleties of interpretation, whereas on the subject of the nineteenth-century missionary, no matter how important he may have been or how interesting his career, there is very little secondary literature of consequence. The biographer, therefore, has to attend to such obvious chores as locating scattered and neglected documents, establishing chronology and narrative, disentangling misdated materials, and deciphering abominable handwriting.

In these diverse duties I have received assistance from a number of very gifted people. I was especially fortunate in my summer research assistants: Vita Bite, Jane Cohen, and Vivien Tsu, each of whom made distinctive and valuable contributions over and above their routine handling of harassing problems of detail. Their presence was made possible by grants from Wellesley College, the American Philosophical Society (Johnson and Penrose Funds), and the Public Health Service, for all of which I am immensely grateful.

Among many who have given knowledgeable help on diverse points of scholarship I wish particularly to thank the following: Robert Irick of Taipei; Marion Brewington of the Kendall Whaling Museum; Francis B. Lothrop of Boston; W. B. McDaniel, 2nd, Curator of the Historical Collection, College of Physicians of Philadelphia; Crosby Forbes, founder-curator of the Museum of the American China Trade, Milton; Walter Liebenthal, German savant; and Joseph Needham of Gonville and Caius College, Cambridge University.

Catherine Cadbury gave me otherwise unprocurable books dealing with Dr. Parker, one of them the private copy of her husband, William W. Cadbury, distinguished mission successor of Dr. Parker. Suzanne W. Barnett clarified for me the Chinese materials relating to the policies and actions of Lin Tse-hsü in

Canton. Former students of mine have generously checked materials in distant collections: Nancy Baker Metcalf (in London), Harriet Bryan (Washington), June Dreyer (Hong Kong), and Dale Hellegers (Japan). Among the archivists whom I have consulted, three were unusually helpful in steering me through complex collections: Mary Walker of the United Church Board; Madeline Stanton, Librarian of Historical Collections of the Yale Medical Library; and Irene Fletcher, who had reorganized the London Missionary Society archives shortly before my work there in the summer of 1964, and who had a remarkable grasp of the materials in that collection.

Among the doctors who have helped me on various points I am especially indebted to the late Professor G. Payling Wright and Dr. G. A. K. Missen of the Department of Pathology, Guy's Hospital Medical School, London; to Richard M. Robb of the Children's Hospital, Boston, for his careful corrections and suggestions regarding a medical chapter; and to Linda Pessar, for her skill in dealing with medical aspects of the Lamqua paintings of Dr. Parker's patients.

Two friendly, flint-hearted critics read and criticized almost all of the emerging account: Paul Cohen of the Wellesley faculty dealt with it in a much longer and cruder version and offered a host of penetrating suggestions for improvement; and John Cooper, of the University of Wisconsin, undertook the same chore for a later and better version. My wife, Betty Gulick, contributed very helpfully in a number of ways, especially with expert suggestions on organization and on how to strengthen the manuscript by cutting it radically.

I wish to thank the following for permission to examine or quote from materials within their purview: Yale University Library (letters of S. Wells Williams to Dr. Peter Parker); United Church Board for World Ministries (the American Board archives at Houghton Library, Harvard University); The Library of Congress, Manuscript Division (Caleb Cushing Collection); Peter Parker III (the Peter Parker Collection of Yale Medical Library); R. Forbes Perkins (Captain R. B. Forbes' 1840 diary to his wife); London Missionary Society (letters of Dr. Benjamin Hobson and others);

Franklin D. Roosevelt Library, Hyde Park (Edward Delano diaries); and Matheson and Co. Limited, Lombard St., London (materials in the Jardine Archive of the University Library, Cambridge); and Commonwealth Relations Office, London (miscellaneous materials in the India Office Records).

Finally, many thanks to my daughter, Susan Gulick, who took tangled and often appalling manuscript pages and somehow converted them to the clarity of typescript.

Edward V. Gulick

Wellesley, Massachusetts
1972

◆

Contents

◆

Peter Parker and the Opening of China

1 ◆ The Rough Road to Commitment

Peter Parker came from a long line of Yankees. The Parkers in the United States generally trace their ancestry to Thomas, who came over from London in 1635.[1] Peter's father, Nathan Parker, born in 1764 on the family farm in Framingham, Massachusetts, grew up there in the years before and during the American Revolution. His marriage in 1791 brought Catherine Murdock of Newton to the farm, where the couple remained. They had six children, of whom Peter — born on June 18, 1804 — was the fifth. Harriett (1793–1861), the eldest, married Josiah Bigelow, a carpenter of Framingham, and lived to witness the fame of her youngest brother, although she does not appear to have been particularly close to him. Two of the boys — the second and fourth children, both named Preston — died in infancy. Of Maria, born 1799, little is known beyond the fact of her marriage to Abijah Fay of Southborough and that she received only an occasional letter from her brother during his years in China.

Catherine, two years younger than Peter, provided the warmest and dearest family tie, as evidenced by his loving solicitude in various scattered references. Troubled with chronic ill-health, she did not live beyond her mid-thirties. Peter, however, was to survive all his siblings by a comfortable margin, his brothers by nearly a century.

Parker's early years appear to have been structured by the triangle of farm, school, and church. Coming from a devout family

solidly grounded in New England Calvinism, he was himself
relatively untouched by family devotionalism until the "goodness
of God" (as he later put it) brought him at age fourteen or fifteen
"*to a solemn pause* and to reflection." This was for him the third,
and most serious, episode of religious concern up to that time. His
account continues: "When, as a man awakening out of sleep in a
strange place, I looked around me & silently exclaimed with
astonishment, where am I! — How came I here! What am I here
for & what have I been doing since I have been in the world!"
Reflection brought him momentarily to a sense of sinfulness, but he
soon relapsed. In the ensuing year, however, a conviction of sin
returned several times, gaining in intensity and frequency, so that
he would sometimes exclaim, "*Oh. that I never* had been *born!*"
Resolving never to sin again, he was at the same time continually
frustrated in his attempts to live without breaking any of God's
laws and began to find his difficult resolutions an insupportable
burden. Working in the field one day with his father, he broke
down "weeping in despair" and exclaimed, "*What shall I do to be
saved?*" [2]

His mother directed him to rely on Christ as his Saviour and sent
him to read Romans 8:1 ("There is therefore now no condemna-
tion for those who are in Christ Jesus"). In this he found great
consolation and passed from despondency to joy and a sense of
forgiveness. Belief in this kind of religious conversion was characteristic of much of rural New England from the time of Jonathan
Edwards well into the nineteenth century and was commonly
considered the "normal entrance into the religious life." [3]

Of formal schooling he was relatively innocent by our standards.
Framingham then offered its children elementary training at
several scattered district schoolhouses with secondary work at the
academy on the green. Having had this exposure and having
completed the course at the academy, he divided his time between
summers of farming and winters of schoolmastering. He started
teaching in a "common school" in nearby Holliston at the age of
fifteen. At sixteen he taught in Westborough and Grafton; then
repeated in Westborough before continuing at a schoolhouse on

Salem End Road near the family farm in 1821 and 1822 and in the eastern part of Framingham several times.[4]

It is likely that these teaching experiences made clear to young Parker his desire for a college education. Not daring to take such thoughts seriously, he muffled them until a chance mention to W. P. Temple, neighbor and friend, set off a chain reaction that was to have consequences seven thousand miles away.[5] When Peter had overcome his father's objections, his pastor, Dr. David Kellogg, encouraged him to go to college and recommended Day's Academy in Wrentham, sixteen miles away, for preparatory work.

Parker entered Day's in March 1826. In August he was summoned home by the illness of his father, who died soon thereafter. The decision to return to Wrentham cannot have been an easy one, but he did go back and complete the term before transferring to Framingham Academy. Enrollment at the latter meant also that he could resume teaching in east Framingham. He received a tuition scholarship and was "gratuitously boarded" by a series of families, among them his own. His preparatory training in Wrentham and Framingham in 1826–27 was sufficient for accept ance at Amherst, that "inexpensive school of the prophets," [6] which he entered in the fall of 1827.

Amherst College in the late 1820's was only a pale tincture of its colorful present self.[7] Its student body of approximately 200 was instructed by a hardworking, unrenowned faculty of less than a dozen, most of them ministers, solidly trinitarian in their theology. The distinctive characteristics of the college at that time derived from its newness, rural isolation, religiosity, and a recent faculty tempest in deciding not to combine with Williams College.

Amherst's grades, based on a scale of twenty, show Parker to have done adequately in Math and Latin, well in Greek, better in Natural History, and best in Rhetoric, where he received an eighteen for the first term of his sophomore year.[8] Toward the end of that year he recorded dissatisfaction with the slender resources of the library and referred without explanation to "very unpleas-ant" circumstances concerning the literary societies.[9]

A revealing, oblique light is cast on Parker in this period by one of his few friends, Thomas M. Howell, Amherst '31, subsequently a New York State lawyer:

Parker made a confident of me. He was much older than myself and was the oldest student in college. We called him "pater omnium." He was short, fat. Those who did not know him intimately regarded him as mentally and bodily sluggish. I found that he was warm hearted, kind, benevolent, and when roused . . . "quick as a toad." . . . One day, after appointments had been made for our Junior Exhibition, I was in his room in Middle College and Parker said, "Howell, I am going to leave. . . . The Faculty do not notice or appreciate me. No one except yourself and my room mate has any regard for me. Now mark my word, you will all hear from me and regret that Peter Parker's name is not among the graduates of Amherst College." [10]

Having had a taste of higher education, Parker now sought it in a yet higher form. Thinking of transferring to Harvard, he attended Commencement in Cambridge in 1830, but he found it an unsuitable place for pious students[11] and decided instead upon Yale, where he would be safely distant from the disquiet of Cambridge Unitarianism.

The city he had chosen, originally a Puritan Bible Common-wealth, had by 1830 become a flourishing town of over ten thousand — largely Anglo-Saxon, Protestant, and transitionally industrial, a town more renowned for its piety and scholarship than for sauciness and bright lights.[12] The Yale College of that time was largely confined to the Old Campus, with its four brick dormitories, chapel, a dingy dining hall, and two steepled classroom buildings. Only one of these structures now remains — Connecticut Hall.

Peter Parker's mid-October arrival in New Haven was exhilarating and nerve-wracking. By luck he found a room at the home of the brother of S. J. Mills, who had participated in the founding of no less than four missionary societies — American Board, American Bible Society, United Foreign Missionary Society, and the American Colonization Society. On his very first Sunday at Yale, at the urgent request of a Sunday School superintendent, Parker addressed that individual's school, but he felt he had spoken stiffly and without adequate confidence.[13] Within two weeks of his arrival he was characteristically attending the annual meeting of the Foreign Missionary Association of one of the local churches.

It was awkward for a reserved, older student to be arriving at Yale as a senior, years after his contemporaries had consolidated their camaraderie; and his diary reveals how grateful he was for small, friendly overtures by faculty and classmates. His waiting on table seemed to isolate him too much, and he apparently abandoned it in favor of boarding at the home of Miss Sarah Hotchkiss, principal of the Female Department of the Lancasterian School. This proved to be a very pleasant arrangement. Peter helped Miss Hotchkiss at the school later on and did some of the gardening for the household. They must have become close friends. In the spring when the Parker exchequer was even more depleted than usual, Miss Hotchkiss reduced her charge from $1.25 per week to $1.00 and told him that "if he had money and could pay one dollar, that was well; if he couldn't, he should nevertheless remain and not feel troubled." [14]

In spite of the availability of several journals which he kept during this period, one gets only the most disjointed glimpses into his academic life. Having received full credit from Yale for his courses at Amherst, he was able to complete during this first year in New Haven the requirements for his B.A., but his records disclose few reactions to the academic experience itself. What really enthralled him about Yale was the galaxy of opportunities for religious development and activity. The personal account of these matters is very full. He conceived his voluminous journals as a religious device, like the diary of a monk. For the first term of the first year at Yale, there is a relatively garrulous entry about arrival in New Haven. Most of the other, nonintrospective entries deal with various meetings, usually religious, the funeral of a pious freshman, a day of fasting set aside by the churches, the formation of a Yale Bible class, the establishing of a committee to call on church members among the student body, mission lectures, and sermons. The method was as un-Pepysian as could be; the deadly serious product becomes interesting only when it is accepted on its own terms, as a record of the spiritual life of a passionate religionist. We find in it much Calvinist self-excoriation, some records of religious ecstasy, and repeated self-exhortations like "I desire to be more *holy,* more like Jesus." [15] Entries of self-examination appeared throughout each year, predictably achieving their fullest dimensions in the major evaluations before New Year's and on June 18, the time for Birthday Reflections.[16] It is clear that one of the central functions of his diary in this period was a recording of the criteria by which he felt he should live, and then a systematic following along with frequent entries so that he had a record of his own performance, construed usually as shortcomings.

Although Amherst had sustained Parker's piety and nourished his general interest in the foreign mission movement, it wasn't until this senior year at Yale that he wrestled with the decision over investing his own career in the demanding and hazardous occupation of foreign missionary. Today, one can easily underestimate the adventurousness of such a choice. Travel to China took four months one way, with accompanying hazards of lightning, scurvy, piracy, and high seas; the isolation from home was extreme and was enhanced by a sense of possible finality since life expectancy was very low on the China coast. Foreign missions were young and mission boards in the United States were fewer, less experienced, less well financed than in later decades, and correspondingly less able to protect their personnel. Although the profession of foreign missionary was as old as Christianity itself, the circumstances of communication in 1830 were still such as to make the decision that of a pioneer.

Parker's teenage call to the ministry in 1820 was accompanied by the thought that, since he expected to have no college education such as would fit him for overseas work, he might possibly be used as an evangelist or teacher to the American Indians. His birthday reflections for 1828, at age 24, referred to foreign missions, as did his journal several weeks later.[17] One can be sure that for a considerable number of years he had felt a deep interest in the cause of foreign missions. Nevertheless there was still an appreciable distance between deep interest and self-commitment, and it was difficult for him to come to a crisp decision. He did take a giant step toward the latter at a moment which eludes precise dating but which probably occurred in 1830. He imagined himself before "the

Tribunal of God" looking back over his own life and asking how it should have been invested. "Reason and . . . the Holy Spirit, suggested to me that it would then afford me the highest possible felicity, to remember that I had spent and been spent, in the service of God. All human pursuits that did not tend directly to promote the divine glory, seemed unworthy my regard." [18] At a mission meeting in December 1830, his resolve momentarily seemed almost definite. Later in the month he reported a sermon by Professor Eleazar T. Fitch in which the speaker was so animated by the subject of missions and the millennium that sweat flowed down his cheeks.[19] Deeply moved, Parker was nevertheless not fully clear as to his own stand during the winter months.

To him the most stirring event of the second term was the religious revival which took hold of Yale in February 1831 and to which his journal refers for a number of weeks. President Jeremiah B. Day and members of the faculty were active participants. The effects of the Yale revival were also felt in the Lancasterian School. At the height of the revival, when Parker had been asked by Miss Hotchkiss to meet with concerned students, he found himself in the midst of a group of thirty girls who sobbed so loudly they nearly drowned out his voice. Such an experience was for him more moving, exciting, and relevant than the classroom. Even after this notable spring revival, he was confiding to his journal that "whilst my duty to preach the Gospel . . . appears plain, I have not a little solicitude whether it shall be as a missionary to foreign lands or as a minister at home." [20] He was conscious of great deficiencies for either.

The April visit of Rufus Anderson to New Haven proved to be important for Parker. Coming from the American Board, Anderson exuded evangelism. Parker heard him preach a "most excellent" evening sermon on "we walk by faith and etc." In the evening Peter talked and prayed regarding missions with a small group which included Anderson, and he wrote of this visit: "It may be the present day is a crisis in my existence — the leadings of Providence have never appeared so plain to me as they have today, as it respects my duty and *privilege* of becoming a foreign missionary. I have felt and felt deeply upon this subject often and for a long time, but seldom with more intensity than today whilst addressed by Rev. Mr. Anderson." [21]

This contact with Anderson began Parker's long connection with one of the most influential Protestant missionary enterprises and thereby launched him on the mainstream of modern mission activity. Until about the time of his birth there had been markedly different missionary emphases by Catholics and Protestants. For Catholics foreign missions were characteristically a bigger and more impressive set of operations, as shown by Jesuit careers in many parts of the world. China serves as an illustration. Francis Xavier had initiated a drive into the Orient but died off the Chinese coast, never having seen the interior. Matteo Ricci penetrated the periphery of China and finally, in 1601, established the Jesuits in Peking. The aim of their successors evolved as an attempt to ingratiate themselves with the court and with prominent literati in Peking in the hope that by those agencies Christian influence would percolate down through Chinese society. This Jesuit effort in China was ultimately destroyed but it shows how overseas Catholic missionaries were carefully chosen, well financed, well trained, and solidly backed for many decades.

Protestant missionary activities in the same period of the seventeenth and eighteenth centuries were more miscellaneous, more scattered, and much less steadily nourished than the Catholic. In North America, the chief scene of their labors, there were some individuals, like John Eliot, Jonathan Edwards, and Eleazar Wheelock, who evangelized among the Indians, and there were a few mission societies which sought converts either among the Indians, the slaves, or — on behalf of the Church of England — among the dissenting sects. In general, the pieties of Old Calvinism did not include missionary zeal, and churches were usually indifferent, if not opposed, to it. Not until the early decades of the new American republic did an upsurge of Protestant missionary fervor in America become widely based and significant, this roughly coinciding with Peter Parker's early years.

At that time several energetic missionary organizations took shape, among them the American Board of Commissioners for Foreign Missions (variously referred to as the ABCFM, ABC, or

American Board). From modest origins in 1810, it flourished and soon possessed quite astonishing dimensions, as indicated by the figures for both money and personnel. Annual receipts for 1811 were $999.52, with expenditures of $555.88.[22] By 1820 revenue was up fortyfold; that figure of $40,000 was doubled in the next decade and nearly doubled again by 1834, the year of Parker's departure from Yale. From 1837 on it levelled off for most of the century at about $250,000. Personnel increased at the same time, as did the scope of operations. During the headlong fiscal advance between 1810 and 1834, the number of American "preaching and doctoring missionaries" rose to nearly 100 in 60 stations. If one adds "teachers, printers, farmers, and females" as well as "native preachers and assistants," the total was 328 for January 1834.[23]

The intent of the American Board was clear enough. In the words of the Act of Incorporation, it was "propagating the gospel in heathen lands, by supporting missionaries and diffusing a knowledge of the holy Scriptures." [24] The ABC regarded itself as an "agency for prosecuting foreign missions," that is, as a mechanism for assisting a number of churches, *not* as an arm of the Congregational Church.[25] In this way it served not only the Congregationalists but, for varying numbers of years, several brands of Presbyterians as well as Dutch Reformed and German Reformed churches. The type of man which the ABC sought was someone of appropriate piety and sound theology, good health, and sense of adventure. It may be significant that there was only one Harvard man on the ABC mission roster down to 1840, whereas the less elegant Yale and Williams colleges of that period had each produced 21 of the 170 college graduates who had become missionaries.[26] The Harvard educational product was too sophisticated, too Unitarian, too skeptical, too cosmopolitan, and therefore above the necessary singlemindedness and fervid certainty of the missionary.

During the spring of 1831, after having established contact with Rufus Anderson and the American Board, Peter Parker found considerable help in religious journals with their captivating excerpts from mission diaries. In his journal he recorded that he felt a fire burning within him when he read or thought on the subject. He sought to stand with other missionaries "at the Judgement-Seat of Christ, surrounded by ransomed heathen who shall bless God forever for having made them, and disposed them to obey the Saviour's dying mandate, 'go — *teach all* nations.' " [27] Part of the confusion of mind and spirit in his critical decision derived from puzzlement over which mission field was most appropriate. During the winter of 1830–31 when he thought about this problem, his mind turned more often to the Mediterranean than to China. Professor Chauncey A. Goodrich, the most interested among the faculty in Parker's destination, favored the Mediterranean region.

Parker's dilemmas persisted, and when, even by late spring, he felt that he had no clear lead from God as to a ministerial or missionary career, he set aside a vocation day, May 24, 1831, to fast and pray and examine into whether it was his "*duty* and *privilege*" to become a foreign missionary.[28] This private retreat proved very useful but it did not settle his mind, and the torment continued. Moreover, the latter was compounded by the results of a trip to New York in mid-May to attend "anniversaries of Benevolent Societies"; he there developed a "very acute" pain in his side.[29] At the end of June he reported he was still unwell with headaches, stomachaches, and general debility, which in July escalated to violent pain lasting several hours each day.[30] One gets the distinct impression that his ailments were more mental than physical and derived from the throbbing anxiety of indecision. Thus the summer term began with ill-health, with gloomy entries in his journal revealing how remote he felt from God, and with worry about which way he should turn after graduation. He was not, to be sure, always despondent and tense in this period. His annual Birthday Reflections were particularly radiant in their references to the fullness and excitement of his religious experience at Yale. "Had some angel been commissioned at the commencement of this year to draw aside the veil of futurity and to disclose all these things at once to my view, it had overcome me. I could not have contained myself." [31]

Although he found occasional diversions, such as a pleasant walk to West Rock with some twenty others, he remained in a state of deep unrest as he continued to wait for some clear indication from God as to where his career properly lay. At the end of August, although still pleading with God for some sign,[32] he was nearer to a resolution than he realized and may indeed have been helped by the excitement of graduation.

The terms of Yale College in that academic year ran from late October into January, from early February through April, and from early June to Commencement on the second Wednesday in September. Under such an arrangement students from farm communities could go home in May to help with the spring planting and possibly the early haying; they would be free most of September and October for the late harvest and for bedding down the farm for the winter.

Parker was home by September 19, 1831. Disclosure to members of the family of his thoughts about a possible mission career evoked tears — and agreement. His sister Catherine observed that "if she were to consult her own feelings she should say to me *stay,* but when she thought of *perishing heathen* she would say *go.* The Lord direct me and bless me." [33]

Family support gave him immense relief. From this point on, one can witness the quick slaying of the dragon of indecision. Within a week after his return he wrote of "great delight in a conscious submission to the will of God." [34] He was prepared to go or stay, but the overriding conviction was that he should become a foreign missionary. There remained only the immediate decision as to where he should study theology. He went to Andover to see Rufus Anderson, who expressed great joy at his decision, said they needed someone like Parker in China, and urged him to stay in New Haven for further training.

The Andover conversations led to the fully crystallized decision by the end of September or very early October. The decision, once made, was consolidated with a long and revealing letter of application to the American Board in which he went over numerous matters relating to his background, health, piety, and attainments.[35] Declaring himself fond of study and blessed with a good memory, he still believed he had but mediocre natural talents. In many ways the most important and interesting parts of this intimate document are those which relate to his motivation. He alluded again to the experience of his imagining himself before the tribunal of God looking back over his life and wishing to spend and be spent in the most effective way in the service of Christ. There was no longer any real question in his mind but that he could be most effective in the sphere of foreign missions. "I have often felt my soul go forth in longing desires for the conversion of the *whole world*. What a *privilege* will it be, if before I leave the world I may but kindle up one Gospel fire on some morally frigid and benighted shore, which shall continue to burn when I am dead, and light up the way to glory to many a heathen who shall survive me." [36]

No great subtlety is evident in Parker's self-analysis, but we do find abundant commitment and dynamism. It becomes very clear that behind his words lay the influence of Samuel Hopkins, as transmitted and interpreted by the modified Yale Calvinism of that period.[37] To Hopkins, a disciple of Jonathan Edwards and minister of the First Congregational Church of Newport, Rhode Island, from 1770 on, it was axiomatic that the heathen were doomed to hell's everlasting torture unless they were reached by Christian missionaries. A stern sense of duty supplied the missionary with the necessary willingness to confront hardships as a soldier of the cross. Thus it was neither romance nor adventure that impelled them to abandon family and friends and go to inhospitable lands, where privation and perhaps martyrdom awaited them. Their conception of duty in the spirit of disinterested benevolence was the real compulsion. Their tasks were undertaken with the joyful abandon of a medieval saint or a Jesuit missionary as they sought to transmit the best in America to the heathen world.

In mid-October, Parker returned to Yale to begin the graduate studies that would prepare him for missionary work. By the twenty-fourth he was established in his room in the seminary and was ready to confront his bifurcated academic duties in the "Theological Department of Yale College" and the "Medical College." For this first graduate year he planned to study Greek Testament and Hebrew at the seminary, attend medical lectures, learn to read and speak French, and teach for Miss Hotchkiss.[38]

His studies were basically in the Theological Department, then located at the site of Battell Chapel. This branch of Yale had been founded nine years before he entered it, in part to sponsor the New Haven theology.[39] The latter retained a stark Hebrew moralism, yet favored a cast of mind which, rejecting both skepticism and mysticism, sought a rigorous testing of traditional dogma through the application of common sense to the Bible. Professors Nathaniel W. Taylor, Fitch, and Goodrich, all ardent apostles of the New Haven theology, had been the chief architects of this divinity school, the seventh in a list beginning with Andover in 1808. The founders were still there in Parker's day. Taylor, a powerful preacher, was the outstanding Yale theologian of the early nineteenth century and the first incumbent of the new chair of theology. Fitch held the chair of homiletics. Goodrich, professor of rhetoric on the Yale College faculty and subsequently professor of practical theology at the Divinity School, was editor of the *Christian Quarterly Spectator*, the organ of the New Haven theology. A strong revivalist and an enthusiastic supporter of missions, he exerted an evident influence on Parker, as did Leonard Bacon, pastor of the Center Church, statesmanlike Congregationalist and eloquent controversialist. Willard Gibbs, who taught Greek and Hebrew, was their top scholar and their most tentative divine. Gibbs helped keep the theologians limber in their testing of traditional creeds, a function in which he was joined by Benjamin Silliman, the College's first professor of chemistry and natural history, who played a major role in the medical program as well. These were the individuals who figured with special prominence in Parker's graduate training in theology. One might add President Day, one of Parker's close ties to Yale.

The theological pattern and emphases which Parker evolved under the training and influence of these men are quite clear. He believed in a Triune God steady in his unfailing promises and an Arch Fiend ever near at hand (but not repetitively emphasized in his journals). An enormous stress was placed on the bleakest aspects of Calvinist devotionalism: "The whole world lieth in wickedness. For all have sinned and come short of the glory of God". Trusting in the atonement of Jesus Christ as his only hope, he believed that a Day of Judgment lay ahead with its consummation of unspeakable felicity for ransomed sinners. His ardor admitted no genuine sense of proportion: "There is not in the Universe of God any such thing as a small sin for every sin is a transgression." Occasionally a more positive motif enters: "I never saw or heard of a fellow creature that I could not love with the love of benevolence." For him, revivals seemed the most exhilarating of human inventions, and he rejoiced in the fact that, as of the summer of 1833, he had shared in eight of them.[40]

Parker's journal reveals a mind which, possessing no theological subtlety, was straightforward in its conventional emphases, among them a powerful, unrelenting sense that he was himself a kind of spiritual weakling, unworthy and wicked. He used the journal partly as a confessional device to knit up the sleeve of his despair when he could hardly live with his own presumed sinfulness. It never reveals him as a "ruthless lover of the five senses," and indeed the latter-day reader creeps through the pages, stifling in the fetid atmosphere of this brand of religiosity, rarely daring to hope for the blessed relief of one tasty act of genuine wickedness. Parker seems doomed throughout to be the captive of his own unavoidable discretions. His method of therapy constitutes a Freudian horror: "When tempted by wicked thoughts or unholy and fleshly desires," he wrote, go at once by prayer to the "pavillion of God, and there remain till the soul becomes absorbed in the contemplation of heavenly things" and temptation subsides.[41]

His extracurricular activity during the years of graduate work fitted his theological concerns very closely and served as a needed supplement to the formal, academic commitments in the Theological Department. He continued to teach Sunday School and did an increasing amount of pastoral visiting, to the jail, the city alms-house, and to troubled families of Irish immigrants. His most interesting and impressive set of visits occurred during the cholera outbreak of 1832 when he called on several families suffering from this terrifying epidemic.[42] He also continued to associate very closely with those who were deeply committed to planning and propagandizing for foreign missions. He was a charter member of the United Band, a student missionary society founded late in 1831[43] that appears not only to have been tolerated on campus but to have enjoyed some measure of heroic stature. The Yale testimonial to the American Board in support of Parker's reactivation of his formal candidacy for an appointment illustrates the value which prominent members of the Yale community placed on such missionary activity. Signed by President Day and Professors Taylor and Fitch, the letter stated that he had "manifested ardent and active piety, united with sound judgment and discretion. His labors to promote the cause of experimental and practical godliness, in the college and in the city, have been almost incessant." [44]

Peter Parker's entry into medical work was influenced especially by the counsel of Professor Goodrich in May 1831, when the latter spoke of the importance of medical and surgical knowledge to the overseas missionary.[45] The advice was reaffirmed early in September before Parker left New Haven for his autumnal weeks of clarification at home and in Andover. Upon returning in October he buckled down to attending medical lectures as a part-time, first-year student. The medical training consisted of attending two years of lectures (three years, if no B.A.); it was academic, nonclinical, nonlaboratory and thus in line with the standard practices of good medical schools of that day. Although in general there is disappointingly little in the Parker journal on his medical studies, one gets some tantalizing glimpses into the classroom, as when Dr. Eli Ives, professor of the theory and practice of medicine, ended the term by holding up the Bible to his students as containing the principles which were sufficient to regulate all their future course.[46]

It was very difficult for Parker to reconcile his chosen professions of medicine and theology; and at times he was nearly overcome by the weight of responsibilities that his contemplated career involved. "How great! How numerous! the qualifications indispensable to a missionary to China. A sound theology, a thorough education, a very practical knowledge of Medicine and Surgery." His priorities ordained that medicine and surgery, much as he liked them, were only auxiliary to a more effective preaching of the Gospel among the heathen.[47]

The busy first year of graduate work, crowded with extracurricular activities, brought ill-health. Although he had spoken of his own physical fitness in a letter to the American Board early in March 1832,[48] he was shortly thereafter recording a major setback: on March 24, 1832, he "was seized with an affection of the lungs accompanied with a slight hemiptysis." When he finally sought medical help from Dr. Ives, he was ordered to keep to his room and avoid all excitement of body and mind. More distressing than his pains was the thought that all his plans might be "forever blasted." [49] He had been caring for others with tuberculosis and had probably picked it up from them. It is likely that some of his subsequent illnesses were really recurrences.[50] Convalescence in West Haven was followed by recuperation in Framingham, where by late May he had largely regained his health,[51] although still experiencing depression.

During the following year, his physical health appears to have been relatively good, but he experienced a different type of difficulty at the end of February and early in March of 1833. He had set aside February 28 for fasting and prayerful self-scrutiny. "Immediately the neglect . . . of my duties came up before me to my utter confusion. During the preceeding week I had felt an exceeding pressure of my studies upon me . . . [and] had taken license to neglect my duty to Christ. . . . As I was upon my knees before God the conviction struck my mind that I had deliberately and knowingly neglected my Savior . . . with a secret presumption that I might do it till I had accomplished a given end (i.e. my Medical Lectures)." [52] Hoping after that to be forgiven for his acknowledged delinquencies, he realized that God "could not be deceived and would not be mocked." For more than a day his pain was constant and his wound seemed incurable. He found no solace in portions of Job or the Psalms to which he turned and felt utterly cut off from God and from Christ. However deep his penitence, he felt it could never be enough.

In this state of despair he attended public exercises led by President Day and Professor Goodrich, where he wept and sobbed during most of the meeting. Afterward, he sought help from Goodrich, who did all he could to guide Parker out of the dismal slough into which he had sunk, but with no success. While with Goodrich, he experienced great distress over the problems of life after death and God's judgment. Goodrich knelt and prayed on his behalf, and they parted.

Beset with unrelieved agony, Parker stayed up all night praying. Friday morning he requested Professor Taylor's help but still found no relief. He tried various hymns and passages in the Bible, to no avail. Evening found him at church again. Later three friends accompanied him to his room and prayed with him. Luckily, one of the friends directed him to part of the First Epistle General of John ("My little children, these things write I unto you, that ye sin not. And if any man sin, we have an advocate with the Father, Jesus Christ the righteous" [2:1]). This reassuring passage occurs in a context which deals at some length with sin and forgiveness, and it spoke quite perfectly to his condition. Suddenly feeling that God had triumphed and at the same time pardoned him, he was once again able to pray.[53]

Whereas Parker often had used his journal as a confessional device to work out problems, on this occasion he did not write during the week of torment. His distress seems to have been too great to allow it. The journal entry thus became a record rather than a therapeutic act. There is even something warmed-over about it, as he savors his pious distress. It has a slight suggestion of God's compromising a bit: in effect, Parker was receiving God's forgiveness for a shift in priorities as medicine was placed above regularity of devotions. Once the crisis had been resolved, he was freer to admit his growing commitment to medicine. The shift represented a step toward a new inner poise.

After this late-winter depression Parker enjoyed the tentative consolidation of a framework within which he could live and act effectively. His willingness to admit a somewhat higher priority for medicine did not diminish his desire to spend and to be spent in the service of God nor weaken his sense of obligation to preach the Gospel. He was genuinely in fear of God's judgment, should he fail to do the latter. More positively, he was set aflame by a great event in August when, after examination, he was licensed to preach the Gospel. Within a short time he was off to Philadelphia for a pleasant week at the annual meeting of the American Board, where it was suggested to him that he attend the medical lectures in

Philadelphia for the coming winter. This plan would also enable him to work at a hospital. The idea was most attractive, especially since he had heard all the medical lectures at Yale. But the Philadelphia plan fell through when Anderson and Benjamin Wisner, the two corresponding secretaries of the American Board, agreed on Parker's superior usefulness in New Haven, since he was an aggressive evangelist with active contacts in undergraduate Yale, the Seminary, and the Medical College.[54] So back he went to New Haven, for a medically repetitive experience and the completion of his degree requirements at both graduate schools.

In October 1833, just two years after submitting his candidacy to the American Board and with the end of his graduate preparation in sight, he reactivated his formal application with the expected iteration of a Hopkinsian sense of the duty and privilege of going on a foreign mission. "I feel the worthlessness of the offering, but . . . had I a thousand lives I would rejoice to give them all to the same object." [55] The American Board acted favorably on Parker's reapplication, appointing him missionary to the general field of China. This decision left scant choice as to the particular mission station to which he should be assigned. To go to China in that period was to go to the Macao-Canton complex. As to the precise location and shape of his work, Parker hoped that the Prudential Committee would "leave it discretionary" with him.

On a trip to New York City in January 1834, he met and spent an evening at the home of D. W. C. Olyphant, one of the most interesting of the contemporary American merchants in the China trade. Olyphant, who had already spent several years in Canton, was planning to sail for China with two members of his family on the *Morrison* in May or June. He electrified Parker with the offer of passage. "The Lord be praised for raising up such friends." [56]

For each graduate degree, a student would normally have spent two years — a total of four in Parker's quick-step situation. Thus, his plans for further work at Yale were suddenly thrown into disarray by this invitation. He pushed his college medical training to completion with an appearance in early March 1834 before the Board of Medical Examiners of the state and the medical school. Duly examined in medicine and surgery, he was shortly writing to the American Board of his success in obtaining the degree of Doctor of Medicine. His teachers urged him to supplement it by spending as much time as he could in New York City attending the eye infirmary and hospital. Although he managed only one week there, it was a very helpful one.[57]

For years Parker's acquisition of the B.D. and M.D. degrees has been spiced by the legend that the faculties of medicine and divinity, although granting his request to telescope his course, recommended that he receive his graduate degrees with the restriction that he neither practice nor preach in this country.[58] Although he never held a pastorate here, he did preach in this country — often, and doubtless at length — beginning very soon after he was licensed in August 1833.[59] However, he never settled into a medical practice in the United States. One is therefore confronted with his puzzling nonpractice of medicine after his ultimate retirement from the mission field as one of the internationally famous doctors of the nineteenth century. So far no one has demonstrated the validity of the restriction theory. There is no reference to a restriction on his medical degree either in his correspondence with the ABC or in his Yale journal. The records of the Medical Institution of Yale College show that at the examining sessions of March 6–8, 1834, eleven medical students, including Parker, "were found duly qualified for the Degree of Doctor of Medicine and were admitted to the same by the President of the College." The record divulges the added information that Parker's dissertation was upon "Purulent Ophthalmia." [60] The rush to leave on the *Morrison* does lend tepid circumstantial support to the restriction tradition, because completion of a four-year program in three years by a sound but not brilliant student suggests the cutting of enough corners to trouble some members of any faculty. Nevertheless the evidence so far available suggests that he was awarded a perfectly normal degree.

Early in the spring of 1834 Parker visited Samuel Russell of Middletown, Connecticut, a veteran trader who had spent thirteen years in the Far East. He arranged for the departing Parker to take along a Chinese youth then living with Russell, one Ah Leang, aged about seventeen, who could start Parker on his Chinese lessons during the voyage out. Briefly in Framingham toward the end of April, Parker found his mother in relatively good health, much improved over the previous January when he had rushed home during one of her serious illnesses.[61]

On May 16, 1834, he was ordained in the First Presbyterian Church at a special meeting of the Second Presbytery of Philadelphia.[62] Parker's choice of conservative Philadelphia was a bit odd for someone who had been trained by leaders of the New Haven theology with its emphasis on revivalist spontaneity, missions, and disinterested benevolence; but it is explained by the sympathetic response to New Haven theology of that particular Philadelphia church and especially of its energetic pastor, Albert Barnes. The sermon in Parker's ordination service was preached by Benjamin Wisner of the American Board, and Barnes delivered the exhortative "charge." The high point of the Presbyterian ordination service is the laying on of hands. After this, the newly ordained minister gives the benediction. These steps were inexpressibly moving for Parker, and his journal entries reflect his ecstatic condition.[63]

A set of experiences in New York City was almost equally exhilarating. Parker remained the central figure in a round of prayer meetings, services, and sermons. On June 1, 1834, at a service in the Bleeker Street Presbyterian Church he received from the Prudential Committee of the American Board an elaborate formulation of Instructions. These informed him he was not to expect or seek the sanction of heathen governments in his efforts to extend the Gospel. He was to go directly to the people, wherever he could find them,[64] persevering though laws and magistrates forbade, even at the expense of life and liberty. But he was not to court persecution; if persecuted in one city, he was allowed to flee to another. He was to concentrate his efforts on *"the circulation of the Scriptures, & other religious books, & tracts, & the direct preaching of the Gospel."* The practice of medicine and surgery and the communication of Western arts and sciences, they stressed, "are to receive your attention, only as they can be made handmaids to the Gospel. The character of a physician, or of a man of science, respectable as they are, & useful as they may be in evangelising

China, — you will never suffer to supercede or interfere with your character of a teacher of religion."

Parker's first concern should be to acquire both written and spoken Chinese, accurately and thoroughly, possibly investing two or three years in the process. At the same time he was to acquaint himself with the people, their manners, and customs. When he had mastered the language, the mission would determine his assignment. That same June evening, Parker's farewell address revealed a serenity of spirit most unusual for him, as he hailed his departure with devout gratitude.[65]

Finally, on the sunny morning of June 4, he attended a farewell prayer meeting at the home of a friend on Bleeker Street, going thence by carriage to the waterfront, where thirty or more friends of missions had assembled to celebrate his departure. Together all proceeded by harbor steamboat to the *Morrison*, an American merchant-vessel flying the house flag of Olyphant and Co. The ship had moved into the bay on the previous day, and was now towed by the steamboat the twenty-six miles south to Sandy Hook. On the deck the well-wishers and crew crowded around Parker, all joining in a service at eleven-thirty as he "ascended an elevation near the cabin door, and made a feeling and beautiful address, and then offered a fervent prayer." [66] He and his fellow passengers were introduced to the officers and ship's company, Parker voicing the hope that they all might "have *Christ* for . . . [their] pilot." [67] After further prayer and some remarks by the Episcopal minister, James C. Richmond, the latter read aloud the words of a hymn newly composed and dedicated to Dr. Parker. Sung to the tune "Heber," the verses asked God's protection until "that which now doth blossom/Shall ripen" and "China shall be free." [68] By one o'clock in the afternoon guests were boarding the harbor boat for the trip back to the city.

No breath of wit had ruffled the mood, such as Sidney Smith's brash and brilliant remark on a similar occasion, when he hoped his departing missionary friend would agree with the man who ate him. Parker's departure was a sterner event, there being a dimension of sorrow for him at leaving very dear friends whom he did not expect to see again.[69] He found it hardest to part from Dr. Wisner, whom he admired and loved. Earlier that morning he had prayed "with great tenderness and affection" for his mother — then sick at home — and his sisters,[70] but the dimension of religious buoyancy was predominant. To one of the visitors, who had met him for the first time on that day, Parker appeared "calm and tranquil, and happy in the great mission he was about to undertake. He was collected in all things." [71] Inwardly, however, he floated on ecstacy, experiencing "emotions that angels might covet," and feeling this to be the happiest day of his life. A week later he wrote "I had the sweet consciousness that I was in the way of my duty, was obeying the *will* of God, and beyond this felt there was no need for solicitude." [72]

The occasion reveals him as unselfconscious in his deeply felt pieties, but wearing his conscience like a crucifix, on guard equally against temptations to sinfulness or laughter. He appears good-humored but outwardly unbent in his fixity of purpose, with something rashly Faustian in his will to transform the earth.

In mid-afternoon the vessel stood out to sea under a press of canvas and was soon beyond the sight of land. "The pleasantness of the morning continued till evening — when a heavy sea from the East set in, attended with thunder and lightning, rain, and much wind." [73] From a pinnacle of ecstasy the only road is down, and to descend to seasickness is to go all the way down. This nearly all the passengers did, not excepting Olyphant and Parker, and departure ended in wretchedness.

Looking back over his Yale years, it is clear that Peter Parker had to grope for an energizing identity among a whole field of vexing perplexities. His decision in the fall of 1831 to become a missionary, although settling some matters, obviously had not completed the search for his new maturity. He had yet lacked a demonstrated prowess and persistence in graduate training and a convincing incorporation of medical work into his daily enthusiasms and routines. By early 1833 it had become clear that he could do well at medical work, but, as has been noted, he still regarded medicine as possessing a somewhat lower priority than his spiritual life. When end-of-term medical pressures required a skimping of private devotions or reduced time for evangelical activities, his journal immediately registered the inner depression. He had not wholly emerged from a phase of his life where medicine seemed an unworthy catering to the body as opposed to the loftier attending to the needs of the spiritual life of his fellowmen. These sensations of inner disarray diminished with the resolution of his religious depression in the spring of 1833 and the up-grading of the importance of his medical training; they finally dissolved and fell away in the spring of 1834 with the approach of an agreed-upon-departure, with the absorbing routines of packing, medical examination, ordination, goodbyes, preparation of a farewell address, and special religious services. In 1834, these multiple activities helped transform him from fluid to solid, leaving him at departure time on June 4 in a remarkable state of newly crystallized wholeness, with the promise of enormous latent energies for the uncharted, beckoning, menacing task that lay ahead.

2 ◆ Arrival in China and the Singapore Internship

The empire of China which Peter Parker and David Olyphant approached was one of the distinguished centers of civilization in 1834. With a population officially set by census that year at 401,000,000; with a tradition of sophistication in the arts; and with a centuries-long record of cultural domination of eastern Asia, the Middle Kingdom stood in remarkable contrast to a United States of 15,000,000 inhabitants, brief history, and scanty artistic achievements.

The Manchu government of China, originally rather tolerant of contact between Chinese and foreigners, had in recent decades generally forbidden intercourse between its subjects and outsiders. It was normally impossible for Chinese to deal with Westerners, to trade with them, teach them, visit them, sleep with them, or worship with them. One of the exceptions to this policy of exclusion was the port of Macao. Long under joint Sino-Portuguese control, this settlement occupied a beautiful, hilly isthmus, projecting southwest from one of the largest islands of the Pearl River delta on the South China coast. Macao in the 1830's had a population of some 35,000, most of which was Chinese.

Foreigners could live there relatively unmolested by the Chinese or Portuguese authorities. Except for the typhoons, a menace from mid-June to September, the climate was soft, fragrant, and captivating, its heat requiring one to accept the siesta as a way of life. People emerged from the shadows of their homes and gardens

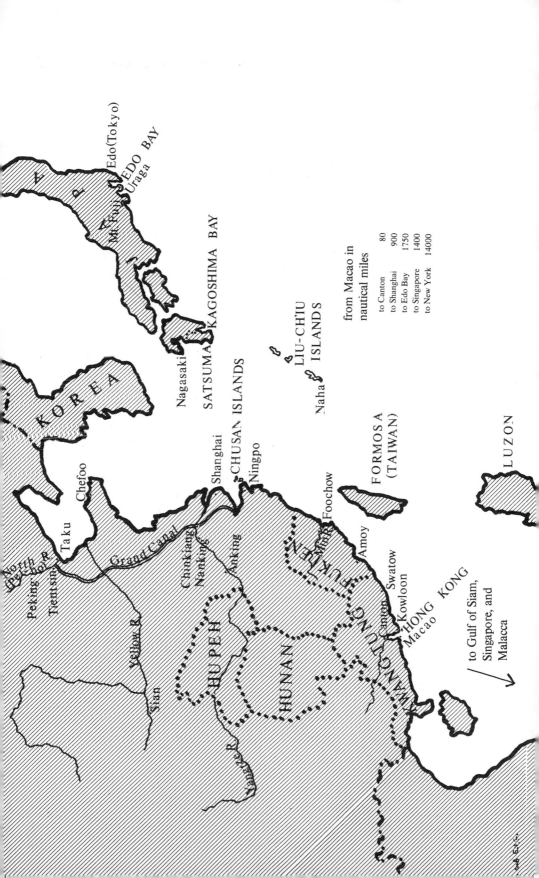

Edo(Tokyo)

EDO BAY

Uraga

Mt Fuji

KAGOSHIMA BAY

SATSUMA

Nagasaki

CHUSAN ISLANDS

LIU-CH'IU ISLANDS

Naha

from Macao in
nautical miles

to Canton 80
to Shanghai 900
to Edo Bay 1750
to Singapore 1400
to New York 14000

KOREA

Chefoo

Shanghai

Ningpo

FORMOSA
(TAIWAN)

LUZON

North (Pei-ho) R.
Peking
Tientsin
Taku

Grand Canal

Yellow R.

Sian

Chinkiang
Nanking

Anking

Yangtze R.

HUPEH

HUNAN

KIANGSI

FUKIEN

Foochow

Amoy

Swatow

Canton
Kowloon

HONG KONG

Macao

KWANGTUNG

to Gulf of Siam,
Singapore, and
Malacca

for the evening stroll, the English and Americans in a favorite area
of their own, the Portuguese along the curving waterfront espla-
nade.

Not only could one study Chinese here but both Catholic and
Protestant evangelists could proselytize discreetly. Since both of
these acts were forbidden to foreigners elsewhere in China, Macao
assumed a role of unusual importance in China's mission history.
Catholic mission headquarters for the Far East were permitted to
remain there for many years. Elijah Coleman Bridgman, the
founder of the American Board mission station in Canton, reported
in 1830 that there were in Macao twelve to fifteen chapels, not well
attended, and forty to fifty clergy for the Catholic community.[1]
Macao was similarly a haven to Protestants. Dr. Robert Morrison
lived here for over twenty-five years while compiling the first
Chinese-English dictionary and translating the Bible into Chinese.
Other Protestants soon came, unwelcomed by the suspicious
Catholic fathers, suspicious of them in return, the two groups
thoroughly alienated from each other by cultural and language
barriers.

A necessary port of call for vessels en route to Canton because
clearance papers had to be secured from the Chinese authorities,
Macao was the long-sought destination toward which the *Morrison*
labored,[2] although on this occasion Peter Parker would merely see
the town from the water. Olyphant and Parker had determined to
press on to Canton, seventy miles to the north, the only other spot
in China which could legitimately be visited by an American in the
1830's. Toward it the two travellers, having transferred to the
schooner *Union*, now proceeded, across Canton Bay, past moun-
tainous Lintin Island, center of the opium trade, and up toward the
Ch'uen-pi fort at the Boca Tigris (the Bogue) — the narrow mouth
of the Pearl River. This first half of the journey from Macao to
Canton gave them no difficulty, although this stretch was often
rendered precarious by the prevalence of pirates, who traditionally
have flourished off the South China coast, tempted and protected
by its jagged indentations.

Safely past the Boca Tigris, the trip, a leisurely one of several
days, took them up a famous, inland artery. The delightful,
humped hills of the bay islands had given way to blander river

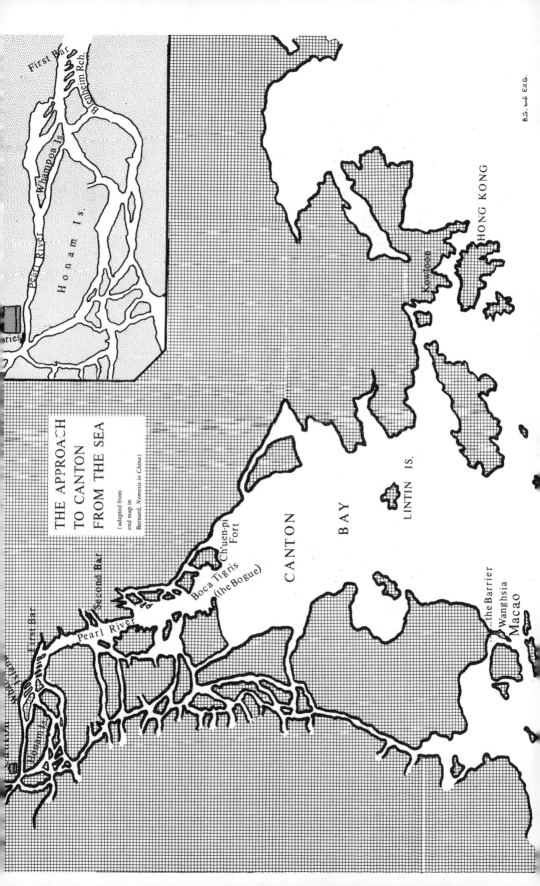

THE APPROACH
TO CANTON
FROM THE SEA

(adapted from
end map in
Bernard, *Nemesis in China*)

First Bar

Benheim Rch.

Whampoa Is.

Pearl River

Honam Is.

ries

Second Bar

First Bar

Pearl River

Ch'uen-pi
Fort

Boca Tigris
(the Bogue)

CANTON

BAY

LINTIN IS.

HONG KONG

Kowloon

the Barrier

Wanghsia

Macao

B.S. から E.K.G.

vistas as they sailed north up the Pearl. At the First Bar the course shifted almost due west for the run to the anchorage at Whampoa. Foreign ships were forbidden to approach closer to Canton. In due time the thirteen miles to Canton were covered in one of the small Chinese craft which swarmed in that region.

After a trip of 144 days from New York, two or three weeks longer than the average, Parker was finally put down at Jackass Point, the boat landing on the southern side of the zone for foreign personnel. His journal was effervescent as he recorded: "At half past 11 o'clock at night *Oct. 26th.* I arrived to my very great joy at *Canton.* As I stepped ashore, the ejaculation *instinctively* and fervently arose *God be* merciful to this Empire." [3] In a few minutes he was pleasantly accommodated in Olyphant's living quarters where among other Americans he was introduced to E. C. Bridgman, by whom he was received as a brother and with whom he offered up his first prayer in China.

Foreigners in Canton were confined to one of the best-known waterfront areas in the entire world,[4] stretching about 1000 feet east to west along the river and inland about the same distance. The section next to the river — nearly half of the fifteen or more acres — was somewhat open and contained both an attractive English garden and walks crowded with peddlers and city folk. Foreigners could not normally leave this restricted area, but Chinese could freely enter it. The inland half of the property was for the most part covered with the so-called factories or hongs, thirteen long structures of granite and stuccoed brick lying at right angles to the river.[5] From Thirteen Factory Street at their rear, three lanes — New China Street, Old China Street, and Hog Lane (just north of Jackass Point) — passed through the factory area toward the water, dividing the hongs into four blocks. These short streets were lined with shops and drinking establishments which were accessible to, but neither run nor controlled by, the foreigners who lived in the thirteen factories.

The American Hong at which Peter Parker took up his residence was quite typical of these structures. Three hundred to 400 feet long, it possessed an open passageway running through its center

from number 1 in front, on the riverside, back through number 3.
From the ground floor of storerooms and servants' quarters, one
ascended to an upper floor with drawing rooms and spacious
chambers. The top of the building afforded space for a promenade
at the edge of evening when a good breeze enhanced the view of
river and city.[6]

Immediately to the east of the factory area and across a creek,
were further hong establishments stretching for some distance
along the river front. Here, officially out of bounds to the
Europeans, were the Chinese warehouses where trade goods from
the interior were weighed, packaged, and stored. Their boats, the
"melon boats" or "chop boats" of the Canton waterfront, were
circular-decked craft, neat and efficient. The owners of both the
hong establishments and the thirteen factories were the hong
merchants, a group of about a dozen very rich Chinese who
manipulated the Canton monopoly of foreign trade and with whom
the foreigners had surprisingly good relations.

Under the control of the Hoppo, an appointee of Peking who for
three years held this most lush of customs posts in the Kingdom,
these merchants were organized as a kind of guild. Since foreign
traders could do business only through one of the security
merchants, the latter were unique among Chinese in having
extensive contacts with outsiders. The foreign community with
whom they had their dealings in the mid-1830's numbered about
150, a third of them Parsees. The overall group was divided into
some twenty mercantile houses, the most prominent of which were
Russell and Co., Dent and Co., and Jardine, Matheson and Co.

China was of keenest interest to these foreign merchants because
of the black teas of Fukien, the silks, and export porcelains.
Autumn was the time of the most spirited activity, when ships were
crowding into Whampoa Reach; shipmasters were daily dealing
with their hong merchants; goods were being moved down the
Pearl to the rumbling innards of merchantmen; and sailors were
jamming the gin shops and gutters of Hog Lane. Adding to the
frenzy, most firms observed no Sabbath, since most Chinese had
none. Each captain sought to complete his cargo early, clear port

quickly, and crowd on canvas to get home first with the lucrative early tea crop.

Although the foreign community reacted to the factory area with varying blends of frustration and enthusiasm, the two pioneer American missionaries, who resided there, regarded it as "a selfish and gain-greedy community," [7] corrupt and corrupting — where honest men had difficulty remaining so.[8] It was a kind of weird mercantile cocoon in which a foreigner could live for years and be almost unaware of the Chinese parts of Canton; and, so effective was the isolation, a Chinese could live out his industrious destiny a mile away from the river and be unaware of the foreign community.

The city of Canton itself, an ancient, large, and important administrative center, was wholly Chinese. S. Wells Williams, one of Parker's colleagues, estimated that both inside and outside the walls Canton had roughly a million inhabitants. The inland parts of the city, in his view, had their attractions, but flatness, congestion, the monotonous "expanse of reddish roofs relieved by few large trees" rendered the city, when viewed from the wall, "insipid and uninviting." [9] Its glory lay in its waterfront; there each shore of the river for several miles was lined with tiers of craft.

In the factory area, Bridgman, Williams, and Edwin Stevens were the American Board men. Peter Parker, joining their household in "A" Hong, unavoidably saw a great deal of them after his arrival. Anyone familiar with remote mission stations will know the sense of mingled pleasure and anxiety with which resident missionaries await the arrival of a novice with his new energies and rough edges. Of the threesome who now awaited Parker, Stevens had been a companion of his at Yale. The two had many friends in common, and their reunion in Canton was most cordial.[10] Stevens had come out under appointment to the Seamen's Friend Society and had been engaged in pastoral work at Whampoa.

Bridgman, aged thirty-three years to Peter Parker's thirty, was the pioneer and senior member. He had preceded Parker at Amherst (class of '26) and gone on to Andover for his theological degree. Devout and guarded in his speech, he was very hard-working, with an unusual singleness of aim.[11] The diary of his trip to China shows him to belong, with Marco Polo, to the broad genus of basically dull men who were enlivened by remarkable experiences. His arrival at Macao and Canton in February 1830 had given him a period of intimate and cherished association with Dr. Morrison in the years just before the latter's death. These had been, on the whole, very lonely years. Depressed by a vast job and too few colleagues, an evangelist cut off by the Canton arrangements from evangelizing, Bridgman had subsided into attempting to learn Chinese, to operate a tiny school,[12] and to edit a monthly journal, the *Chinese Repository*, which in time became a valued historical record.

Much younger and less well educated than Bridgman, devoted to him, and looking up to him as to an honored, older friend was Williams. Trained as a printer at Rensselaer Institute, he joined Bridgman in 1833, at once taking over the printing of the *Chinese Repository*, then almost a year old. Cheerful, healthy, and industrious, he proved a first-rate member of the mission group. A fine linguist, he too was hard at work at the language.

Peter Parker fitted in well with these men. Just two days after his arrival he was confiding to his journal: "Were I to give a definition of happiness on earth, without the help of language I would introduce the person requiring it into the room of four missionaries on the borders of China — at their hour of devotion." [13] The records suggest that Parker liked Stevens very much, began here a close friendship[14] with Bridgman, and was somewhat less attached to Williams, although on good terms which improved with age. One of his primary tasks, indeed the chief usefulness of his medical degree in the eyes of the American Board, was his care of the health of the other three. And he at once reported to the Board that he found Stevens well; Williams, active and in fair health; and Bridgman in rather poor condition.

Stevens and Williams had solved the problem of how to secure adequate exercise in the confining conditions of the factory area by resorting to rowing their own boat on the river, in violation of the letter of the law but disregarded by the authorities. Parker's first glimpse of the up-river waterfront came during this welcome release on the second day after his arrival. He was much struck by the astonishing numbers of people that lived in boats.

The following day he was taken by Stevens and Williams to a temple where he watched for the first time "a female worshipping before an idol." [15] It was colder than usual in the subtropical city, and "one poor creature having terminated his wretched existence here below had left his cold remains upon the pavement of the yard — and several others lay near who probably did not live the day out, and some with hardly strength to stand were collected around a little smoking straw, with a piece of mat to cover them. To see the unburied dead in the streets in the morning I am informed is frequent." [16]

Parker's arrival came at a time of tension when the mission work was being buffeted from several directions. Against the background of an unusual incidence of piracy and shipwreck had come the death of Morrison and the trouble caused by Lord William Napier, who had inevitably failed in attempting the hopeless task of altering China's centuries-old pattern of conducting foreign relations. Since his activities in Canton had kindled official Chinese displeasure and retaliation, it was a period of dark clouds for the little mission. In sadness they received news of the murder of two of their friends who had gone to Sumatra. Bridgman felt that these very severe trials should not dampen the ardor of missionaries and their supporters; on that principle, "Christianity would have become extinct at the very moment our Saviour expired on the cross." [17] To this end he was heartily glad of the arrival of Peter Parker as a new recruit.

To Elijah Bridgman and to Parker the Middle Kingdom was a benighted land desperately needing to be saved by the healing touch of Christianity. In Bridgman's words: "Darkness covers the land, and gross darkness the people. Idolatry, superstition, fraud, falsehood, cruelty, and oppression everywhere predominate, and iniquity, like a mighty flood, is extending far and wide its desolation." [18] Nations of the East, Bridgman believed, sat in the shadow of death, "without hope, without God, the willing slaves of

Sin and Satan." [19] He was fecundity itself in the ready flow of
dramatic excoriations, asserting that his poor heart withered with
grief at the very thought of the forlorn state of China,[20] whose
unconverted citizens were "going down to hell, on account of the
negligence of Christians." [21] Only Christian faith could penetrate
"the filth and debasement . . . and see under it all, the priceless
soul, accountable, progressive, immortal." [22] It was, therefore, the
duty of western churches "to pour the light of the glorious gospel
on this dark empire." [23]

Parker's journals and letters rang with bitter severities about the
"moral wilderness" in which he found himself, although there was
some observable restraint, in that he used less than the full
Bridgmanesque orchestration.[24] Indeed, his first reactions to China
were relatively wan compared with those of Bridgman. However,
restraint of manner did not mean restraint in yearning for "the full
triumph of the gospel." [25]

One of the captivating aspects of the relationship between these
self-assured fellows and their chosen imperial target was the
mutuality of the fanaticisms. For every bristling insult uttered by
the young missionaries there was an answering Chinese arrogance.
The classic expression of the official policy of exclusion and
exclusiveness had been enunciated in the letters and mandates of
the aged Ch'ien-lung Emperor to Lord Macartney in the 1790's.[26]
Those lofty attitudes were then reiterated in state papers and
official correspondence during subsequent decades.

What lay back of such joyless counterblasts of egocentrism and
condescension was China's historic size, her cultural self-image as
the Middle Kingdom, and a unique system of international
relations. At the basis of the European system lay the great fact
that there existed states which were competitive equals — sovereign, independent units, theoretical peers before international law.
The history of East Asia had been utterly different. There China
had been the dominating power, the biggest, oldest, strongest, and
most advanced. The Chinese had tended to regard themselves with
deep and understandable pride as the exemplars of a superior
Middle Kingdom, the source of true culture toward which the eyes
of the non-Chinese, "barbarian," outer world were naturally drawn

in fascination. Moreover, these facts and attitudes had been institutionalized in Tribute Relations, the East Asian system of international relations, symbolizing the superiority of China and the inferiority of the suppliant societies which wanted a formal relationship with China.[27] Limited trading privileges and certain fringe benefits were extended by Peking, if one followed with traditional and impeccable correctness certain time-honored procedures.

As a type of state-system, this Confucian familism, and its inequality of brother-states, was older than the Western system of sovereign equals. It had the great advantage of giving a certain homogeneity to international relations. Also, since China did not normally interfere in the internal affairs of its tributaries, the classic tributary relationship did not make of these areas colonies or protectorates in the European sense. It was thus a good working relationship for large and small without a compromising and repellent domination.

In the duel of missionary challenge and Chinese response, if the Confucian literatus was "the uncompromising guardian of values obsolete but irrefutable," [28] the missionary was a sour devotee of a dreary, cultural barbarianism. East-West relations had been much more satisfactory during the seventeenth century when most of the contact between Jesuit and mandarin was mutually tolerant. The reciprocal intolerance of the 1830's made for an unfortunate beginning to the Protestant mission movement.[29] Both the denunciatory charity in the mission outlook and the equally denunciatory condescension in the Chinese view invited an increasing involvement by Western governments, prodded by their nationals who had settled in the Orient. Bridgman, among others, felt that the stalemate of relationship was about to change, that the haughty mandarins and their government were riding for a fall,[30] and that Western governments should more directly confront the Chinese.

As a participant in the prickly dialogue between Chinese and American, and prepared as he was to treat both the body and the soul, Dr. Parker needed now to think out carefully the strategy of how and where he should commit his time and energy. Among his first impressions were the obvious medical opportunities in Canton.

He talked to Drs. James H. Bradford and R. H. Coxe, residents in the factory area, about his tentative plan of having a certain hour of the day, or day of the week, when he would attend to such as might seek medical aid.[31] He was still innocent of any clear idea of how easily medicine could engulf a career. In actual fact, he had already begun his medical work on Chinese soil (although not yet with Chinese patients) by attending two Lascars from the schooner *Union* which had brought him up from Macao.

But he was, equally clearly, devoted to the profession of evangelist which he had chosen and been chosen for. The instructions which accompanied him, substantially the same as those given to Bridgman five years earlier, did not allow much latitude for medical work. In addition to this central dilemma there were certain nagging considerations which had to be confronted at once. On the evening of October 31, 1834, he read to his mission brethren his instructions and raised especially the questions of what dialect he should study, where he could best acquire it, and whether an immediate beginning of medical practice among the Chinese would be consistent with his instructions.[32]

It seemed best, as they talked these matters over, for him to remain at Canton, to begin studying both Cantonese and Mandarin, and to delay any systematic medical practice until solid progress had been made on the language. Consequently he settled quickly into language work, for which he fortunately had both aptitude and liking. There were interruptions, as when his Chinese tutor had to absent himself during the days when the government clamped down on Co-hong personnel, and people were jittery about Sino-foreign relations. Nevertheless, November 1834 must have been on the whole a very happy month for Peter Parker. He was content with his decisions, was finally embarked upon the career for which he had spent some years preparing, found friends and hospitality at hand, and enjoyed the rich chutney of sights, sounds, and smells of Canton.

Early in November he was taken by Bridgman on a visit to a vaccinating establishment.[33] The Chinese doctor was polite and attentive. There were about 100 Chinese mothers present with their children, of whom more than two dozen were to be vaccinated, the others to supply the vaccine. The institution was one of the offshoots of the work in innoculation which Dr. Alexander Pearson of the British East India Company had begun at Macao in 1805. Dr. Parker was informed that the Chinese authorities supported the work by offering bounties for successful cases. He observed that there was systematic registration of the patients and that about half a dozen men were taking the vaccine and doing the vaccinating.

Although Dr. Parker had previously attended patients who were natives of Ireland, Scotland, Sweden, Goa, Bombay, and Malacca[34] and had seen and prescribed for a Chinese from the American Hong, not until mid-November did he treat a Chinese unconnected with the foreign community. A ten-year-old boy was brought in by his father. Bridgman and one of his pupils translated; Parker examined, diagnosed dysentery, and prescribed. He received also the comprador of the American Hong and then, by indirection, a woman. For the latter he had to prescribe without seeing the patient.[35]

This happy context of language study and minuscule medical practice, quickly and efficiently established, might have continued through the winter and beyond, had it not been thrown askew by the appearance of the demanding and unsettling Dr. Karl Friedrich August Gutzlaff. This individual was by 1834 the most experienced Protestant evangelist on the China coast. A Pomeranian by birth, an aggressive linguist by avocation, and a meteoric Christian propagandist by profession, he had been sent by the Netherlands Missionary Society to Siam in 1824. He learned Fukienese, left that mission, and embarked on a series of voyages along the China coast, using Macao as his base and occasionally visiting Canton, as at the time of this encounter with Parker. Gutzlaff regarded the Chinese as semibarbarous idolaters;[36] the Chinese, in turn, viewed him as a swashbuckling barbarian. To Parker he was eccentric, remarkable, puzzling, and somewhat grotesque.[37]

Gutzlaff at once advised, and probably ordered, Parker to withdraw to Singapore, where he would find an accessible community of Fukienese. He could mingle freely with them, learn their dialect, and be prepared linguistically for the impending opening of new missionary enterprises up the coast to the east. Canton itself was most unpromising at that time as mission territory; Bridgman had been there for five years and had not seen a single soul converted.[38]

By the end of November Peter Parker, shaken by Gutzlaff's advice, was also suffering from the violent diarrhea which periodically attacked foreigners in China. If he remained in Canton he could study Mandarin and open an eye infirmary, but Singapore, needed medical work and was open to preaching. The pros and cons were carefully weighed at a meeting in which Parker, Bridgman, and Williams were joined by Olyphant.[39]

The language question was a poser. Official documents were in Classical Chinese (a rough counterpart of our Old English). The local spoken language was Cantonese, but would not be useful in other provinces until missionaries received permission to work in them. The coastal areas to the east and northeast, the most likely areas of penetration in the not distant future, were themselves riddled with local languages which did not apply to any very large part of the Middle Kingdom. A mastery of Mandarin was the way to converse with the largest number of Chinese, except that from the mission point of view in 1834 it applied to central China, the North China plain and Peking, all safely beyond the reach of missionary activity in the foreseeable future. There was also some practical difficulty at Canton in securing a teacher, technically forbidden to foreigners, and in finding flesh-and-blood Chinese to talk with. Moreover, the dilemma over how much medical work to do pressed in on him. The outcome of the agonizing reappraisal was an acceptance of the Gutzlaff thesis and departure by Parker on December 6, 1834, for Singapore with plans to return to Canton in April or May.

At first Singapore seemed unusually attractive to him. Arrival on the day before Christmas revealed gardens fragrant with flowers, the Union Jack flying over elegant buildings, and horse-drawn carriages moving along spacious streets.[40] Residing initially with Ira Tracy, evangelist of the American Board, he was soon able to move into the building known as the Morrison House. The property of the heirs of Dr. Robert Morrison, it was in the midst of the Chinese community with no European very near.[41]

There was from the start the expected involvement with attending or preaching at various church services, assemblies, and prayer meetings. Parker sometimes attended the Episcopal church but concentrated on the activities of Mr. Tracy's small Chinese congregation, which appealed more to him since such a church could not yet exist under the segregated conditions of Canton.

What was missing was the ability on his part to evangelize in Chinese. Accordingly, language arrangements were quickly made with a private teacher-interpreter for ten dollars a month,[42] and daily work was begun on Hokien, the language of the Fukienese immigrant community. As the teacher himself did not know the written characters, they confined themselves to spoken Chinese.

Parker also began to accept patients, hoping to confine this activity to a small and manageable part of each day. The routine seems to have been to see them first thing in the morning, often starting at sunrise. He took some patients into his house to keep them under constant care. The practice increased steadily, with patients assembling before dawn and the doctor busy with them until noon, sometimes with no time for breakfast or morning prayers; he was also called out to attend them at night.[43] Care was gratuitous and generally well received. Dr. Parker was frank in recording deaths of several patients. Medical work soon absorbed so much of the day that he was quite unable to devote adequate time to language study, and this development bothered him a good deal.[44]

Near the end of April he interrupted his Singapore routines with a side trip to Malacca, where he wished to study for several weeks with the scholar who had taught Chinese to William Milne, Walter Henry Medhurst, and other representatives of the London Missionary Society (LMS).[45] During the second day of the voyage three local *praus,* manned by oarsmen, were observed putting out in the direction of Parker's ship, the *Catherine.* On the latter no suspicions were aroused and they commenced dining as usual, soon to be interrupted with the panicky cry of "pirates" from on deck. With the *praus* in pursuit of the *Catherine,* all women and children were ordered below. Cannon were loaded; steel ramrods rattled in the muskets; swords and spears were produced. Since the *Catherine* was nearly becalmed, the pirates gained until a light breeze arose to which the *Catherine* unfurled every sail. Half an hour from the first alarm it was pulling away from the pursuers, leaving them far astern by evening. During part of the chase, Parker could hear the gongs with which the pirates were said to inspire each other. By eight o'clock, when all was still and his heart overflowed with gratitude to God, he read from the Book of Psalms and led his fellow passengers in prayer.[46] When he finally reached Malacca, he stayed with the superintendent of the British East India Company and his wife and devoted much of his time to discovering a good site for a "Christian colony."

Return to Singapore early in June found him resuming his practice, but with lassitude of mind and body[47] and a growing desire to leave. Although some of Parker's South China brethren favored his remaining longer at Singapore,[48] he was himself moved by strong reasons to return to Canton. He had been longer in Singapore than originally planned; there were now many newly printed tracts waiting to be taken to Canton; both Stevens and Olyphant had expressed the wish that he return, the former feeling that he could be immediately useful there. He also thought that with his present teacher he could pursue Chinese studies in Canton nearly as well as at Singapore. Moreover he had suffered a good deal from the climate, and his health troubled him. Feeling even worse during August, it was with pleasure and relief that he unexpectedly encountered Captain James Neish of the *Fort William*, recently arrived from Calcutta en route to Macao and Whampoa.[49] The captain immediately offered him passage, saying that he had ample space as well not only for the teacher and dresser who were to accompany Dr. Parker but also the voluminous baggage of all three. The dresser was a Chinese assistant who administered prescriptions.[50]

After a flurry of farewells to his patients and to several candidates for baptism who had studied with him, he spent such furiously busy hours in getting his belongings onto the *Fort William* that the exertions brought him near to collapse.[51] However, the weather of the first few days at sea was delightful, permitting him needed rest. By sharing a stateroom with the teacher and dresser,

Dr. Parker was able to continue his language studies, the teacher adding immeasurably to Parker's joy by joining him in prayer.

Their good weather disintegrated in the Gulf of Siam. Parker first became aware of the change at two in the morning, when the noise from the ship's keel wakened him. He went on deck where with solemnity and awe he beheld nearly constant blue lightning as thunder pealed and the sea ran high. Some abatement by day was followed at night with a more savage gale, during which they feared the ship might founder. Another lull was also followed, again at night, by a tempest in which the main topsail was riven from the yard. Relative calm finally returned to their world, pleasant weather prevailed, and the first of September found Parker as happy in approaching Macao as someone arriving home. The authorities cleared his baggage with its large number of mission tracts without objection. And his attempt to settle with Captain Neish for the voyage was met with a cordial note in which the Captain, not a pious man, begged him to accept a free passage as a small mark of his esteem.[52] These happenings were somewhat offset by the bleak discovery that he had been duped by the Chinese teacher from Singapore. The latter, having gambled away the money advanced by the doctor to enable him to return to his home, became a conspicuous beggar in the streets of Canton until Parker succeeded in getting him on board a later ship.[53]

Peter Parker's return from Singapore to Canton settled the language question, since, despite his willingness to go on with Hokien after his return to Canton, residence there inevitably dictated setting Hokien aside and reviving his study of Cantonese. But the special significance of the Singapore period was his medical experience. Those months comprised his internship, a period which not only enhanced his skills and confirmed his self-confidence but prepared him for a quick, efficient start in a much more important medical practice.

3 ◆ A Hospital for Canton

As of 1830, Chinese medicine, like almost everything else to which
Peter Parker was going to be exposed in the Middle Kingdom, was
at once ancient, elaborate, and based on a doctrine largely at
variance with the one in which he was trained.[1] Chinese practitioners were relatively sophisticated, but there was no recognized
system of medical instruction, no required diploma, and doctors
had little status.[2] A physician simply read what he could, the
medical lore often being handed from father to son to grandson
like treasured family recipes.

Many scholars who failed the imperial civil service examinations
fell back on medical careers. In the role of physician, although
sometimes men of substance and gentry status, they labored under
the disadvantage of their patients being as empirical in selecting
doctors as doctors were in choosing their medications. Dr. William
Lockhart, Parker's friend in the London Missionary Society,
writing out of experience in Canton, Macao, Chusan, and Shanghai, pointed out that when a person was sick his friends consulted a
physician, who examined the case, gave his opinion and plan of
cure, and then often found that the case was left in his hands for
only a day or two. If it did not follow the course expected, another
practitioner was sent for, sometimes six or seven physicians
successively taking charge of the patient.[3]

Along with acupuncture and the use of an astounding variety of
drugs, Chinese practitioners depended mainly on the doctrine of

the pulses. In each wrist the pulse could be variously read over a zone nearly two inches long, which was divided into three sections, each of which was held to possess an external and internal pulse.[4] Thus every person had twelve pulses, each being diagnostically related to a definite internal organ. Pulse theories dealt much with "rate, character, rhythm, volume, tension" and exphasized four principal pulse readings: "a light flowing pulse like a piece of wood floating on water," a deep one, a slow one, and a quick one with six beats to a cycle of respiration.[5] Many subsidiary readings were often added: typhoid, for example, was held to be not dangerous with a superficial pulse but to become dangerous when the pulse shifted to a "thready, small, and soft" one.[6] Peter Parker's friend, Dr. Lockhart, believed that the endless variations in pulse interpretations were largely fanciful.[7] Dr. Benjamin Hobson, his colleague in the London Missionary Society, was denunciatory. With regard to the circulation of the blood, Chinese physicians were, he wrote, "preposterously confused and erroneous," making no distinction between veins and arteries, having no knowledge of the heart's proper function, nor of the change in the blood in capillaries and lungs. It seemed ridiculous to him to have "a pulse for every organ but the brain." [8] Although Chinese doctors made excessive claims for their ability to read the pulse, their success with it was indeed remarkable.[9]

The size and quality of the materia medica at the command of Chinese doctors was impressive. They used several thousand herbs, powders, and concoctions many of undoubted efficacy. Some, such as ephedrine and kaolin, have become well known in the West. Dr. Hobson successfully used chaulmoogra, which he believed to be an old Chinese prescription, in the treatment of leprosy.[10] Lockhart recorded that the Chinese were acquainted with the power of arsenic in checking the periodicity of ague.[11] Ginseng was considered the ultimate medication, the sulfa and penicillin of premodern China. The wild variety, *Panax ginseng,* was held to be the best and was accordingly reserved for the Emperor and his household, but any kind of ginseng was regarded with awe. Presumed to be helpful during pregnancy, it was also recommended during many serious ailments, but cost was prohibitively high, Lockhart recording that it might run to $400 an ounce.

The mystifying and ancient practice of acupuncture was commonly used. A stunning product of a daring empiricism, this therapy dealt with "rheumatism, deep-seated pains of all kinds, sprains, swellings of the joint," [12] cholera, cough, and colic. The specialist, having memorized 365 exact points on the human body where puncture might be made, had at his command nine different kinds of needles, usually of steel, copper, or silver, rather oddly shaped. One or more of the needles was dexterously introduced into the patient's body superficially or even deeply, in the latter case often driven in with a hammer. No antisepsis was used, and the instruments might be left in for days. Today, antiseptic precautions are often taken; low-voltage, electronically charged needles may be employed; and acupuncture is routinely utilized as a type of anesthesia for major operations. Its undoubted efficacy may derive from stimulating the body to produce and release its own cortisone. [13]

Despite many successful medical therapies, Chinese surgical techniques in Peter Parker's time were extremely rudimentary. None but the most trifling operations were attempted, according to Lockhart, and "surgeons" were assigned a lower status than internists. [14] There seem to have been available very few surgical procedures other than the dramatic and exotic operation of castration, presumed to have been introduced by Hua T'o, a renowned physician and surgeon of the early third century A.D. [15]

On the whole, one may conclude that as of the period of Dr. Parker's residence an intelligent empiricism spread over many centuries had evolved a large number of sophisticated Chinese treatises, drugs, and therapies. Chinese medicine did not have antisepsis, so far as we know, nor did Western medicine; neither had anesthesias; [16] neither could cope with dozens of ill-understood maladies. Chinese medicine may have been more effective with typhus, fevers, and midwifery. Indeed, Lockhart reported a fairly good public health record in Shanghai, with few cases of cholera and no epidemics, and also praised the work of Chinese medical

clinics in the major cities.[17] Western medicine was in all probability
superior in eye treatment and anatomy, because the Chinese did
not perform autopsies or dissections and thus had a very limited
knowledge of physiology and anatomy. Western methods also held
out the promise of greater, more abundant, and earlier improvement in therapy and technique. The West had a demonstrable
superiority in surgery: cataracts responded readily to relatively
simple surgical therapy, tumors of the surface of the body and of
the extremities could be removed, as could some stones of the
urinary tract, by a standardized procedure familiar to Parker. The
Chinese did not treat any of these conditions surgically.

Prior to Dr. Parker's arrival in the Orient there were three main
points of entry for Western medical influences: Peking, Macao,
and Canton. In Peking the Jesuits were the most important source.
Beginning early in the seventeenth century several medically
trained Jesuits were sent there.[18] Later, other Catholic orders sent
missionaries to Peking who served as incidental disseminators of
Western medicine. To Peking also came occasional physicians
attending the tribute missions, but these figures played no significant role in the transmission of the healing art. On the whole,
Peking seems to have made little use of these possible sources of
information on Western medicine.

Macao had readier access to the outside world and proved to be
a more important point of entry, but one does not find significant
and demonstrable examples until the contributions of four able
physicians early in the nineteenth century: Drs. Alexander Pearson, John Livingstone, Thomas R. Colledge, and James H.
Bradford, the third of these being a friend of Peter Parker's. The
first, Pearson, was senior surgeon in Macao of the British East
India Company. He had served as ship's surgeon on the *Arniston*,
became a member of the Royal College of Surgeons in 1801, and
was appointed to Canton, taking up residence there in 1805, the
year in which he also received his M.D. from St. Andrews.[19] In
1805 Dr. Pearson, newly assigned to Macao as a resident Company
surgeon and interested in Jenner's new method of preventing
smallpox, began to vaccinate Chinese patients successfully. Vaccination proved far superior to the traditional Chinese method of

treating smallpox, which involved inserting smallpox scales in the nostrils.[20] Pearson's success was a notable event in the history of the modern Orient. His published tract was both widely circulated and very useful.[21] Parker, unfortunately, never met him.

Pearson's work was effectively supplemented by Dr. Livingstone, who had served as surgeon on the *Lord Thurber*, the *Cirencester*, and the *Coutts*[22] before settling in Macao as the British East India Company resident in 1808. A dozen years later, Livingstone joined Dr. Robert Morrison in opening at Macao a joint Sino-Western dispensary for the relief of afflicted Chinese and for the purpose of garnering some knowledge of traditional Chinese therapies.[23] Dr. Lee, a respectable Chinese physician, was in charge and Dr. Pearson assisted at the clinic.[24] They appear to have gone about their business with energy and effectiveness. Having stocked a large assortment of Chinese medicines as well as a library of 800 volumes of Chinese medical literature, they worked at the dispensary one to two hours each morning. The enterprise was probably abandoned when Morrison went on furlough in 1823. Livingstone left Macao in 1827 and died at sea two years later.[25]

The third member of this quartet of inadvertent, part-time Westernizers was Dr. Thomas R. Colledge, whose career had evolved in much the same way. He had studied medicine at Leicester Infirmary and St. Thomas's Hospital in London, was a surgeon's mate and then a ship's surgeon for five years before settling in Macao[26] in 1826. Beginning in 1831,[27] he acted as Company surgeon at Canton and then when the Company monopoly was terminated, as surgeon to the British superintendency of trade. In 1827, responsive to obvious need, this energetic and generous man had opened a dispensary in Macao, available to all patients but principally intended for those suffering from eye diseases. Colledge became a direct influence on Peter Parker's subsequent work. Having little or no professional assistance, he soon found himself immensely busy. In all, about 4000 indigent Chinese were treated for a large variety of maladies.[28] This labor, added to his regular medical duties, became too much for him, and he was forced to discontinue it after four years.[29]

Colledge's success at Macao led to the establishment of similar work in Canton in 1828 in collaboration with Dr. Bradford, who was chosen to open a hospital there and take charge of it.[30] The fourth physician to play a significant role as a forerunner of Dr. Parker's work in Canton, Bradford received his M.D. from the University of Pennsylvania in 1823, and shipped to China as surgeon on the *Caledonia*. After a second voyage he was chosen by the Americans of Canton as their physician. For this he received a salary and gave free medical attention to foreign residents or transients. According to the American merchant John R. Latimer, who gave much of his leisure time to helping Dr. Bradford, the hospital had been established six or seven years by the time of Bradford's departure for home in 1834. Although transient surgeons helped Dr. Bradford, and although he often had assistance from Dr. R. H. Coxe,[31] the work overtaxed him. Falling ill himself during a season of great sickness, he was forced to leave. By 1835 he was back in the States.

The institution in Canton of which Colledge had been the architect and Bradford the builder probably saw little activity after Bradford's departure. Evidence is sparse on this point, and occasional items do testify to a longer existence.[32] Whatever its exact duration, it served for Peter Parker as a clear demonstration of the feasibility of medical work among the Chinese by a missionary.

One now comes to the heart of Peter Parker's career — the nature of the role he chose for himself in Canton, the way his choice enabled him to transform mission activity in China, and the place his endeavors won for him among mission pioneers. The mission station he joined, one of the smallest and most recently established by the American Board, had its origin in 1824 in the action in the Prudential Committee, specifying that suitable persons be sought as missionaries to China, one of whom should be a doctor.[33] When a suitable physician could not be found, E. C. Bridgman and David Abeel were sent out in 1829, the latter for the *American Seamen's Friend Society*.[34] When Parker arrived in 1834, the Canton missionaries were housed rent-free by David Olyphant at number 2, American Hong. They found their quarters comfortable and agreeable, although removed from society and normal domesticity.[35] Their daily regimen consisted of rising as soon as it was light, breakfasting substantially at 8:30, dining at 3:30, with tea soon after lamplighting. Their group devotions were at 8:00 A.M. and 9:00 P.M., with additional time for private prayer, a social-religious meeting on Friday evening, and a biblical exercise at the end of Sunday afternoon.[36] In its moral corsetting the household was straightlaced in the extreme. When Bridgman found his aged Chinese tutor playing cards, there was a household crisis.[37]

The missionary stance of this Canton station prior to Dr. Parker may be outlined as follows: a tiny group of alien Protestant evangelists seeking the conversion of China, confronted with difficulties of communication and access, and misidentified by the Chinese with the opium traders, had adopted first a strategy of preparation and marking time, and then, sporadically, one of limited activism. Preparation chiefly revolved around language work (study, dictionaries, translation of scripture), writing tracts for distribution, and producing the *Chinese Repository* as a means of educating foreigners about China. Limited activism involved the actual distribution of scripture and tracts, various probing trips to forbidden spots along the coast, the beginning of mission schooling in China, and the grandiose aberration of urging (unsuccessfully) the planting of Christian colonies.

In their work in China the missionaries were increasingly caught in a strategic dilemma over whether to remain in a pallid state of perpetual preparation or venture into a gauche activism, these extremes being symbolized, from the early days of Protestant missions to China, by Morrison and Gutzlaff — the linguist in "the day of small things" [38] and the Victorian Viking who undertook to annihilate difficulties by saying there were none.[39] Williams wrote with unusual tartness some years later that one of their activist colleagues, totally disregarding the feelings of the Cantonese, talked publicly with women, forced tracts into the chair of the governor as he was passing through the streets, and perpetrated other similarly rude acts, whereas Bridgman, never opening his mouth, seemed unable to exert an influence for the good on anyone, anywhere.[40] Bridgman, himself, wrote sadly that the work was so great and the laborers so few, that they would need a troop of men to accomplish anything.[41] Thus, given such facts confronting the Canton mission, what were they to do?

In a sense their health problems supplied the answer. These held a special urgency since the health of mission personnel in other areas had been disastrous — forty-five deaths abroad since the founding of the American Board, plus fifty-three returnees, thirty-one of which were for reasons of their health or the health of members of their family.[42] As a consequence, one of the standard protective devices of the ABC was to train some of its evangelists in medicine as well as theology, on the premise that Hippocrates would sustain Paul. With this in mind a number of doctors were sent to various missions in the 1819–1834 period [43] to care for their colleagues, the Prudential Committee expecting that such doctors would devote only small amounts of time to medical work among the "natives." At the same time the missionaries themselves, notably those in Ceylon and Canton, were arguing that medicine was a valuable adjunct to evangelism and requesting medically trained workers. Bridgman, for example, stressed the advantage of medical knowledge for mission work.[44]

Initially the Board responded to such suggestions with the dispatch of nondoctors S. Wells Williams and the Reverend Ira Tracy, who arrived at Canton together in October 1833. Then Peter Parker had been sent in 1834. The following year, with his Singapore "internship" behind him, Parker was ready to test whether or not Bridgman had been right about the usefulness of a mission doctor.

Parker was himself in poor condition.[45] His symptoms, in his own words, were "languor, imbecility of mind, and at times difficulty in breathing; pain in my breast and between my shoulders, & these indicate the commencement of the liver complaint so common in warm climates." [46] At one point he thought that his earthly prospects were dim. When Parker was no longer able to prescribe for himself, Dr. Coxe had come to his aid.[47] It was during these weeks of ill-health that the decision was made to open a dispensary. Encouraged by the success at Singapore and

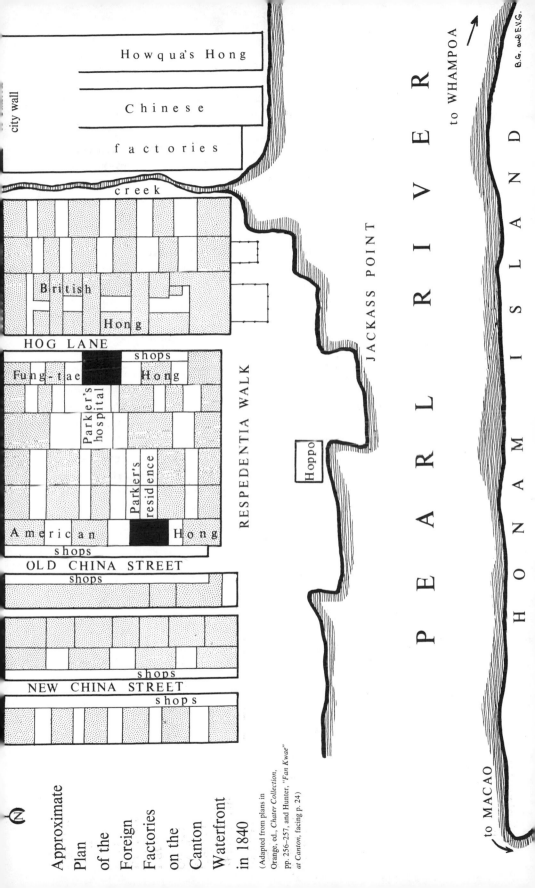

Approximate
Plan
of the
Foreign
Factories
on the
Canton
Waterfront
in 1840

(Adapted from plans in
Orange, ed., *Chater Collection*,
pp. 256–257, and Hunter, *"Fan Kwae"*
at Canton, facing p. 24)

city wall

Howqua's Hong

Chinese

factories

creek

British

Hong

HOG LANE

shops

Fung-tae   Hong

Parker's
hospital

Parker's
residence

American   Hong

shops

OLD CHINA STREET

shops

shops

NEW CHINA STREET

shops

RESPEDENTIA WALK

Hoppo

JACKASS POINT

P E A R L   R I V E R

to WHAMPOA

H O N A M   I S L A N D

to MACAO

B.G. and E.N.G.

by the work of his predecessors in Macao and Canton, Parker believed that the Chinese would welcome such an attempt.[48]

Given the stark facts of low budgets and high rents (usually somewhere between $1200 and $3000 per year for each establishment),[49] some form of subsidy was necessary, in addition to Chinese willingness, to enable Parker to secure the use of rooms in the Canton factory area. The initial support, which he so much needed, came from Olyphant, who, after considerable difficulty,[50] secured a suitable building from Howqua for the very reasonable rent of $500 per annum.[51] This mention of Howqua conjures up one of the great figures of the period, the elderly Howqua II (Wu Ping-chien, 1769–1843), inheritor of the I-ho Hong and creator of one of the world's large fortunes of the nineteenth century.[52] As a brilliant merchant prince, long a member of the Co-hong, he was admired for his honesty, generosity, and incredible success as a trader.

Peter Parker's residence and the newly rented building for the dispensary, although on different streets, were within the same block of hongs, on opposite sides of it. To go to the new rooms, Dr. Parker turned left at his own doorstep, walked a few dozen yards past Chinese shops on Old China Street, turned left onto Respedentia Walk, walked about 150 yards past half a dozen hongs, and turned left onto Hog Lane. Halfway up this tiny street, the hospital was at number 3, Fung-tae Hong.[53] Hog Lane, some seven feet wide, was jammed with liquor shops which catered to the foreign sailors. Though a tough and disorderly area, this location seemed promising to Parker, who liked its direct communication with the street, which allowed patients to enter and leave without either annoying foreigners by passing through their hongs, or exciting curious Chinese by being seen to resort to a foreigner's house. Besides possessing a large room in the second story where two hundred could be comfortably seated and prescribed for, the house afforded temporary lodgings for forty or more patients.[54]

There, in early November 1835, the great moment arrived for Dr. Parker. In the words of his own journal:

Nov. 4th. Commenced an Ophthalmic Infirmary in Canton. Four presented themselves. The first a female perfectly blind, with

Amaurosis of both eyes, which commenced in the right eye five years since after a fever. . . . The second, also a female 25, with Chronic Ophthalmia. A third with Pterygium of both eyes and Entropium of the right. A fourth Amaurosis of both eyes. The first and fourth far from being desirable cases to commence with. Unwilling to refuse them the only possible chance of recovering sight, without much exciting their expectation I told them I would do the best I can for them.[55]

The following day he operated for the Pterygium on one of these patients, who submitted to the operation with entire confidence. Parker thought it worthy of notice that the three female patients had been brought by a Chinese physician and a government official. By the ninth of November he was recording a large increase in the number of his patients. On that day alone he treated twenty-one additional patients, embracing a great variety of eye diseases. There were men, women, and children, rich and poor, from the suburbs, from the city itself, from different parts of the province, and even from others. Among various treatments, he bled two of them, one being a person who was said to hold a high office in the salt department. The other was a young lady, which was the first instance of a Chinese female in Canton being bled. He had a case of especial interest on November 10 when he treated a lad of seventeen who had been born without external ears. There were slight "excrescences" where the ear should have been but no opening whatever into the internal ear. The patient could hear best with his mouth open when very loudly addressed. The Doctor, having satisfied himself on the propriety of perforating the obstruction with caustic potash, and with Dr. Coxe and the boy's family concurring, undertook treatment — the patient finding it like fire in his bones. "May the Great Physician render the case successful — . . . & not unto me but onto *thy* name O Lord shall be all the praise." Ten days later the Doctor reported his expectation of complete success.

In repeated instances he found the most ingenuous gratitude.

On Thursday a patient who came first the day before — affected with opacity & vascularity of the cornea of both eyes, had found perceptible benefit — I give his own story — . "My father &

mother are aged & depend upon me for support. I was fast becoming blind & unable to work — I felt bad that I could not then support them or myself. I heard of the new Dr. & I have come only one day & am better. He is all the same as our josh (God) to me." I then corrected him & told him of the God of Heaven — & his goodness in giving us all our mercies, & especially his Son to die for us. This conversation excited the attention of the bystanders who also listened to my remarks — This first opportunity (however imperfectly I was understood) of pointing these benighted men to greatest of all good refreshed my spirit. An[d] these are the opportunities that I anticipate with great joy.

Fitch Taylor, a visiting naval chaplain, wrote of a grateful father whose daughter had had the sight of one eye restored. The father came with the recovered patient plus a younger daughter of thirteen, both of whom kowtowed with two knocks on the floor, while patients and Europeans looked on. Dr. Parker tried to stop them, saying that no gifts were allowed nor any kowtow, and that "it was abundant reward that the treatment of his daughter had been successful." [56] Dr. Parker found it embarrassing when grateful patients kowtowed to him — "the knee that should be bowed in homage only to their creator"; and he invariably tried to get them at once back on their feet, lecturing them a bit.[57]

The gratitude of his patients repeatedly merged into adulation. In a "Note of thanks to Dr. Parker" we find: "To be blind in both eyes is a great misfortune; but to meet with an excellent physician is a heavenly favor. I am under great obligations to you, Sir, for your kind attentions." [58] Dr. Parker reported on himself, that people were saying, "Canton no have got another such pigeon!" [59] a rare glint of humor on the dark armor of his sobriety.

Confidence and gratitude are repeatedly corroborated by the growth overnight of a full-sized new practice, and the overwhelming daily work load for Dr. Parker which went with it. Of his torrent of patients he wrote, among other things, "On going to the Infirmary this morning I found the house so full that I was apprehensive of the consequences, fearing the gravity of so many upon the floor. One hundred and fifty tickets had been given at the door before I came — more than 100 new patients had presented themselves — which together with old ones have made the number full two hundred today — It was quite dark this evening before I had completed my day's work." [60]

As the initial hurly-burly of the opening of the Canton hospital and the waves of patients were being dealt with, November 22, a Sabbath, began placidly with Dr. Parker looking in on the hospital and then preaching to some forty or fifty Europeans in number 2, American Hong. That same evening the New City of Canton was in flames. Parker later recorded "the sea of fire & smoke, the distress of animals perishing in the flame — the crash of falling roofs, explosion of gun powder, the pitiable condition of the women and children fleeing from the general conflagration — the fearful anticipation of Foreigners of being themselves among the sufferers, and the bustle from preparing for the approaching catastrophe." [61] The distance from the factories at which the fire commenced gave the foreigners time to make some preparations. Medicines and patients were first removed from the Eye Infirmary, which was closer to the city than the American Hong. Some of Parker's books and apparel were put in readiness for removal. During that sleepless night he was tormented by the fear that the operations just commenced must so soon be interrupted. His journal, with suspense worthy of a temple storyteller, does not tell what happened to the factory area, but the *Repository* account describes how the firefighting apparatus at the southwest corner of the city, assisted by opportune changes of wind direction, was used doggedly in repelling the fire at the wall. Howqua's plan to sacrifice some of his buildings in order to save several of the factories never had to be put into effect,[62] but an estimated 1400 buildings were destroyed.

Dr. Parker, proud of the success of his hospital, was also full of admiration for the courage, cultivation, and good manners of his patients. Right from the opening he found that the "patients submitted with all desirable fortitude and have been most punctilious" in following his directions.[63] He admired the courage of a woman upon whom he operated for a cataract.[64] She neither groaned nor moved a muscle during the operation. When it was over she pressed his hand and for a moment said nothing. When Dr. Parker raised her eyelids, she said "I see a little light," which was all they could hope for in her case.

About three months after the hospital's opening he recorded in his journal how:

Feb. 11th. [1836] Among the patients operated upon today was an interesting young woman Ae. 21. who had been afflicted with dropsy of the abdomen (Ascites) for three years — She has been under treatment at the Institution for 10 days — This afternoon performed the operation of Paracentesis and took away three gallons, lacking three pints, of a dark thick fluid — of a chockolate color — and thus far with the most gratifying success — After the preparations were all made the case was stated to the husband — that the consequences of the operation were sometimes fatal — and that it might be so now but I had no particular fear of it. Yet when I had done the best I could he must be satisfied whatever might be the result — To this he objected, saying I must secure that it should be successful — and but for the resolution of the patient — He must have gone away and abided the consequences — The fortitude and strength of mind of this young woman has been remarkable as well as her industry. To my surprise the day after she came to the Hospital I found her at work as tho she were well and not under the influence of medicine, and today tho expecting every hour the operation — She did not lay aside her needlework till the moment I entered her chamber for the purpose — The husband after some delay refered the decision of the question to her — She resolved at once — and not withstanding the quantity of fluid removed, she complained of no pain, . . . [nor] faintness and was cheerful and animated during the whole and most heartily grateful when all was over — and the sentiments of her husband were quite changed — I embraced the *feeling* moment to remind her of the Goodness of God — She was quite lavish in her encomiums. . . . The manner in which she acquitted herself excited the admiration of all present.[65]

A fortnight later she returned, apparently cured, and remarked that "the doctor had been as a father to her." [66]

Parker did have to contend with an occasional maverick — one such was an elderly Buddhist priest who came to the Hog Lane dispensary within its first month. He was treated for cataract and subsequently behaved so like a child that the doctor spent the whole night taking care of him. The vigil was particularly upsetting for Dr. Parker, because the patient in his restlessness repeatedly called on Buddha, "his idol god [in the doctor's narrow phrase] . . . who neither heard nor pitied." [67] When the morning revealed that the eye was doing well, Dr. Parker gave instructions for further care, entrusted him with some medicine, and agreed to his leaving. At this point, the patient expressed his sorrow at having caused so much trouble and was much pleased later on to be visited by Dr. Parker at the temple.

A considerable number of mandarins became his patients. He understood that one had resigned the office of district magistrate to put himself under the doctor's care. The Hoppo himself indicated that he expected to visit Parker's clinic for eye treatment but was waiting for a propitious day.[68] Later in the year a relative of the new Hoppo was under treatment by Dr. Parker, as well as a secretary of the governor.[69] And so it went, with "the rich and the poor — the officers of rank and destitute beggars all coming for relief and showing by their words and actions their thankfulness for the benefits conferred upon them." [70]

Thus was launched what became an immediate and extraordinary medical success. Within the first seventeen days, 240 patients were received — this in a land in which previous contacts between local citizens and Protestant missionaries had been rare. By establishing his hospital, Dr. Parker not only created in China a new type of mission enterprise which became a staple among mission institutions, but opened up new kinds of relationships with the Chinese. The new institution was variously designated by its founder the Infirmary, Hospital, Ophthalmic Infirmary, Eye Infirmary, and more permanently — Ophthalmic Hospital. The Chinese name at the entrance was P'u Ai I Yuan (Hospital of Universal Love).[71] They were one and the same; all eventually became the Canton Hospital.

Our chief sources on Dr. Parker are from his own hand. Although we find numerous corroborative statements by contemporaries, mostly foreigners, there is generally a lack of direct, unmediated testimony from the doctor's patients themselves. We know of effusive scrolls which were presented to him or to the hospital, but we have no diaries, articles, memoirs or letters of theirs, and we lack testimony which gives the subsequent experience of patients regarding the relative permanence or impermanence of the benefits bestowed by Dr. Parker's surgery. For all we know, the original and apparent success of the treatment may have been more short-lived than one is ever likely to think from reading Dr. Parker's hastily recorded accounts. The unearthing of supplementary documentation on these points is now highly unlikely. Our resources are further diminished by Dr. Parker's having limited his testimony for the most part (but not exclusively) to recounting his successes. It seems reasonable to assume that there were more failures than he records, as well as unreported facets to the relationship to him of his patients. For example, the tone of the relationship probably levelled off on a lower and less ecstatic key; it must have been partly characterized by suspicion, malice, and contempt, particularly in the years after the British had made such a wreck of public relations in Kwangtung by their actions in the First Opium War. Hobson in those later years reported of medical work in Canton that "using the knife among a people so suspicious and fault-finding requires unusual caution." Hobson found some "very grateful; the greater number are unthankful or indifferent, and a few make the obligation to appear to be on our side." [72]

The series of Quarterly Reports which Parker began in February 1836 and continued, with interruptions, until the 1850's gives a good picture of his medical work in Canton. He recorded how he kept the hospital regulations few and simple. The porter was furnished with slips of bamboo, which were numbered both in English and Chinese. One of these was a passport to the room above, where the patients were treated in the order of their numbers. The name of each new patient, his number, time of admission, residence, and occupation, were recorded sequentially in case ledgers. A card containing these particulars was given to the patient, who retained it until discharged from the hospital, as it always entitled the bearer to one of the slips of bamboo from the porter. A prescription was filed with a record of the treatment. In this way about 200 patients could be prescribed for in a day.[73] The system of registration by numbered card, today nearly universal in modern medical practice, may have been invented by Dr. Parker.[74] His reports give no indication of whether he felt he was originating a method or copying one.

Diseases of the eye were chosen for treatment not only because of their prevalence but because Chinese practitioners were generally impotent in handling them. Thursdays were soon designated for surgical cases. In these he found ready assistance at various times from: Dr. J. Cullen, surgeon on the *Lord Lowther*;[75] Dr. Augustus Alvery Adee, fleet surgeon in the United States Navy, and his assistant, Dr. W. J. Palmer, both of the United States sloop *Vincennes*;[76] an unidentified doctor named Bonsall;[77] especially Dr. R. H. Coxe, who, a year later, was described by Peter Parker as having regularly aided him on each day for surgical operations since the opening of the hospital;[78] and also "Dr." William Jardine, who from his earlier incarnation as ship's surgeon had retained an interest in medicine.[79]

Dr. Parker recorded how difficulties were anticipated over receiving females as house patients, since it was illegal for a female to enter the foreign factories. These worries proved more imaginary than real. Those whose cases required that they remain were attended by relatives. Although many more males than females were treated, it was astonishing to find 270 females in the total of 925 patients during the first quarter, a ratio of 2:5.

There soon developed traffic jams of patients. Dr. Parker repeatedly recorded such events as his Chinese servant reporting at ten o'clock in the evening that about 100 men with eye trouble were already at the infirmary door awaiting morning admission. Patients were so eager to enter the hospital that, when Dr. Parker suspended admissions, they asked hong merchants or Americans or Parsees to intercede with him.[80]

He received no fees for his services, a fact which evoked suspicion among the hong merchants, who appeared to feel that so purely benevolent an object, involving such expense of time, labor, and money, must have some objective which needed watching. They therefore placed him under official surveillance from the beginning. The person who acted as their observer came to be regarded as a member of the hospital family and was put to work for several years as a linguist's clerk.[81]

The courage and good manners of the Chinese did not dissolve Dr. Parker's dismay over their heathenism. Less fanatic in his utterances than Bridgman or Williams, he was, nevertheless, saddened by Chinese ignorance of Christianity, critical of the "priest of idolatry" (that is, a Buddhist), and contemptuous of "the idol's heart of stone" [82] (a reference to an often worshipped religious statue on his street). He was caught in a dichotomy of admiration and denunciation of things Chinese. The ultimate purpose of the hospital was to demonstrate to the Chinese the practical benevolence of Christianity by healing their sick and to create an opportunity for preaching and teaching the assembled patients the doctrines of Christianity. Parker postponed the distribution of tracts until the institution could become well known, not wanting Howqua to cancel the lease and make it impossible to procure another building.[83]

There were not enough hours in the day to allow the doctor more than marginal moments for evangelism, but he made a notable supplementary arrangement by attaching a well-known local convert, Liang A-fa, to the hospital as an evangelist, and allowing him to address the crowd of new patients on Monday just before they were admitted. Liang A-fa gave a tract or scripture to each and conducted a Sunday service at the hospital, as well. Lockhart's experience was that under such circumstances patients for the most part received the tracts with "attention and respect." [84] Given the segregation within Canton, and the general futility of mission activity theretofore, the sudden accessibility of literally thousands of grateful Chinese constituted a dramatic addition to mission endeavor. The Canton brethren were lyrical over the vistas which opened toward the future.

For Parker a role had emerged which was substantially different from the one he would have played had his practice been in New England. In Canton he was greeted with a more lavish gratitude; he had to transcend language and cultural barriers; he was a revolutionary in his medicine and therefore a subverter of the Chinese medical establishment. He practiced outside the law in a technical sense, since patients were not supposed to go to him. Although numerous patients could have paid handsomely, he received for his medical services no presents or fees from Chinese. He worked almost exclusively at his clinic, could not move about freely to visit patients because of the Canton restrictions, and tended to work on an assembly line basis. Finally, he regarded his patients as a captive audience with whom he could not only "communicate instrumentally" [85] as a Christian surgeon but to whom he could convey, as occasions permitted, the Word of God. It was very tempting to use the hospital for purposes of evangelization, and Dr. Parker had no doubts about the wisdom of doing so.[86] However, Parker's work load at the hospital so interfered with the duty of acquiring the language, a necessity for effective evangelism, that he wrote Anderson if the necessary physicians, apothecaries, and assistants for the hospital could be found he would be willing to diminish or even discontinue his practice in order to devote his complete attention to the "welfare of their souls." [87] Fortunately, Anderson took no such stand in that period.

Parker's untiring efforts at the hospital, both medical and evangelical, soon took their toll of his health. Although well during the first weeks of the hospital's existence,[88] he was overcome by exhaustion during the second quarter of the hospital's first year. Left without his Chinese assistant and then without the European who had taken the assistant's place, Parker was desperate for help and forced to turn away large crowds of patients just at a time when his fame had spread and increased numbers of patients were seeking admission. Even so, he was often at the hospital all day and sometimes in the night.[89] At the end of the second quarter, the need for repairs in the hospital gave him a chance to escape to Macao to replenish his energies.[90] Warmly received at the Gutzlaff home, he took great pleasure in the cordiality and attentiveness of new English acquaintances. He was twice invited to preach, once at services held at Sir George Robinson's, superintendent of trade and leader of the British community. Dr. Colledge showed a keen interest in Parker's new labors. Greatly refreshed, Parker was able to return to Canton at the end of May and reopen the hospital. But between the inevitable overwork and the hot, humid, Canton weather, which rusts instruments, mildews leather, and frays tempers, Parker was soon reporting a recurrent fear of fainting from exhaustion before leaving the hospital at night. "My spiritual health & strength have equally declined." [91] So went, with a frenzy of ups and downs, the strenuous first year of his hospital.

Remarkable as was this initial year of the Ophthalmic Hospital, Parker was not the first missionary to venture overseas, nor the first Western doctor to go, nor the first evangelist who was also trained as a doctor, nor even the first "medical missionary" (defined as the possessor of a medical degree who spends at least half of his time on medical work among the indigenous population).

Expressed positively, he was the fifth American Protestant to go as missionary to China, Bridgman, Abeel, Williams, and Stevens preceding him; he was the second resident American physician to practice in Canton, the nonmissionary Dr. James Bradford antici- pating him by some years; he was among the first eight appointed, Protestant evangelists who had medical degrees as well as theologi- cal degrees and who were sent out to various parts of the world to protect the health of their fellow American Board missionaries. The tally here is somewhat more complicated: John Scudder (1819ff.) and Nathan Ward (1833ff.) to Ceylon; Thomas Holman (1820), Abraham Blatchley (1823–1826), Gerrit P. Judd (1828ff.), Dwight Baldwin (1831ff.; no medical degree), and Alonzo Chapin (1832– 1835) to the Sandwich Islands; Asa Dodge (1833, died 1835) to Beirut.[92] He was also among the first three significant, full-time or nearly full-time physicians in the Protestant mission field (Judd, Baldwin, and Parker — Scudder not qualifying as full-time).

Among these possible founding fathers of Protestant medical missions, Scudder in Ceylon, Baldwin in the Sandwich Islands, and Parker in China appear to be the most important figures to consider. Because Judd seems to have practiced primarily among the scattered mission families, he is less important as a founder. Of the leading three, Scudder was chronologically the first by many years. Possessing a medical degree, evolving a practice among the indigenous inhabitants of his regions in Ceylon first and later India, and spending more than half time on their medical needs, he clearly qualifies as a "medical missionary." Baldwin lacked the medical degree and must have been largely self-trained, but he appears to qualify under the other parts of the term. Parker fitted all the requisites of the definition and, in distinction to Scudder, evolved a full-time medical practice among the local inhabitants.

What Scudder lacked in international renown, Dr. Parker fully enjoyed. Dr. Scudder was hidden away in areas unvisited or less visited by world shipping and treated with virtual silence by an embarrassed Board, unsympathetic to his maverick way of intermingling medical care and evangelism, whereas Dr. Parker opened his hospital in one of the most notorious port areas in the world and created an enormous publicity for his new type of career. The passivity of the Board was in Parker's case irrelevant, so successful was he in broadcasting news of his practice and evoking enthusiastic approval of it. Thus one can understand how Dr. Parker, by being timely, well located, and unafraid to dramatize his own activity, was able to do more than any other physician anywhere toward creating acceptance, approval, and support for the new profession of medical missions.

4 ◆ A Parcel of Shipwrecked Japanese Sailors

The Canton mission had probed eastward at various points along the Chinese coast as well as southward to Singapore, Malaya, and the islands by the end of 1836. In 1837 it had the extraordinary opportunity of trying its luck on the Japanese coast in a very precarious mission adventure which aimed at no less a goal than opening Japan. This was sixteen years before Commodore Perry's black ships arrived on a similar mission with guns run out and decks cleared for action.

Forbidden to outsiders, this coast was one of the most formidable in the entire Orient. Although the Japanese had as recently as the sixteenth century nurtured a restless and adventurous sailing tradition which sent shipping into distant arms and reaches of Far Eastern waters, her Tokugawa rulers, fearing foreign intercourse might develop into imperialism at the expense of Japan, had undertaken to seal off the home islands and their inhabitants from the cultural contagions and pressures of the outside world. Foreigners were expelled; Christian converts, persecuted; Japanese ships, confined to home waters; vessels of ocean-going design, destroyed; contacts with foreigners, rendered illegal; and Japanese sailors who had the ill-fortune to be carried by gales into foreign waters were henceforth regarded as outside the law and forbidden to return to Japan.

The Japanese authorities did make a significant exception in allowing the isolation to be punctured at one point. Fearing the matter-of-fact Dutch least, Tokugawa officialdom had permitted a tiny group of these traders to reside under conditions of harassment and constant surveillance on the edge of the Nagasaki waterfront, rather after the Canton pattern. Foreign contact was concentrated here.

The general system of exclusion, whatever its advantages and disadvantages, had been effectively enforced for two centuries up to the time when the ABC was looking with a gleam in its evangelical eye on the untouched, well-ordered, beckoning, heathen soil of Japan. The outside world, although vaguely familiar with the Japanese arrangements, was somewhat unsure about how firm their enforcement remained. The contemplated missionary voyage sought to probe some non-Nagasaki part of the Japanese carapace by returning to Japan seven Japanese sailors who had been shipwrecked in foreign waters. Their opportunity came when C. W. King, partner of Olyphant and Co., offered the *Morrison* for such a voyage.

Finding immediate support among friends in Canton and Macao, the decision was swiftly put into action. So that the expedition might take advantage of Japanese esteem for foreign medical and surgical skill, Peter Parker was asked to join it.[1] King decided to go himself, and decreed that the *Morrison*, under Captain D. Ingersoll, should be divested of all ship's armament. The pacific nature of the voyage was underlined by the inclusion of Mrs. King, whose readiness to go helped overcome her husband's initial reluctance. It was hoped that Gutzlaff, busy on an assignment as interpreter for a coastal voyage of HMS *Raleigh*, might join them in the Liu-ch'iu Islands. Williams was asked to go as naturalist. The vessel, with its "parcel of shipwrecked Japanese sailors," had a total of thirty-eight crew and passengers.[2] It was decided, to Gutzlaff's disappointment, to take no tracts. Few were available at that time, but, more important, members of the group decided that the voyage would do better to de-emphasize that aspect of its intentions. They did carry some documents, prepared by Bridgman and John Robert Morrison, which explained in Chinese the object of the trip, one giving the names and residences of the seven shipwrecked passengers with some details of their adventures; another presenting a short account of America and its commercial policy, with the reassurance that it possessed no colonies. Not wanting to overlook an honest dollar, they took along a small assortment of cotton and woolen fabrics to entice the Japanese into trading with them.[3]

Exhausted by overwork and still depressed by news of the unexpected death of Stevens while on a trip to Singapore, Parker was clearly in need of a release from his labors, but was in sufficiently poor shape to hesitate over undertaking a trip of this nature. A timid sailor after his wretched experience returning from Singapore a year and a half earlier, he was fearful of a voyage in the typhoon season. Knowing something of Japanese policy and proclivities, he also seems to have been very uneasy about the safety of the ship once it should reach Japanese waters. An agony of indecision roiled his peace of mind for some days, as he weighed the pro's and con's, and prayed for divine guidance. Once having decided to accompany the expedition, he took the precaution of drawing up his will before leaving with King for Macao.[4] He had provided himself with medicines, instruments, and a number of anatomical plates and paintings which he thought would command attention. He was also furnished with a document stating his profession and his willingness to practice gratuitously on all who had diseases.

As they descended the Pearl River, he had time to read "Capt. B. Hall's glowing account" of the Liu-ch'iu Islands and brood about what the expedition might encounter en route to Japan. When the *Morrison* sailed on July 3, Parker was apprehensive and dejected.[5] Light headwinds and cross currents (referred to as "chow chow" water in Parker's journal) tethered them within sight of Macao until mid-afternoon, July 4. Generally uneventful, sluggish sailing, punctuated with a single storm off Formosa, finally gave them their landfall in the Liu-ch'ius on Wednesday, July 12. By the end of the morning they were at anchor in the harbor of Naha, within view of crowds on the beach and some very striking limestone formations. Parker's mind was busy with dark ruminations on the moral condition of the inhabitants and with prayer for their deliverance from paganism.[6] At 3:00 P.M., twenty rather official-looking men came alongside. They could speak Chinese; and one, broken English. Parker produced his paintings of medical cases, whereupon some sat down and gazed at them with amazement.[7]

After dinner that evening when some of the travellers went ashore to test relations with the local inhabitants, they encountered generally good-humored behavior, spiced with special curiosity over Mrs. King, and the evident desire of local officials to have them return to the *Morrison*. When provisions were supplied them on the thirteenth with the information that a vessel resembling theirs, no doubt the *Raleigh*, had come and gone the day before, they decided to leave on the following day for Edo (Tokyo).

Parker, having loaned one of the islanders his copy of the tract by Dr. Pearson on vaccination, returned the next day to recover it, accompanied by Captain Ingersoll and armed with vaccine and lancets. He relates in some detail how he had given the tract, virus, and lancets to an old man who, he thought, was a physician. When the old man asked to be shown where to stick the lancet, Parker vaccinated him. "The assembly burst into a hearty laugh to see how the fox had been taken, & the old man perceiving his predicament enjoyed the joke equally with his countrymen." [8]

Parker's first impression as a doctor was surprise at the general healthy appearance of the Liu-ch'iuans, especially their eyes. He did spot a few cases of lippitude, entropion, leukoma, hypertrophy, and staphyloma; noted further some cutaneous diseases, scabies and ichthyosis, as well as bladder stone, smallpox, and syphilis. He was told that leprosy existed. Altogether he regretted that the stay was to be so brief. "Never have I seen an uncivilized people for whom I felt such a sympathy as for this people — & thrice happy will be the man who shall reside among them, & impart to them the blessings of the Gospel." [9]

Departing from Naha, now with the added presence of Gutzlaff, the *Morrison* had a slow passage of fourteen days to Edo Bay. On Friday, July 28, land was sighted at 4:30 A.M., but approach proved slow as they struggled against a headwind for sixty miles. The seven Japanese sat on the long boat or out on the bowsprit, eagerly watching the shore and bursting with delight, as they spotted familiar landmarks. By Saturday they could see Fuji in the distance.

As the *Morrison* moved slowly up the bay, they heard cannon and supposed this was a signal that a foreign vessel was approaching. Heavy fog and clouds preventing them from seeing the location of the guns, they continued up the harbor. When the weather cleared, they could see that from a fortification just south of Uraga cannon balls were still being fired and were falling into the water a mile or so from the vessel. Captain Ingersoll immediately made for land, four miles west and south of the fort, and cast anchor. The Japanese ceased firing when the sails were furled.

Fishing boats soon approached from all parts of the harbor and, finally overcoming their fears, men climbed aboard and crowded the deck. They were treated with sweet wine and other refreshments. Following requests for medical aid, Parker prescribed for a man with rheumatism and others with skin diseases. He also extracted a molar. A total of about fifty boats came during the afternoon. One craft with about twenty men took in sail and rowed around the *Morrison* but would not approach. They were thought to be spies from the fort. Cards were distributed to the more influential visitors requesting in Chinese — a few in Japanese — that an officer might come aboard. Wishing to communicate with someone in authority, they withheld information from their visitors, even to the extent of sending below the seven Japanese shipwrecked passengers. Saturday, after having been sufficiently successful for a first day of human contact, ended on a note of optimism and thanks: "Bless the Lord oh my soul & all that is within me — for this day's mercies." [10]

Sunday (July 31) began briskly on a different note: cannon which had been brought from the fort and planted on the shore opposite commenced firing as soon as it was light. Captain Ingersoll gave orders immediately to weigh anchor and hoist a white flag, but they fired faster than before. The balls whizzed fiercely about, falling a bit short of the ship, passing over it as well as through the rigging. One pierced two deck planks, glancing through the side of the long boat, and narrowly missed several men at the ropes and two of the Japanese passengers. A ball passed so close to the men working the windlass that they felt the wind of it distinctly. With the anchor up and the vessel under sail, they experienced a momentary panic when the Captain exclaimed, "We are becalmed!" It lasted only a moment. Soon all sails were full, & the shore rapidly receded.[11]

Indignant at the barbarism of the rebuff, King was unwilling to accept this answer as final and determined to try again at some port on the southern coast. After considering two ports and then rejecting them because of weather conditions, he resolved to sail for Satsuma and, as a last resort, to Nagasaki. Ten days later, on Thursday, August 10, at 3:00 A.M. they arrived off Kagoshima Bay and lay to until morning, when they sent off a gig with officers, crewmen, and two of the Japanese passengers, the latter immediately transferring to a local boat with the stated intent to go to the nearest village.[12] Waiting for the return of the two Japanese, which some doubted would occur, they moved up the bay until they were abreast of the village. At eight o'clock they saw people assembling on the beach and a boat load of men coming toward them with their two Japanese and a dignified, middle-aged individual with "sword & sabre" at his sides. He proved to be quite obliging and had brought a pilot to conduct them to a temporary anchorage until communication could be established with higher authorities. They learned that the area belonged to Satsuma, and that word had already been dispatched to Kagoshima. The official took King's dispatches, including those previously prepared for the Emperor and said a reply would be received in three days.

Friday, August 11, was a day of waiting. An officer visited them, displaying curiosity about the vessel. Water was brought to them, but the supervising officer would permit no one to go on board the *Morrison*. A fresh gale having rendered their anchorage unsafe, a pilot directed them to the inner harbor for the night.

Saturday morning their suspense was over. At 7:30 a fishing boat with half a dozen men came out and, from a distance, told the Japanese on board that the *Morrison* should put to sea. They said something about officials firing upon the vessel. Gutzlaff, who overheard the conversation, described it as a bluff, but Parker disagreed. Almost immediately activity was observed on the shore in the form of the erection of special portable forts of mail, recognized by the Japanese on board as "the accompaniments of war" and impermeable to cannon ball. The suggestion that what they saw was merely preparation for the arrival of an official somewhat diminished the fear of hostilities. But all doubts were soon dispelled when a troop of several hundred soldiers rushed to the shelter of one of the forts and commenced a promiscuous fire of musketry and artillery. The situation on the *Morrison* was critical. They were anchored in a small bay, had seventy-five fathoms of heavy chain cable to take in, and were nearly becalmed. What little wind existed was directly against their getting out. Finding themselves fired upon from several directions, unable to anchor or get away, nearly caught on a rocky shore, they somehow endured eighteen hours of hair-raising misadventure before miraculously escaping without injury.

The question of whether or not to make a third try, perhaps by going to Nagasaki, the usual spot for Japan's foreign contacts, must have been automatically answered by the reactions of the seven Japanese. The double repulse had been enormously disturbing to them, and they asserted to a man, that they would neither go to Nagasaki nor be put ashore. One of them later reversed himself and asked to be left on some neighboring island, but that apparently was not done.

The mental strain of the attack in the bay of Kagoshima produced in Dr. Parker, according to his own diagnosis, symptoms of arachnitis (inflammation of a delicate membrane covering the brain) which were aggravated by fear that they might try for Nagasaki. In that port, he felt, the same "spirit of extermination" would confront them, but be more efficiently realized. When it was decided the next day to sail for China, the symptoms were allayed.

The return voyage was blessedly uneventful and they reached Macao safely on August 29. So great had been the shock to Dr. Parker's nervous system that the foundations for a violent sickness had been laid. That autumn he descended into such bad health as to lead him secretly to long for death. Under the influence of a raging fever, all motivation for his career seemed to drain away, but upon recovering he resumed his accustomed duties with fresh delight — only to be saddened by the news of his mother's death.[13] Owing to wretchedly slow communications that information reached him nearly a year after the event.

A significant part of Dr. Parker's reactions to the double rebuffs on the voyage — at least if the account in his journal is given priority over the different, published version[14] — was substantially balanced and sane. Religiously radical in the sense of being a mission activist, Parker nevertheless was in this matter a political moderate,[15] forgiving the men who fired on them as tools of despots and rejoicing that no blood had been spilled. This was much to his credit because the second repulse, when the *Morrison* was under fire for so many hours, gave rise within him to wild, turbulent emotions. It is not possible to tell from the various, tidied-up accounts of the voyage to what extent he hid his inner turmoil from the others at the time, but his feelings are clear enough in the disclosures of his journal, where he wrote some of the most passionate prose of his entire life.

O Lord my God, I cried to thee, and thou hast healed me. O Lord thou hast brought up my soul from the grave; thou hast kept me alive that I should not go down to the pit. Sing to the Lord O ye Saints of his, & give thanks at the remembrance of his holiness. For his anger endureth but for a *moment;* in his favor is life; weeping may endure for a night, but joy cometh in the morning. . . . Like a drowning man I felt that my end might have come, but that if by any means God should effect my deliverance *all* that he should add to my life would be peculiarly his own.[16]

This final resolve he incorporated into an elaborate vow, rededicating himself to the service of God. With parts underlined and underlined again, the passage is so intimate as to embarrass the intruding reader.

A considerable ambivalence of motivation existed among all the notables on the trip. Oddly enough, each one was led during the voyage to Japan to disavow to some extent his real calling. King, the man of gain, claimed not to be going solely for pecuniary advantage; Williams and Gutzlaff, men of God, went respectively as naturalist and translator; and Parker suppressed his mission impulse to serve merely as a secular physician — and came back with a budding interest in what might be achieved through a career in diplomacy.

The fact of these multitalented men joining in a multipurpose trip suggests a fundamental mutuality of interests and beliefs within the group. Symbolized in their persons and through their multiple roles was the growing consensus within the society whose outriders they were — especially the Protestant concern with salvation and conversion, the acceptability of the entrepreneurial spirit, and the feeling that the flag had a right to go virtually anywhere. They were advocates of material progress, of Christianity as an automatic improvement, and of rational, eighteenth-century ways of reforming men, religions, and governments. An effective consensus, so symbolized, meant among other things that Parker was soon to be listened to in Washington, as one cannot imagine men of his calling being listened to today.

Demonstrable results of the voyage to Japan — in the sense of those events leading directly toward the opening of Japan to commerce and evangelism — were minimal. The journey did mark a microscopic beginning for Protestant evangelism there. The rebuffs by the Japanese government meant the return of the seven shipwrecked Japanese to Macao, where two remained with Gutzlaff and two worked in the ABC printing office. These four aided Gutzlaff and Williams with their language, so that the books of Genesis and Matthew, and the Gospel and Epistles of John, were translated into Japanese for the instruction of these Japanese expatriates. Rikimats, the youngest man, went to Nagasaki with Admiral Stirling in 1855 as his interpreter. According to Williams, he and Otosan, who lived at Shanghai, both demonstrated in their lives that the faith which they had professed was a living principle. For nearly two years five of the seven maintained daily prayers in Williams' house at Macao.[17] In sum, the expedition cast a modest pebble into the international millpond, and ripples were felt both in Edo and Washington. The trip clarified the situation for Westerners and performed its bit toward ultimately creating and shaping the Perry Mission of 1853–54.

5 ◆ The Institutionalization of Medical Missions

Peter Parker having brought in a medical gusher in 1835–36, he and others sought to relate it properly to mission activity and at the same time exploit it by adopting an institutional mechanism which would encourage and assist the expansion of this new and exciting mode of missionary activity in China. In October 1836, Colledge, Parker, and Bridgman issued a public statement in which they called for the founding of a society to raise money and assist newly arriving medical missionaries who would be sent out by English or American societies. "Those who engage in it must not receive any pecuniary *remuneration:* the work throughout must be, and appear to be, one of *disinterested benevolence.*"[1] In addition to the Ophthalmic Hospital already established, they wanted to encourage specialties in surgery, ear treatment, cutaneous affections, women's and children's diseases.

In terms of immediate response, not much happened. The year 1837 came and went, with Dr. Parker absorbed first in his hospital work and then by the trip to Japan and its aftermath. Early in that year he had answered an ABC cautionary letter by agreeing that in the event of more hospitals being opened "the danger should be guarded against of their becoming institutions for the relief of bodily evils merely, and not tributary to the good of the soul as they *ought* to be."[2] Finally, everything was ready for a public meeting called by Colledge, Parker, and Bridgman for February 21, 1838, in the rooms of the General Chamber of Commerce, at

Canton to establish "the Medical Missionary Society in China." Their stated motive in so doing was "to encourage the practice of medicine among the Chinese, to extend to them some of those benefits which science, patient investigation, and the ever-kindling light of discussion have conferred upon ourselves." [3] Fifteen or more men came. William Jardine was asked to take the chair, and the meeting briskly set to work to consider and adopt a constitution of eleven articles and eleven by-laws. The following officers were elected: President, Thomas R. Colledge; Vice-Presidents, Reverend Peter Parker, William Jardine, Robert Inglis, Alexander Anderson, G. Tradescant Lay, Reverend E. C. Bridgman; Recording Secretary, John Robert Morrison; Corresponding Secretary, Charles William King; Treasurer, Joseph Archer; and Auditor of Accounts, John C. Green.

No sooner was the Medical Missionary Society (MMS) formed to embody his idea than Dr. Colledge, who had not attended that initial meeting of the Medical Missionary Society, left China, never to return — and only with death in 1879 to relinquish a forty-one-year presidency of the Society. The swift changes in personnel on the China coast were also reflected in Jardine's departure the following year, Parker's absence during his trip home in 1840–1842, and J. Robert Morrison's premature death in 1843. Colledge's position as surgeon to the British factory was filled by Alexander Anderson, one of the Society's most energetic supporters, who had been in private practice in Canton and Macao and who remained in China until about 1845.[4]

Support for the Medical Missionary Society was essentially Anglo-American, there being but one Chinese (Howqua) and one Parsee (Framjee Pestonjee) listed among the subscribers in the 1836–1838 period. The group of officers was suitably diverse, including Englishmen, Americans, and a Parsee; traders who trafficked in opium and one who did not; a doctor-divine and two establishment surgeons; an editor-divine and an interpreter.

At a second meeting, April 24, 1838, the Society voted to request Dr. Parker to open and operate a hospital in Macao during the several months in 1838 when repairs and improvements were underway in his Canton hospital. Parker went down to Macao with his pupils, hospital coolies, porter, comprador, and even some current patients. On July 5, 1838, he opened this second hospital. The purchase of the building for $5000 and its preparation had been handled by Dr. Colledge before he left China.[5] According to Parker, the spacious rooms of this well-built brick structure could accommodate 200 patients.[6]

Patients were slower in Macao than in Canton to overcome their suspicions and take advantage of a new medical institution. Moreover, fewer important surgical cases presented themselves, but Dr. Parker was aided in reducing local diffidence by the arrival from Canton of some of his patients, of others who had been successfully treated and discharged, and of still others who were acquainted with his work. During his three months in Macao he treated 700 patients, diseases of the eye preponderating.[7] Committed to reopening the Canton hospital for the last quarter of 1838 and without a replacement at Macao, he was forced to close this newly opened establishment in October.

The Medical Missionary Society did not pretend to include in its membership all the early successors to Dr. Parker, some of whom arrived in the interval between the opening of Parker's first hospital and the founding of the Society. Three men fell into this category, all representatives of the American Board (and therefore indicating an early commitment to medical missions by that board). Primarily based on Singapore, they were men of short, truncated mission careers: James T. Dickinson, 1837–1840; M. B. Hope, 1837–1838; and Stephen Tracy, 1837–1839.

Dyer Ball, who worked with them briefly, was in a different category by virtue of the length of his mission career and his later affiliation with the MMS. After taking graduate work in theology at both Yale and Andover and an M.D. degree from a medical institution in Charleston, he arrived in Singapore in 1838. He worked in Macao in 1841–1843, where he probably assisted in the Society's hospital, then moved to Hong Kong (1843–1845) to work in the new MMS hospital there, and finally to Canton (1845–1854, 1856–1866).[8] His tie with the Society was apparently not established until he began to work in Macao in 1841, and he was not, therefore, the first doctor after Peter Parker to be formally sponsored by the Medical Missionary Society.

Advance information had meanwhile reached Macao in August 1838, that "a medical gentleman of experience" was then on his way out from England under appointment to the London Missionary Society. The rumor proved correct, and Dr. William Lockhart arrived early in 1839. Born in Liverpool, he had taken his medical training at Guy's Hospital in London. He remained only briefly at Macao, and was soon at the American Hong in Canton, a guest of Dr. Parker. Planning to associate himself with the Medical Missionary Society, he also hoped to remain some weeks in Canton to familiarize himself with Dr. Parker's hospital routines. Only when that had been accomplished did he expect to return to Macao, accept a very few patients, and devote himself chiefly to language study. Meanwhile he reported to London very favorably on Parker's work.[9]

Despite the opium crisis blowing wide open in March, Dr. Lockhart went ahead with such parts of his plan as seemed feasible. Disregarding the urgency of full-time language work, he reopened the Macao hospital on July 1, 1839, thereby becoming the first doctor to begin his work assisted by the MMS. Lockhart's arrangement with the Society specified that there would be no interference with his instructions from the London Missionary Society; that the MMS would supply him a hospital and residence; and pay for his hospital servants, medicines, and instruments, while the London Missionary Society would pay his personal expenses. Lockhart expressed some fear of the arrangements working out differently because MMS funds might dry up during the heat of the war crisis.[10]

This first working arrangement between the MMS and a newly arrived doctor showed very clearly the invaluable type of reciprocal assistance which might be evolved, but the arrangement was almost immediately postponed when Lockhart was forced by the authorities to close the hospital on August 13, 1839, and join the exodus of the English from Macao as the opium crisis deepened. He left for Batavia to continue his study of Chinese under the supervision of

W. H. Medhurst of the London Missionary Society, a study which would have been seriously inhibited by the irresistible pressure of hospital duties in Macao. Able to return in the following June, he helped reopen the hospital on August 1, 1840.[11]

Dr. Lockhart turned out to be an excellent person for the Medical Misionary Society to have among its associates. During parts of 1840–41, he followed the British forces onto Chusan at the mouth of Hangchow Bay;[12] he assisted again at the Macao hospital which Parker had established; supervised the building of a new MMS establishment in Hong Kong (1842–43); returned to Chusan; and then went into the new treaty port of Shanghai in 1844 to found yet another hospital. He was the first mission doctor to settle in Peking, where he founded the hospital which later became the nucleus for Peking Union Medical College, the elite medical school of twentieth-century China. His example and his writing were both very influential. All in all, he built, as did his friend, Peter Parker, one of the great nineteenth-century careers in medical missions.

Parker and Lockhart were soon joined in the MMS by Dr. William Beck Diver, sent by the American Board.[13] Arriving in September 1839, shortly after Lockhart's departure, he was the victim of such poor health that, although a participant with Lockhart in the reopening in 1840 of the Macao hospital, he was soon forced to leave for home. An eighth mission doctor, Benjamin Hobson (1816–1873) had the health which Diver so seriously lacked and managed to sustain the work in Macao before pressing on to a remarkable career in other Chinese cities as a pioneering medical missionary.[14] A graduate in medicine from University College, London, he was accepted by the London Missionary Society and dispatched to Macao, where he proved to be the mainstay of the second reopening (1840) of the Medical Missionary Society hospital. He initiated similar work in Hong Kong, but was forced by the ill-health of his wife to return to England, Mrs. Hobson dying during the voyage. Dr. Hobson returned to Hong Kong where he married the daughter of Dr. Morrison, moved to Canton (1847) not far from Parker, and settled into a busy and difficult medical practice, later moving to Shanghai. Completing his China career in 1859, he returned to England. During his two decades of service in the Orient, he treated a vast number of patients, trained young Chinese doctors, and wrote a series of influential, illustrated works in Chinese.

The eight medical missionaries down to and including Benjamin Hobson were supplemented by six others within the first decade of medical missions following the opening of Dr. Parker's hospital. The six men were: James C. Hepburn (Singapore, 1841–1842, Amoy, 1843–1845[?]; later to Japan); William Henry Cumming, Amoy, 1842–1847, not connected with any mission board and therefore not officially recognized by the MMS, although mentioned in their reports; Daniel J. Macgowan (Hong Kong, Chusan, Ningpo, 1843–1859; later in private practice, China); D. Bethune McCartee (Ningpo, 1844–1862, Chefoo, 1862–1865, Ningpo, 1865–1872, Japan, 1872–1881); T. T. Devan (Hong Kong, Canton, 1844–1847); Andrew [?] P. Happer (Macao, Canton, 1844–1851[?], 1859–1862[?]).[15]

At least half of these fourteen pioneer medical missionaries had mission careers of five years or less, while five had relatively long careers of nineteen years or more. Most of them were affiliated with the MMS. Dickinson, Hope, and Tracy were not, since they had arrived in the field before the founding of the MMS. By the time the Society had begun its operations, each of the three was already established in medical work at a considerable distance from the MMS base in Canton and therefore somewhat out of touch with that situation. Moreover each was in the process of being divorced from his mission career by health problems. The fourteen were bi-national (partly British, mostly American), tri-denominational (Congregational, Presbyterian, Baptist), and miscellaneous in their professional training. It is noteworthy that the Anglo-American cooperation which was central to the MMS played a similar role in the formation of two other mission enterprises of that era, both well known to Dr. Parker — the Morrison Education Society and the Society for the Diffusion of Useful Knowledge among the Chinese.

One of the basic questions, wrestled with by Parker and others, concerned how desirable it was for doctor and divine to be united in the same person. Dr. John Scudder, long antedating the discussion of this dilemma in the 1830's and 1840's, was for decades a living example of someone somehow maintaining both careers, though it is impossible to determine from the available evidence whether his medical work suffered because of the demands of evangelism. Dr. Colledge was one who felt strongly that the all-absorbing duties of an active doctor left too little time to devote to any regular form of religious instruction. Moreover, the profession of medicine was replete with responsibility and required unremitting attention. Dr. Parker seemed to him a rare exception, not normally to be imitated. It was better to avoid the risk of injuring the medical missionary cause, which could easily happen at the hands of a missionary who pretended to a knowledge and skill in medicine which he did not possess.[16] There was ready support for Colledge's position from Bridgman,[17] Dwight Baldwin, and William Lockhart, himself the prototype of the full-time, nonministerial physician.[18] Lockhart argued the case with great force, urging that in every case the medical missionary be a layman.[19] The Jesuit evangelists, with their smattering of medicine, had represented the opposite end of the spectrum.

Peter Parker represented a blend of Scudder's art of combination, with its fairly heavy emphasis on evangelism, and Colledge's insistence on separation, with full-time performance as a doctor. In effect, Parker committed himself to the theory of the former and the practice of the latter. A stubborn man, believing in medical missionaries with both theological and medical degrees, he stuck with this construct throughout his life. It pleased him to receive ardent backing at the other end of the earth from Sir Henry Halford, president of the Royal College of Physicians and prominent member of the English medical establishment of that period.[20]

In the long run the tendency of medical missionaries has been to settle more in the Colledge-Lockhart position, but the question of who was "right" has never been finally resolved. Despite their differences over how best to utilize the medical opportunity, they all appear to have believed that, "no earthly, temporal enjoyment should be put in competition with the redemption of the soul and its eternal felicity." [21] The points at issue were merely disagreement within the guild.

A larger problem remained, however: that of persuading a public in the West, and especially the mission board establishment, of the propriety of medical missions. It was no trivial matter to evolve a persuasive philosophy in dealing with the theologically minded bureaucrats at home. Colledge, Parker, and Lockhart all played significant roles in this drama, powerfully assisted by others.[22] They based their case fundamentally on scripture and access to potential converts. To them it seemed especially significant that before the Sermon on the Mount Jesus went about Galilee, taught in the synagogues, and healed all manner of sickness. After the Sermon, he first healed a leper, then the Centurion's palsied servant and Peter's mother-in-law. In the evening he treated many that were possessed with devils, casting out the spirits with his word. Later he sent his disciples out not merely to preach, but to "heal the sick, cleanse the lepers, and raise the dead!" For Lockhart the conclusions to be drawn were self-evident: "To the various missionary boards, whose co-operation is sought, we would respectfully say, 'Imitate Him whose Gospel you desire to send to every land.' " [23]

The appropriateness of medical missions in terms of scriptural precedent was reinforced by their practical success. They opened a way to the Chinese who were otherwise inaccessible. This point needs no further proof here beyond Dr. Parker's breakthrough, but the matter of access did have to be demonstrated in that period to church audiences who were unfamiliar with Parker's triumph. Lockhart believed that in opening a new station where foreigners had not previously resided it was important speedily to win the confidence of the people. No technique had been found more likely to effect this than the opening of a dispensary and a hospital. He spoke from repeated experience, having opened hospitals in several cities in the course of his twenty-odd years in the Orient and attended over 200,000 patients in them.[24]

Access opened up corollary advantages which were less readily apparent. These were eloquently described by G. T. Lay at the November 29, 1838, meeting of the MMS, just before his departure for England.[25] He found that in the unique relationship of a physician to his patient much was revealed of the Chinese mind and character, just as missions enabled the Chinese to become better acquainted with westerners. "We have societies for giving the Bible, the Gospel, useful knowledge, and so on, to the world, — we will also have a society for giving the benefits of rational medicine to the world. Humanity shall be taught to flow in new channels, and to wear names and designations unused before."

Access also created the opportunity for a philanthropy with both physical and spiritual facets. In much of the literature dealing with the rationale of medical missions runs a concern with the dualism of body and soul and the need to minister to both simultaneously through science and religion. To Peter Parker there was a wisdom in the wholeness of the medical missionary approach, which fitted nicely within his overall conception of medical missions as a device "to liberate man from physical, mental, and moral vassalage, and to disseminate the blessings of science and Christianity all over the globe." [26]

6 ◆ Opium and the
Approach of War

For the foreigner, life in China has always demanded constant adaptability. In Dr. Parker's case the great medical expansion of 1835–1838 had required that he accommodate himself to the Chinese scene, to its exhilarations, health hazards, and exhaustions; that he fit in with the curious, alienated culture of the Canton factories; and that he relate himself effectively to the demands and corollaries of a new mode of evangelism. In addition, 1839–40 exacted adjustments to the outbreak of a Sino-English commercial war and the resulting gross disarray of the foreign settlement on the Canton waterfront.

As previously noted, Sino-barbarian difficulties had long existed. The closed society of China had for many decades confined and isolated the westerner, badgered him with the threat of an alien jurisdiction, and subjected him to the chafing tribute relationship. Outsiders had, for their part, compounded the intrinsic difficulties of that situation by developing the narcotics traffic to a point where, in the 1830's, opium was entrenched as one of the key commodities in China's foreign trade.

The reason for this dismal development was essentially simple. When Portuguese, Dutch, and British merchants had begun trading with China in the seventeenth century, they had been powerfully attracted by the luxury items of the China market — silks, porcelains, and tantalizing teas of extraordinary variety and subtlety. Coveting all of these items and at the same time lacking commodities which the Chinese wanted, the foreign traders had increasingly turned to transporting Indian and Near Eastern opium to China. By the late 1830's the hong merchants were importing annually over 30,000 chests of opium, each weighing substantially more than 100 pounds and with a total worth of about $15,000,000.

The smoking of opium, although habit-forming and possessing manifold disadvantages, is at least one of the less dangerous forms of drug indulgence. If the user stays close to the level of intake to which his system has become accustomed and smokes opium of good quality, he may encounter few ill-effects. He gains a sense of adequacy and well-being which enable him to cope with the day's problems. With slight oversmoking, he experiences great clarity of mind, elevation of spirits, deep composure in the face of difficulties, the certainty that he can perform superbly well. The lassitude and inactivity which accompany this general elevation of spirit mean, in actuality, that the smoker's problems remain unsolved, his scholarship unfulfilled, and his poems unwritten.

Even with discreet involvement and good intentions, the number of "mouths" (roasted smoking-pellets) a smoker needs do mount year by year, and he ultimately cannot avoid very considerable losses of time, money, and energy, which are disastrous for the family of a smoker without ample resources. Moreover oversmoking is tempting, and deep addiction may lead to the most wretched results, repeatedly witnessed by Parker. Delay an addict's smoking and he will begin to yawn conspicuously and his eyes to water, as his spirits rapidly descend into distraction and bewilderment. Withhold the drug and he suffers unspeakable torment. To avoid these calamities a smoker may find himself reduced to irresponsibility, with no face, no honor, no concern for family. From a civic point of view, the smoker is vulnerable and unproductive. His demand for opium can readily serve as the basis for rackets, corruption, and smuggling — which is precisely what happened in China, especially in the population centers of the southeast, where the drug created its first beachhead on the Chinese mainland. The Manchu establishment, not immune to the outreach of the drug, came to have its share of smokers in the land tax and salt offices, the Yellow River Conservancy, and the Manchu banners.

Disquieting as all this was, there were pressures and reasons for Peking to follow a generally apathetic opium policy. Opium smokers in the mid-thirties probably did not total more than 10,000,000 (out of the census total of over 400,000,000 for 1834), most of the former in the south and southeast at a great distance from the capital.[1] Moreoever, addicts in the imperial bodyguard and among the eunuchs of the Forbidden City made their influence felt in maintaining a flow of the drug. In addition the court desired revenue from the Canton traffic and was involved in the appointment every three years of a new Hoppo to oversee the activities of the security merchants in Canton. At such a time bribes must have brightened palace lives like festival fireworks. In Canton, foreign traders of great resourcefulness were involved in the trade, bringing energy and expertise to the task of maintaining and enlarging the traffic.

Opium, jurisdiction, the frustrations of confinement, and corruption were all Cantonese problems which had been satisfactorily and even successfully handled for decades on a muddling-through basis. The situation which had grown up around them had never appeared to be particularly menacing. However, newer elements in the mid and late 1830's were upsetting the older accommodation.

In 1834 the British discontinued the East India Company's monopoly among British traders in the opium traffic between Bengal and South China, removing the Company as intermediary for British subjects and Chinese authorities and thrusting the British government forward into that role. The British created the new office of "Chief Superintendent of the Trade of British Subjects in China," and supplied the incumbent with a small squadron to add to the persuasiveness of his orders to secure equal relations with the Chinese authorities. Thus they made a critical shift in policy from one of accommodation with China's antique type of international relationship, based on inequality, to a pursuit of the purely Western goal of establishing a treaty relationship between theoretical equals. To the Chinese the superintendent of 1839, Captain Charles Elliot, seemed a complete anomaly. Not fully an official and not accused by the Chinese of being a smuggler, his principal job, nevertheless, appeared to them to be the protection of smugglers.

Accompanying these changes and resulting from the increased opium traffic was a developing economic crisis over the outflow of silver to pay for the opium. By 1836 an elaborate inquiry into the opium problem was underway in Peking, with the possibility that, since silver would flow out so long as opium was smuggled, opium might be allowed in on a barter basis and taxed as a medicine. The Tao-kuang Emperor himself took an active part. In the summer of 1838 he received from Governor-general Lin Tse-hsü of Hunan and Hupeh an outline of successful steps already taken by Lin himself against opium trade at the provincial level. The emperor summoned him to the capitol and armed him, as Imperial High Commissioner, with almost unique powers for cutting a way through the Cantonese opium thickets. It is clear that Lin possessed remarkable abilities, was broadly experienced in many parts and problems of the empire, although not yet in Canton, and generally represented the best in the old order. He established his headquarters on March 10 within half a mile of Dr. Parker's hospital. After studying the situation for just over a week, the new commissioner began a series of energetic moves aimed at wiping out the narcotics traffic. He ordered the surrender of opium, ordered foreigners to give bond to stop future importation of opium, and threatened the hong merchants with execution, if they were obstructionist. Lin came to view the opium smugglers as connected with Chinese shopkeepers in the tangle of alleys near the factories, the shops being used as fronts. All trade was temporarily stopped, and on March 21 Chinese troops were moved up close to the factory area, scarcely a minute's march from Peter Parker's residence.

Lin might have made a distinction immediately between the firms that handled opium and the ones which did not, and then allowed the latter to continue trading. Dr. Parker's friends, Olyphant and King, headed such a company and could appropriately have been so rewarded, but Lin — all for quick solutions — neither made nor acted upon such a distinction. When the foreigners were slow to conform with his demands, he stopped all loading and unloading; withdrew Chinese boatmen, compradors, and servants from the service of foreigners; and threatened the permanent end of trade.[2] Doors and street entrances on the north side of the hongs were bricked up by the Chinese, and a triple arc of boats was set up on the river before the factories. Captain Elliot, who had earlier gone down to Macao, managed to get back through this cordon at some risk to himself and settled into the role of one of the principal antagonists of Commissioner Lin, although he did cooperate by ordering the British opium handed over to Lin. It comprised some 20,000 chests.

The fortunes of the Ophthalmic Hospital in 1839 were very closely related to the deterioration of Chinese relations with the English. Full and very busy during the winter of 1838–39, the hospital was "never so prosperous" as on the eve of the March opium crisis.[3] However, with the general clamping down on the foreign community in the latter part of March and the bricking-up of the street ends, that part of the Fung-tae Hong which had for some years been available for Parker's medical work was firmly shut.[4] Repeated requests from many sources for reopening the hospital were invariably rejected in 1839 by the senior hong merchant. The latter did, however, tolerate Parker's limited use of the abandoned dispensary of Doctors Coxe and Anderson, both of whom had withdrawn to Macao.[5] On a diminished basis Parker was able to continue a useful practice. There were clandestine attempts by various officers, officials, and some females to secure treatment by the American doctor. Even a member of the august Board of Rites, citadel of ancient orthodoxies, sought him out.[6] Moreover, Parker received private assurances of the high esteem in which he was held by the Chinese authorities.[7] It was of decisive importance that Commissioner Lin was relatively well disposed toward Parker's medical work and even a quasi patient of his. Parker did lose his medical students at the height of the trouble, but they were later allowed by the authorities to return. On several occasions he took pains to conceal all his Chinese books when searches were being pressed by suspicious officials.

The diminution of his medical practice left Parker in the singular position of having free time in which to rest and indulge himself.

The Canton factories in 1839. The foreign hongs were blockaded by Commissioner Lin from late March to early May during the opium crisis. Artist unknown. *M 4806, courtesy of Peabody Museum, Salem.*

While he was enjoying his involuntary leisure, Commissioner Lin was fitfully busy with problems which were accumulating. In Lin's view, Jardine and Dent were essentially clever villains; Westerners on Chinese soil should be subject to Manchu law; strictly speaking, foreign opium smugglers were liable to the death penalty but by a special act of grace were only being asked to hand over their opium and sign guarantees not to reintroduce it. A complicating factor was that Lin, despite the extravagant powers which had been given him, had to adjust his policies to ill-advised orders from Peking. One such command specified that all the opium be destroyed publicly, even though it must have been evident that the success of prohibition logically rested on smokers tapering off, a process which would require a large supply of the drug. Lin unquestioningly carried out the destruction. He did pray for the region's marine life before the polluting residues were drained into the river. The property loss through confiscation and destruction was immense.

Despite circumstances thus skidding toward tragedy, there were persistent casual aspects, a kind of leisurely desperation, all beautifully suggested in Arthur Waley's *The Opium War through Chinese Eyes.* One observes Lin writing poems, reading the *Peking Gazette* avidly for news of the imperial examinations, resorting to calligraphy to calm himself when beset by hay fever during days of great tension, and visiting the locally renowned Temple of the Five Genii to study its inscriptions. The more serious side of his activities included preparation for the defense of Canton, conferences with Admiral Kuan, constant exchanges with Captain Elliot, and a steady flow of reports to Peking. The bond which Lin had demanded in March, itself a comic product of pidgin English captioned "A Truly and Willing Bond," [8] had caused a great deal of friction. Over fifty barbarian ships' captains did sign such guarantees during the latter half of 1839 and many respected their bonds for several years. With almost no Britishers signing, however, Lin finally stopped all British trade and the situation slipped another notch. When Lin notified the British in May that exit passes would be issued, Elliot ordered a withdrawal to Macao.

Early in July while Lin was trying to disentangle the newly

arrived skein of opium regulations from Peking, an extremely unfortunate homicidal brawl took place in Kowloon between Chinese and an Anglo-American group of sailors, probably drunken. One Lin Wei-hsi, injured in the fight, died the following day. Despite prompt investigation, Elliot was unable to fix responsibility. His decision to fine five men and send them home for short prison sentences (not upheld by the government when they arrived in England) was unacceptable to Lin, who demanded that the murderer be handed over. A scapegoat would have been satisfactory according to Chinese practices of group responsibility. Elliot's refusal to comply provoked the Commissioner into removing the servants from English households in Macao, threatening and finally cutting off food supplies, and exerting pressure through Portuguese governor Pinto on the British adversaries. The murder of Lin Wei-hsi proved a difficult and disastrous case, leading ultimately to an unsuccessful Chinese attempt (four junks sunk) to seize the accused seamen, and to the August removal of British personnel from Macao to Hong Kong. Although this shift gave them sanctuary, it meant that they remained dependent upon foodstuffs from mainland China. Lin's hope to cut off those sources of food led to another small naval encounter, again with disparate casualties.

Nevertheless, the pace of escalation remained leisurely, and the commissioner even had some modest victories. He learned in mid-October that Captain Warner of the *Thomas Coutts* in defiance of Elliot's orders had asked to sign the agreement and secure clearance for the Bogue and Canton. By the end of the month a second British ship, the *Royal Saxon*, had signed the guarantee. Despite these refreshing gains, his mistakes accumulated relentlessly. Having threatened in a September 28, 1839, note to "annihilate the English," he repeated the menace one month later, declaring then that men and ships were ready. On November 2, 1839, the English moved their twenty-eight-gun frigates, *Volage* and *Hyacinth*, to Ch'uen-pi on the east side of the Bogue, only eight miles from a big fleet of Chinese war junks. Next day Captain Smith of the *Volage*, attempting to prevent the *Royal Saxon* from entering the Bogue in defiance of Elliot's strategy, fired across her bow. When elements of the Chinese fleet moved up to protect the errant British vessel, the *Volage* opened fire. Although the Chinese and English accounts vary widely, one can be sure that in the ensuing engagement the two English frigates routed the Chinese fleet. Lin did not report the battle carefully to Peking, although this was clearly something that required accurate analysis and reporting. Viewed from the China end, the Battle of Ch'uen-pi (November 3, 1839) appears to have begun a new phase, the crisis never having been irretrievable up to then.

Actually, the British decision to send out an expeditionary force to blockade Canton had already been taken. Parker's friend, William Jardine, having arrived in England in September, had soon placed the recommendation before Foreign Secretary Palmerston with the result that the latter was writing to Superintendent Elliot on October 18 that an expeditionary force would be sent out to blockade Canton. In effect a decision for war had been made by Palmerston, Jardine, Elliot, and a few others without informing Parliament and with scant reference to the British public.[9]

In June, July, and August, 1839, in the midst of this deterioration of Sino-British relations, Peter Parker had several oblique connections with Commissioner Lin, beginning at a meeting on June 10, 1839, with three of his emissaries. Among other things they dwelt on the subject of geography, chiefly as the result of the curiosity of one of the Chinese.[10] When Dr. Parker offered to place at the disposal of Lin an atlas, geography, and globe, the reaction of that representative was to raise points of protocol: Dr. Parker would have to couple his offer with a petition, a requirement which Parker thought absurd. The obligation, he felt, was not on his side.[11] The offer was subsequently accepted with the assurance that the commissioner would write the doctor and send him a passport so they might get together. Lin was at that time downriver at the Bogue.

Parker's interview with Lin's representatives led to Howqua's agitated intervention. He implored Parker — if he should in the future be granted an interview with the commissioner — to limit his comments to medicine or politically harmless subjects like foreign customs: "*trade* you not understand. Opium ships you not understand." Howqua, despite his contempt for Lin, may have maneuvered successfully to prevent Parker from seeing the commissioner, because the imminent interview seems not to have taken place. Six weeks later we learn from Parker's journal that Lin's subsequent requests were being channelled through Howqua to the doctor.

Two requests of that period sought from Dr. Parker "a prescription for curing all opium smokers" and advice regarding treatment for a hernia.[12] Parker sent an account of the effects of opium on the human system and the principles for treating it; Lin later expressed the hope that Parker could supply him with a "*specific* for opium smokers," [13] "a prescription that would answer for all opium victims irrespective of age & sex and the various other diseases with which it might be complicated." [14] He was once again informed that there was no available medicine which was capable of effecting a quick cure and that the sole hope was the imprecise and complicated method of gradual withdrawal through reduction of intake, a process requiring anywhere from two months to two years.[15]

Parker sent explanations of the hernia condition pointing out that he possessed an instrument by which it could be benefitted, but that he had to fit it to the patient. To this Lin postponed replying.[16] The commissioner ultimately became Dr. Parker's patient number 6565, but only by proxy. To avoid medical intimacies, he initially used as substitutes an official and the senior hong merchant. Later, possibly in mid-September 1839, two men from Lin's staff appeared at the hospital for treatment: one for hernia, the other for a cutaneous facial infection. Parker's servants were convinced they feigned illness in order to spy, but the doctor accepted the reality of their complaints and outfitted one with a truss. Later yet two more men from Lin's staff appeared, one of them the commissioner's younger brother, who claimed that a truss fitting him would certainly fit his sibling. The brother, in order to assure a good fit on the stout commissioner, was entrusted with all of the doctor's trusses, a half dozen or so, none of which was ever returned.[17]

In July 1839, Commissioner Lin asked Parker through intermediaries to translate into Chinese certain passages from Emeric de Vattel, *Law of Nations*, a standard international law handbook widely used by European diplomatists. Lin's interest was focused on certain passages relating "to war, and its accompanying hostile measures, as blockades, embargoes, etc." [18] Parker's journal for August 23, 1839, shows him at work on this task; [19] his September 5 letter to Anderson refers to daily language study with his tutor and to their having "recently translated" the passages. [20] The latter dealt with the right of a state to exclude foreign merchandise, to confiscate smuggled goods, and to wage war. Immanuel Hsü's comparison of an English version of Vattel (orginally published in French) with Parker's paraphrased Chinese translation shows the American to have been somewhat unsuccessful in conveying the lucidity of Vattel. [21] Lin, whether troubled by perceived ambiguities or merely acting out of caution, had one of his interpreters translate the same three sections along with a fourth. [22]

Through the June interviews with Lin's emissaries Parker had become a participant, although probably a marginal one, in Lin's celebrated writing of homiletics to Queen Victoria. These took the form of two basic letters, each passing through several modifications. [23] The first, drafted in the March-April period early in the opium crisis, was circulated in Canton, the imperial commissioner vainly hoping that some ship's captain would agree to convey it to the queen. Dr. Parker appears to have been familiar with this first version, some of the substance of which was discussed at his first meeting with Lin's representatives. Then in the July–August period the commissioner wrote a second version of the letter to Queen Victoria and sent it to Peking for approval. Containing an appeal on moral grounds for help in suppressing the opium trade, its chief purpose was to publicize the new Chinese statute which provided the death penalty in cases involving foreign merchants who were found guilty of importing opium into China. A court interpreter having rendered it into English, Lin so suspected the product that he had it translated back into Chinese to see what resemblance might exist between the double translation and the original. He then through Howqua asked Parker to translate the original into English. Parker's reaction to it was somewhat mixed: "It contained some arguments against the Opium trade which are irrefutable, and much nonsense and insult. It will do no good, I fear, unless it shall be the opening of a correspondence which may result in a better understanding of each other's views and wishes." [24] The commissioner did in this case find someone to take the letter to England, Captain Warner of the *Thomas Coutts,* but the Foreign Office refused to receive it, presumably in retaliation for Warner's having defied Elliot and signed the bond against future importation of opium into China.[25]

Whatever influence Dr. Parker may have had on Lin's letters, he was unconnected with the evolution of Palmerston's toughened policy, although the latter was clearly shaped by William Jardine. After Palmerston's choice in October 1839 of an aggressive policy, an expeditionary force was assembled and ultimately dispatched. For the Emperor of China Palmerston drew up a letter in which he demanded that China pay for the confiscated opium, grant equality in relations, and place an island at the disposal of British shipping.

While the documents embodying this British war policy were tossing about on their briny trip to China, Parker, still in Canton, carried on a private practice and then was permitted to reopen his hospital. The number of patients was again limited only by his ability to receive them. Because of the formalities involved, he found especially burdensome the ever-increasing roster of patients who were holders of high office.[26]

In this first half of 1840 little took place on the surface to mar the relations of the two countries. There were no further bloody encounters; the British expeditionary force had not arrived; British merchants were busy trading, using the Americans as intermediaries to transship goods to them; and there was precious little to suggest that the existing state of nonwar dead-lock should or would be transformed overnight, without intervening provocation or escalation, into a state of war by the mere arrival in June of a particular diplomatic bag containing paper, ink, and sealing wax.

June, though, witnessed the arrival off Macao of the main body of the British expeditionary force. A blockade of Canton was declared, and the war formally began. Peter Parker's hospital was again ordered closed and the doctor, after calling on Howqua and other hong merchants to say goodbye, left for Macao, intending to take an early ship home.[27]

The imperial commissioner still behaved with the penetration of a duckling listening to thunder. When the British fleet put to sea, June 24–25, on its way east and north up the coast, Lin rejoiced, completely missed the point and misinformed Peking about what could be expected.[28] Before the capital received his optimistic report, the British had landed in the Chusan island group off Hangchow Bay. Palmerston's letter to the emperor, delivered up north in August 1840, by one of the English vessels, was read and its demands rejected. With Peking boiling over at the letter, Lin was soon scalded. The Manchu proclivity for government-by-scapegoat was indulged now at the expense of the commissioner, and he learned in October that he had been cashiered. The emperor supported Lin's tough line right up to August 8, 1840, and then suddenly switched to caution toward the British and soon to denunciation of Lin.[29] So quick was the apparent shift that it almost seemed that the emperor went to bed pro-Lin and woke up anti-. The torpid processes of the Middle Kingdom meant that in actuality the former commissioner would remain for some time in Canton: although first ordered to Peking for trial, he was shortly placed under investigation by his successor and told that he should remain there in an advisory capacity. In January 1841 the British forces stepped up their pressure on the Pearl River by attacking and taking the forts at Shakok and Taikok, and destroying the Chinese fleet which guarded the Bogue.

The period of this conflict was clearly, and importantly, transitional in international affairs. In the microcosm of Dr. Parker's career it served more as a hiatus. The First Opium War brought to an end the major period of creativeness in his mission career. The years 1835–1838 had witnessed the opening of his hospital; his breakthrough in Sino-barbarian relations; the height of his impact, reputation, and popularity; his participation in the attempt to "open" Japan; the creation of the remarkable, bi-national Medical Missionary Society; and pioneering the profession of medical missionary. The 1839–40 period had a different quality and thrust. It interrupted the major phase, saw Parker's departure for home, and provided a transition to what happened there. Both periods were interesting and each had its set of demands and strains, but the later one was more transitional than substantive.

With his hospital closed, his health in need of attention, and probably with some unconfessed dreams of finding a bride, Dr. Parker had plenty of reasons for wishing to return to the United States. When the ABC had given its approval of home leave, he was able to take up the generous suggestion of R. B. Forbes that they return together on the *Niantic,* sailing from Macao July 5, 1840.[30] Robert Bennet Forbes was close to Parker's age and the two appear to have been China friends for many years from the late 1830's on. The *Niantic,* Captain L. F. Doty, had a crew of twenty and carried only a handful of passengers, one of them being a Captain Jauncey, invalided and entrusted to Parker's care.

Early on, half the crew was sick, and the captain close to death. "What should I have done without Dr. Parker?" asked Forbes of his diary.[31] Luckily, during the period of greatest disability, they were blessed with good weather and ample sea room in addition to the skilled medical care of Dr. Parker. So fortunate did Forbes find this combination that he was moved to attribute it, quite uncharacteristically, to "the protection of divine Providence." [32] Also, Captain Doty began to regain his health.

As the voyage continued, dragging its weary length through apparently endless weeks, it exposed unsavory nooks and crannies of character and temperament. Forbes' remarks about the other men became shrill. "Parker is full of the *milk* of human kindness though this sometimes curdles a little & wants skimming & boiling over — he is very much wanting in good manners for a man who has been in Canton 6 years — & had the advantage of good Society so long. For example, he eats always with his knife & half the time with the edge, sometimes uses his fingers to blow his nose, and *gulps* at table — he is a great coward and whenever the wind or weather is at all threatning he sleeps but little & asks a thousand silly questions." [33] Forbes also indulged in some gentle baiting of the doctor on the subject of matrimony.[34]

Forbes' blast against Parker's table manners tells something through its implications. The four-tyne fork was the incoming mark of sophisticated table setting in East Coast America, spreading unevenly as Eastern teachers and ministers went west. The older system of eating was to use a two-tyne or sometimes three-tyne steel fork, rather like the kitchen forks of today. The two-tynes were too sharp to eat with, and too far apart as well, so farm folk were apt to use the fork to hold meat as they cut with a steel knife. Then the items were piled onto the knife and the dull side of the knife put to the mouth. This older process, requiring a certain art and dexterity with knife-borne peas, had come to be regarded in many quarters of eastern New England as evidence of boorishness.

Although Forbes laughed at Parker's cowardice at sea, he would have quickly admitted that the latter was no coward as a physician and surgeon. Moreover, Parker had gone to Japan on that hazardous mission in 1837, a decision requiring a good deal of spunk of anyone, and even more from someone possessing his anxieties about ocean travel. There had been already, and there continued to be, occasional periods on his travels when the wrath of the sea would have frightened most people, and those times must have been very disturbing for him.

It is surprising that the confinement of the voyage did not produce bright explosions of anger among Doty, Parker, and Forbes, but it never did. Each must have acted repeatedly with essential restraint, the last week of the voyage squeezing their patience unmercifully. On Thursday, December 3, when they thought the *Niantic* was not over eighty miles from Sandy Hook, a cold northeast gale came up, forcing them to stand away from the land. When the wind subsided, their landfall proved to be Barnegat, forty miles off course. They were all disappointed, and the doctor turned in despairingly. They had a "last" good meal — and then another storm. This gale, also from the northeast, continued from Friday to Sunday while they lay to, drifting to leeward under very short sail. On Sunday, the wind shifted to the south, then southwest, then west, then northwest, and again erupted into a gale. By Tuesday, December 7, they finally took on the pilot who handed Forbes a letter with: "All's well, wife, Boy, Mother & all as when the Panama left, Teas high here & in

Europe." In the last line of his journal Forbes exulted: "the happiest hour of my life . . . Flora [the cat] is glad too."

One of the least attractive entries in Parker's generally unpleasing journal of the same voyage occurs near the end when the *Niantic*'s proximity to Sandy Hook filled them all with effervescent excitement. Parker's apparent sharing in this entirely human effusion led him to write: "I have been grieved to think that I should indulge so much as I have in the common feeling, not maintaining the gravity and seriousness of deportment which adorn the sacred office. This my weakness & sin I have humbly confessed before him who is able to keep me from falling again." [35] He was a prototype displaying some of the unsmiling attributes of nineteenth-century missionaries, this curiously dour, unfunctional sobriety helping to explain his lack of a sense of proportion, as well as the absence of a sense of humor.

7 ◆ Washington, Marriage, and London

Peter Parker's return to the United States in December 1840, six and a half years after a solemn departure with intimations of expendability and finality, resembled a reprieve. His sense of relief resulted in a release of energy, which he directed at once toward friends, travel, and propaganda. Stopping at the Astor House in New York as the guest of J. C. Green, merchant and friend from China, Parker was promptly taken by his host to tailor and shoemaker and newly outfitted. His week in New York was crammed with invitations and effusive encounters with other China friends. A New Yorker who had been treated successfully by Dr. Parker for a dangerous illness in Singapore in 1835 called on him and expressed his profound gratitude for that care. There were many small indications of the way his fame had preceded him and of the way he was going to be lionized by Americans for months. Asked to appear at the Tabernacle Church before a large congregation, he was chagrined to find that he spoke poorly. Only three days off the *Niantic*, he undoubtedly was still groping for a readjustment to America. His culture shock must have been accompanied and compounded by nervousness over the new role of itinerant propagandist. Failure or not, this first venture was followed by dozens of invitations to speak in numerous cities up and down the Atlantic seaboard. He was also cheered by the receipt of an appreciative letter and a donation of $300 from Captain Jauncey, his recent fellow passenger and patient, and on the same day a check for $500 from N. L. & G. Griswold, owners of the *Niantic*.[1]

The message that he proclaimed to his audiences underscored the urgency of evangelization, the duty and privilege of the missionary, the great medical needs in China, the appropriateness of medical missions as a way of overcoming hauteur and suspicion and of gaining the confidence of the Chinese, the specifics of dramatic surgical treatments, and the special role which American diplomacy might play in China. In a number of ways, this message embraced advanced thinking for the early 1840's in the several fields of theology, church history, medicine, and international relations. In that sense it was radically up-to-date.

Leaving New York, Parker spent several days of happy reunion with faculty friends in New Haven, where in Center Church he addressed a meeting so crowded that members of the congregation virtually joined him in the pulpit. Stopping over in Hartford just long enough to speak, sleep, and catch the public coach at seven the next morning, he was by suppertime enjoying a tearful return to the Framingham homestead, with sisters, cousins, and in-laws there to greet him. Neighbors and friends crowded in on subsequent days, much curiosity being evinced over the presence of Chin Sing,[2] his Chinese teacher. He spent much of Christmas Day in a series of interviews at the American Board building, seeing among others Rufus Anderson and Dr. Asahel Grant, who had done pioneering work in medical missions in Persia.[3] The Prudential Committee, he was told, did not object to his plan to go on a publicizing trip to England. After a few more days in Framingham he was off and away on his busy American schedule. Recognized in the public coach, he was invited by a Mr. Ellice to visit the Worcester Lunatic Asylum of about 250 inmates, where he found, to his surprise, "much more happiness" than he could have anticipated in such an establishment.[4] The presence of Dr. Parker's Chinese teacher again diverted bystanders and patients; one of the latter created astonishment by addressing Chin Sing as "Hsien-sheng," the formal courtesy-title in Mandarin for a scholar. After another overnight pause in Hartford, he was back in New Haven, staying first with the Reverend Leonard Bacon and his wife and several days later with the Edward Salisburys for about two weeks. At Yale Parker also had very happy renewals of friendship with Professors Silliman, Fitch, Goodrich, and Gibbs; he greatly enjoyed attending prayer meetings and services, speaking to groups of clergy and students, and talking with new and old friends. The end of these New Haven visits found him at the home of his friend, President Day, a witty and highly intelligent host.

Encouraged by New Haven friends to place at the disposal of federal officials his knowledge and suggestions concerning American relations with China, Parker left for Washington, accompanied by Leonard Bacon. Within a few days he had met there the Spanish, French, Austrian, and Russian ministers and a series of distinguished Americans, among them Henry Clay and John Quincy Adams. The latter, then a member of the House of Representatives, was one of the overflow audience on January 24, which listened to Dr. Parker's missionary sermon on Acts 14:26–27 ("and thence sailed to Antioch from whence they had been recommended to the grace of God for the work which they had fulfilled. And when they were come, and had gathered the church together, they rehearsed all that God had done with them, and how he had opened the door of faith unto the Gentiles").[5] He was offered as a pulpit for the following Sabbath the hall of the House itself, where he enjoyed the glory of preaching — as he described it — to "one of the Most Enlightened audiences of any age or nation, the Senate and House of Representatives." [6] Ex-president Adams and other prominent figures were present, and Parker rejoiced in the feeling that he had spoken well.

When he and Leonard Bacon called upon outgoing President Van Buren and Secretary of State Forsyth, hoping to discuss China, these officials recommended that their visitors approach President-elect Harrison and Daniel Webster of the incoming administration. On January 22 Parker was granted an opportunity to expound his ideas on China to Webster who listened with apparent interest, asking him to formulate his suggestions in writing, and adding that a "strong force would be sent to their seas." [7] Just over a week later Parker left with Webster his written proposals, which argued that the current Opium War between

Manchu China and Great Britain made advisable the sending without delay of an American minister plenipotentiary to China.[8] If the proper man were chosen, he might help the belligerents find a formula embodying a peaceful solution, the saving of face, the cessation of the opium traffic, and the restoration of trade. Despite some Chinese professions to the contrary, Parker believed that there was a desire, both strong and widespread, to continue the foreign trade. To allow the war itself to continue was to risk strengthening a government faction which sought the cutting off of all of China's foreign intercourse and her seclusion from the outside world. Parker argued the advantages to American foreign trade, and the (presumed) moral benefits to the Chinese from their continued contacts with Americans, if only those contacts could be regularized. To achieve that end he believed an American minister had a certain initial advantage because the Chinese knew that the United States sought no colonies and that American merchants participated less than the English in the opium traffic, some not at all. If a minister were sent, Parker felt it was important that he be of top calibre and of an age to match that of the elderly Tao-kuang Emperor, then in his sixtieth year. (Parker mistakenly wrote seventieth.) Parker's preferred candidate was John Quincy Adams, for whom the mission could be an appropriate climax to a long career of great public service. These suggestions were ultimately realized in the mission to China of Caleb Cushing, one of whose preparatory documents was this letter from Parker to Daniel Webster of January 30, 1841.[9] By it Parker established himself as one of the early designers of treaty relations between the United States and China.

Like a colorful thread in the warp of Parker's travel and propagandizing, his introduction to Harriet Webster in Washington emerged into a bright pattern of calling and courtship. They seem to have met during an evening call by Peter Parker at the home of Dr. Harvey Lindsly on January 23.[10] Aged 22, Harriet was good-looking, amiable, pious, and interested in missionary activities. She came from Augusta, Maine, but had been living in Washington at the home of her uncle and aunt, Dr. and Mrs.

Thomas Sewall. Sewall was professor of anatomy and physiology at
the Columbian University, Washington. Harriet and Daniel Webster mutually, but mistakenly, regarded themselves as cousins.[11]

Having met Parker, fifteen years her senior, soon after his arrival
in Washington, Harriet saw him a few times in January before he
left for speaking engagements in various cities and then once early
in February as he interrupted that tour to call on her. She soon
found events rushing toward a climax when he returned on the
twenty-third and was invited to stay with the Harvey Lindslys. He
had himself recently taken a day in New York City for fasting and
prayer in order to decide whether to propose.[12] Having then written
her some form of intimation or inquiry, he was handed an
encouraging written reply when they first met again in Washington.[13] By this time the relatives were a-buzz, variously supporting,
and drawing back from, a marriage which would snatch up a girl
from Maine and drop her on the other side of the globe. When he
formally proposed, on February 25, 1841, she promptly accepted.
On the following day, he sought and received approval from her
uncle. During the next several weeks the two were together much of
the time, sightseeing, calling on friends, and apparently thinking of
an early marriage.

Parker attended the inauguration of William Henry Harrison
and with Sewall called on the elderly president shortly before his
death. Parker discovered him eager to discuss America's relations
with China and prepared to bring the subject before the cabinet.
On the same day Parker spent three-quarters of an hour with John
Quincy Adams, who took a lively interest in American ties to
China, but believed that nothing could be done that year toward
sending out a diplomatic mission.[14] In this same period Dr. Parker
performed his only operation on American soil of which we have
explicit evidence. His patient was "John Kennedy Esq." and the
operation was for cataract.[15]

A short intense set of engagements required travel with his
Chinese teacher to Philadelphia, New York, and New Brunswick
(N.J.). Return precipitated the decision to marry without further
delay, despite the fact that the groom would soon leave on a
projected trip to London, and the further fact that the American

Board had withheld permission for him to take along his bride. They were married in the parlor of the Harvey Lindsly home at eight o'clock in the evening on March 29, 1841,[16] with Harriet's younger sister Priscilla as bridesmaid and the editor of Washington's *Madisonian*, Thomas Allen, as best man. Thus began what Harriet later acknowledged, after many vicissitudes, to have been "a happy union of nearly 47 years."[17] After a day of receiving visitors, they left for Philadelphia where friends held a big reception for them. A host of friends called on them during stops in New York and New Haven, and Harriet quickly experienced what it was going to be like to be married to a public figure with a passion for evangelism, medical missions, and public policy. During her wedding trip she had to share her husband with dozens of friends, aquaintances, and speaking engagements. She may sometimes have felt that she was stuffed into the crevices of a business trip, as Parker was called upon to preach in New Haven, Springfield, and Framingham. In Boston it was much the same. They stayed at the home of Rufus Choate, a relative by marriage of Harriet's, and Dr. Parker preached in the Essex Street Church, the Bowdoin Street Church, and the Park Street Church; visited the Massachusetts General Hospital, Eye Infirmary, the Perkins Institute, and other benevolent institutions. On April 14, he spoke before a heavily attended, special meeting of the elite Medical Association of Boston.[18] The blend of description, piety, and surgery in his talk must have struck just the right note, because the association adopted a series of flattering resolutions, established a committe with special responsibilities for medical missions, and invited men of property to note and assist this medical work in China. The resulting support was more generous here than in any other city outside of Canton itself.

Parker's energy, good humor, technical skill, piety, optimism, confidence, daring, dedication, and acceptance of America's social norms and political establishment, all made him an attractive and practically irresistible symbol at that moment to his contemporaries. Their reception of his message also says a good deal about them. Whereas the very idea of missions had been repugnant to Americans of an earlier generation, missions were now widely acceptable, and medical missions were highly regarded as a legitimate and exciting subcategory.

That one week in Boston burned away like morning mist. Harriet was shortly seeing her spouse off on the *Acadia* on Saturday, April 17, bound for Nova Scotia and an unpredictable reception in England, one of the belligerants in the Opium War. Parker reached England in early May 1841, while Harriet went off on a protracted visit to her parents in Augusta. Before him lay an enviable, and partly desolate, eight weeks in London, with another four given over to a side trip to Paris and brief visits in several Scottish and English cities.

During part of his London sojourn he stayed at the home of the Reverend Andrew Reed, who had been present at his ordination and had more recently served as editor of Parker's journal dealing with the voyage to Japan. On May 16 Parker preached in Wycliffe Chapel and attended St. Paul's, where he was stirred by the realization that here had preached such great churchmen as Cranmer, Wycliffe, and Latimer.[19] He met many other ministers in London among them Dr. Joseph Fletcher of Stepney Meeting, who invited him to preach on the twenty-first at this largest and richest of London Nonconformist churches.[20]

Immensely eager to establish ties with like-minded people, he soon called at the London Missionary Society, bearing a letter of introduction from his LMS friends in Macao—Lockhart, Milne, and Hobson.[21] This visit put him in touch with Arthur Tidman, the Congregational minister who was the society's foreign secretary. Invited to attend the annual meetings of the Society, Dr. Parker visited several sessions.[22] He was probably invited to meet with the Society's Eastern Committee since he reported to Boston that he had had the opportunity of presenting information on medical missions to the LMS directors. They were free and frank in their inquiries and sympathetic to his work.[23]

But Parker was in Great Britain chiefly as publicist and money-raiser and in his energetic attentiveness to duty he began a series of calls on men who might proffer financial support. He visited the Marquis of Lansdowne, prominent parliamentary figure, a former member of Lord Grey's great reform cabinet, and a participant in certain liberal causes. Parker was cordially received, talked about China at some length, and left a copy of his newly printed pamphlet on medical missions.[24] The American Minister, Andrew Stevenson, was repeatedly attentive to Dr. Parker, among other things taking him to call on the Duke of Sussex, who received Parker very warmly. The Duke thought £25,000 could be raised for Parker's work. Promising to take up the matter with the Earl of Fitzwilliam and some wealthy Quakers, he invited Parker to dine with him at Kensington Palace so that the American might meet a number of prominent dinner guests.[25] Parker also received verbal support from the Bishop of London, with whom he had a very pleasant interview. The Bishop declared that the cause Dr. Parker had adopted in China was scriptural and indeed sanctioned by the blessed Savior and his apostles. Nevertheless, as for his own promotion of the cause, he could not "act in concert with independents." [26] Notwithstanding these various supportive hands, it became increasingly evident that the sanguine Duke had badly misjudged the fund-raising possibilities. England was after all at war with China. Moreover, the recent bank failure in the United States had meant heavy losses for British investors and bad repute for Americans.

Financial difficulties, the separation from his bride, and the enormous drain of nervous energy which active travel involves are all possible explanations for the frequent periods of depressed self-obsession which dogged Parker in London. In a typical journal entry he recorded that he "labored under a most painful stage of nervous prostration and discouragement till past noon." [27] Despite the depressions, and helping to hold them at bay, a pleasant trip to Liverpool was undertaken in mid-June. Hospitably received at William Lockhart's home, he attended Sunday morning service and in the evening preached to an attentive audience. One day he was taken by Dr. John Sutherland to visit the Liverpool Medical Institution, then under construction. He visited Birmingham, Coventry, and the ruins of Kenilworth and Warwick castles before travelling by train back to London, where cheering letters from home awaited him.[28]

The most satisfying general contact which Parker made in

London was with a number of members of the medical profession. It is noteworthy that a youngish American doctor who ordinarily would have had no claim upon the time and attention of the English medical great had through his work in Canton, widely publicized by ships' personnel, created an international reputation which gave a ready entry into select medical circles. His chief initial link was with Sir Henry Halford, long-time president of the Royal College of Physicians, who had in a public address spoken favorably of medical missions at a time (1838) when they were especially in need of support.[29] Sir Henry, an eminently successful London doctor, had attended George IV, William IV, and Queen Victoria. This courtly septuagenarian and the young American doctor seem to have enjoyed each other markedly. On Parker's behalf Sir Henry spoke to the Archbishop of Canterbury, the Duke of Wellington, Sir Robert Peel (soon to be prime minister), the Princess Sophia, and the Bishops of Durham and London.[30]

Partly through the contact with Halford, Parker met many other members of the English medical establishment, among them Sir James Clark,[31] a widely traveled Scot, who attended the royal family; William Chambers, physician to St. George's Hospital, London, and to the royal family; Benjamin Travers, eye surgeon and future president of the Royal College of Surgeons; John Forbes, physician to the Queen's household and editor of the *British and Foreign Medical Review*; George James Guthrie, founder and chief surgeon of the Royal Westminster Ophthalmic Hospital, president of the Royal College of Surgeons and author of works on gunshot wounds and on the eye; and Robert Liston, a surgeon renowned for his speed and dexterity. Parker was invited to breakfast at the home of the celebrated surgeon Sir Benjamin Brodie, of St. George's Hospital, an important researcher in physiology as well as surgeon to the royal family. Brodie seems to have given scant time to Parker,[32] who saw more of Astley Paston Cooper[33] and C. Aston Key, both of whom Parker watched operate for stone upon three patients with skill and success.[34]

Parker had been introduced by his friend and part-time host, Andrew Reed, to Dr. Key, and had found in him a cordial supporter of medical missions.[35] With Key he experienced a

moment of glory. Upon the occasion of his first visit to Guy's
Hospital on June 1, having arrived too late to watch an operation
for lithotomy and having met Dr. Key and others, he went with
them to look at the medical displays. "Found a collection of my
patients in the Museum. Copies of the original. But no one
suspected they had been operated upon. I as a stranger asked who
operated. 'Not operated upon etc . . . ' was the reply. 'Yes, they
have, all of them & with success,' I informed them. Much interest
was expressed in learning the history of the etc." [36]

The cordiality of medical men continued when Dr. Parker visited
France in the latter part of June. There, on June 23 Dr. Henry
Jacob Bigelow of Boston took Parker to watch two operations and
also introduced him to Dr. Pierre Charles Alexandre Louis, famous
for his work on typhoid and for his introduction of a statistical
emphasis in medical research. Dr. Louis received him cordially and
expressed approval of Parker's "plan of reaching the soul through
the body." [37] Visiting another hospital next day, Parker and
Bigelow followed a doctor on rounds, attended his lecture, and
watched him operate. "The extractions he performed admirably,
but at couching he was most unfortunate and unskillful, [and]
probably destroyed one or more of the eyes he operated upon." [38]
On the twenty-sixth they visited yet another hospital, where they
saw a distinguished doctor operate "with great skill & modera-
tion." [39] Within the next two days he had bought medical
instruments, admired the equipment at the Orthopedic Institute at
Passy, attended a meeting of the Royal Institute, and made on
Sunday the twenty-seventh a public statement of the objectives and
accomplishments of the Medical Missionary Society. This opportunity was granted him by the Reverend Mark Wilks at the American
Church.[40]

On June 28 he learned from the American Minister, General
Lewis Cass, that King Louis Philippe would receive him in
audience. Court dress was not necessary, but he did need white
cravat, black shoes and stockings. The next evening, accompanied
by the minister, he was presented to the king, the queen, and to
Madame Adelaide, Duchess of Orleans and sister to the king. In
Dr. Parker's letter to his wife that night, he wrote that after his

presentation the king had asked him several questions about China and later sought him out for further brief conversation. At the end of the evening Louis Philippe expressed his wish to see him again, but Parker's plans for departing the following day for England made that impossible.[41]

Back in England early in July, he had an exceedingly pleasant jaunt to Cambridge, where he was cordially received by Dr. John Haviland, Regius Professor of Physic. On his return to London he found a letter from Dr. Colledge containing £70, an unexpected and very moving gift to Parker, then in straitened circumstances. On July 15, 1841, a meeting was convened in Exeter Hall, on behalf of the Medical Missionary Society, with one of Parker's friends in the chair, Sir George Robinson, former superintendent of British trade for Macao and Canton. An invited audience containing many ministers and doctors heard Parker's address dealing with Chinese medicine and his own work in the Orient.[42] After the talk four supportive resolutions were carried unanimously, the first being moved by none other than William Jardine and seconded by the celebrated Dr. Thomas Hodgkin of the University of London.

Parker set off on a swift orbiting of several of the northern cities of the United Kingdom. On July 26 at the Waterloo Hotel in Edinburgh, he addressed prominent academicians, clergy, bankers, merchants, and doctors. The meeting established a large, distinguished committee to cooperate with the Medical Missionary Society in China, placing on it Dr. John Abercrombie, a renowned researcher, William P. Alison, professor of the Practice of Physic at the University of Edinburgh, Professor James Syme, prominent surgeon, and — as treasurer — John Thompson, president of the Royal Bank of Scotland. These were in effect the first steps toward the formation of a noted organization: the Edinburgh Medical Missionary Society. Similar meetings were convened on the twenty-eighth at Carrick's Royal Hotel in Glasgow and on August 2 and 3 in Liverpool. He made a special point of referring to the work in China of Drs. Pearson and Lockhart, both from Liverpool. Each meeting established a committee to raise money and keep alive local interest in his work.[43]

Early August saw him back on board ship headed for his bride.[44]

By September 8 he was in Philadelphia at the Annual Meeting of
the American Board,[45] after which he went to Washington, where
he had another presidential encounter. Harriet's uncle, Dr. Sewall,
took Parker off for an interview with John Tyler,[46] who had
unexpectedly assumed the presidency in April after Harrison's fatal
illness. Although Parker found the new president "exceedingly
affable" in manner and in his inquiries not only about the doctor's
medical practice in China but concerning his recent trip and the
Chinese war, it was clear that nothing had been done about
sending a mission to China. The president apparently felt himself
in a weak position relative to the Congress. When they left the
White House, Sewall took Parker to call informally at Daniel
Webster's chambers, where they had an hour's pleasant conversation.[47] Parker's visits to both these men probably added a timely,
extra push toward the ultimate creation of a diplomatic mission to
the Orient. This president and this secretary of state were the ones
to propose to Congress in the following year that a mission be sent
to China.

In the autumn of 1841 the Parkers visited in New Haven while he
reworked his publicity pamphlet, *Statements Respecting Hospitals in
China*, for publication in Glasgow. They finally settled into rented
rooms of their own in Philadelphia. Although that city could not
match the excitement of London, it was certainly a leading
American medical center and a good spot for the Parkers as an
interim residence while they waited out the Opium War. Their way
was smoothed by an introduction from Dr. Sewall to one of
America's leading medical researchers and editors, Dr. Isaac Hays,
the inventor of a special knife for cataract operations.[48] Displaying
his usual propensity for meeting the most interesting doctors of his
era, Parker now made the acquaintance of the leading Philadelphia
doctor, Nathaniel Chapman, author of a widely used text and
professor at the University of Pennsylvania Medical School. For a
refresher course Parker attended medical lectures at either the
University or Jefferson Medical College.[49] It would be interesting
to know of the interaction between him and the lecturers, since he
had undoubtedly had more clinical experience than they in many
types of cases. His own medical attainments were acknowledged by

his election in February 1842 as an associate fellow of the College of Physicians of Philadelphia. He was, as well, very active as evangelist and public speaker on China and medical missions.

One of the advantages of the sluggish communications of Dr. Parker's era was that he could devote himself to the problems of mission publicity and the delights of matrimonial felicity and remain unaware of the doleful developments of 1841 in Canton. There in March, the month when he was married, the British steamer *Nemesis* under Captain W. H. Hall explored a forbidden, western-channel approach to Canton. This action prefaced the approach in May of the seventy-four-gun *Blenheim* to the south side of Honam Island within four miles of Canton, and its bombardment of the city, that event itself a prelude to an assault by 2000 British troops. An oddity of the war was that such a small force, short of supplies and beset by illness, could nevertheless seize the walls of one of the great cities of the world and extort a $6 million "ransom" before withdrawing. The following month when British troops were on the river, Dr. Hobson made an attempt to reopen the Canton Hospital, but the senior hong merchant refused permission for the use of the building.[50]

Early in May (when Parker was just arriving in London) Commissioner Lin was in receipt of orders concerning his own departure from Kwangtung. With Lin out of the way and the war having shifted east and north along the coast, the British in 1842 moved a small expeditionary force up the Yangtze, seized Chinkiang, strategically sensitive because it lay at the juncture of the Grand Canal and the Yangtze, and proceeded upstream to Nanking. This daring penetration of the interior by naval vessels — unfortunately followed by opium ships — resulted in effective negotiations with the Manchu authorities and the signing in August 1842 of the Treaty of Nanking, which ultimately proved to be the nineteenth century's most important treaty anywhere in the world.

By its deceptively simple terms China agreed to abandon the Co-hong system, open five treaty ports, set fair and regular duties, cede Hong Kong, pay an indemnity of $21 million ($12 million for the cost of war, $3 million for outstanding debts, $6 million for the confiscated opium), and accept part of the Western code of diplomatic equality. With these new general arrangements in effect, new regulations were needed for such practical matters as official papers, measurage, pilots, security, debts, treaty limits, and the status of Hong Kong. Arrangements were successfully negotiated in 1843.

Opium, the ostensible cause of the war, was unmentioned in the treaty of 1842, nor could the British negotiator get the Manchus to accept a formal opium clause in 1843. The Chinese would not legalize it and the British would not agree to suppress it. The one British captain who did act in suppressing it was recalled, Captain Charles Hope of the *Vixen*. Sir Henry Pottinger, acting for Britain, secured an agreed *process*, whereby opium could not go into treaty ports but could be held at certain anchorages out of sight. There, although illegal, it would not be confiscated. This procedure remained in effect for fifteen years.

The treaty arrangements of 1842–43 could not at once overthrow all older practices and substitute new ones, but they did set in motion a train of forces drawing the Middle Kingdom in a new direction. A burgeoning free trade ran counter to the older mercantilist tradition of China and to Chinese assumptions regarding the relative triviality of foreign trade. Increasing penetration by the foreigner of Chinese cities and their environs meant a swelling influx of Western ideas and practices in education, banking, science, politics, military and naval affairs, commerce and industry. But most of all the Treaty of Nanking signaled the beginning of China's eventual abandonment of her indigenous, international system of tribute relations in favor of a grudging half-acceptance of Western treaty relations based on the European assumptions of 1648 and their subsequent elaboration. Upon the Treaty of Nanking was soon built an inverted pyramid of treaties artfully utilizing the devices of extraterritoriality, most favored nation, and the attritive tactics of several active nations.

Manchu obtuseness was remarkable and persistent: even after 1842 one finds self-congratulations over the fact that, despite defeat, they had lost only the bare rock of Hong Kong. Such blindness was matched by foreign myopia concerning the magnitude of the shift which the British were foisting on the Chinese. The kowtow had seemed an obnoxious ritual of essential triviality in Western eyes, but its abandonment shook the Chinese way of life. The emperor himself was expected to kowtow, although — like the Lowells and the Cabots — only to God. To relax this principle was to lose the *Tao*. Multiply the distress which grew out of this single change by the total alterations which were thrust on the nineteenth-century Chinese, and one gets an alarming glimpse into the magnitude of the composite unease and alienation for the Chinese as the century unfolded and a glimpse into the appalling nature and relentlessness of much of the foreign influence.

Parker may have had an authoritative preview in 1841 of the terms of the Treaty of Nanking because of his London encounter with his friend and former medical assistant, William Jardine, potent and effective lobbyist for the East Asian opium establishment. Jardine's communications to Palmerston in the autumn of 1839 had given the Foreign Office its guidelines toward the ultimate treaty terms of 1842.

Some weeks before the actual negotiation of those provisions, Dr. and Mrs. Parker, gambling on the termination of the war, left Boston via the *Mary Ellen*, Captain Henry, on June 13, 1842. They were the only passengers. Each voyage has a quality of its own, this one being shaped by the presence of Harriet Parker, the loss of a sailor overboard, several cases of smallpox, and the grounding of their vessel on a bar in Javanese waters.[51] This last crisis, during which Harriet displayed a cool presence of mind, ended with the freeing of the ship and the successful resumption of the voyage. His wife's composure would particularly impress a man like Parker, so apt himself to become quite unraveled in dangerous situations at sea.

When the Parkers arrived in China after this trip out, the Cantonese situation had changed from one in which a bland good-humor predominated into one taut with tension. Henceforth the whole Protestant experience in China was to be colored by its existing parallel to the unequal treaties with their gunboat and treaty-port base and to the growing Sino-Manchu weakness which made possible the unequal treaties. By late 1842 in five prominent Chinese cities, Canton among them, the missionary could theoretically "select his residence, erect his chapel, open wide his mouth, and scatter freely both Bibles and tracts." [52] In actual fact the Canton scene was in many respects harder to work in than before. Whereas one used to be able to count on a prevailing Cantonese hostility to the Manchus, a marked hardening of sentiment toward the foreigner followed the May 1841 campaign, when English troops raped and looted in the villages north of Canton.[53] The treaty at the end of the war did nothing to mitigate this newer form of Cantonese xenophobia.

At first, when Dr. Parker returned to Canton in late 1842, he left Mrs. Parker in Macao. He reopened his hospital in the building where it had commenced seven years earlier, but this time Howqua renovated the building without cost to Parker and charged no rent.[54] Having reestablished himself at Canton, he brought Harriet up from Macao, arriving on November 5 very early in the morning—"consequence no mob," as recorded with relief by the American merchant Edward Delano.[55] She thereby became, so far as we know, the first Western woman to take up residence in China proper, and the circumstances of this phase of her life are therefore of special interest. Some Western women had preceded Harriet Parker to Canton for short times, but she was the first to reside there on a relatively permanent basis. Unhappily, one gets only tantalizing glimpses into her early weeks in Canton or, indeed, into any part of her life. Delano called on Mrs. Parker once or twice a week when she was in Canton, or when they were both in Macao, and he repeatedly referred to her as "very pretty & amiable," "Mrs. Parker — at home & agreeable," "his pretty wife," and "as comely as ever." [56] Her youth placed her much closer to his age than Parker's, and her presence in that citadel of masculinity on the Canton waterfront seems to have enlivened Delano's free time.

Harriet was forced to leave after a month in Canton because of riot, fire, and looting by Chinese in the factory area; her presence in Canton was possibly one of the causes. Despite his obvious enjoyment of her company, Delano was concerned lest Parker bring her back too soon for her own safety. When she did return, soldiers still occupied the foot of Old China Street, next to the American Hong.[57] On a later occasion "the selfish old doctor" received in Delano's diary a sharp, peevish blast for removing Harriet from Macao, whither Delano had gone.[58]

In the absence of surviving letters or diaries,[59] there is precious little to go on with regard to her state of mind during those weeks of pioneering residence in Canton. It is clear that she had some poor health, since Delano refers to her leaving the city in February for this reason.[60] It is also clear that she had had to endure unusual confinement, even for Canton. Owing to the miserable, tense relations then prevailing with some of the local citizenry, she was imprisoned in an unhomelike structure, taking her outings on the roof in the evening and generally going without the company of her husband whose hospital work swamped him in the way it had in the thirties. As a young and pretty wife, she had to cope with wretched circumstances, to which one should add her husband's rough edges and probably rather domineering ways. "Her spirits and health are not good," reported Dr. Hobson in the following year.[61]

Whether this young wife was happy or not, the period of 1841–42 had been of great importance in her life, as for her husband and for China. Dr. Parker, since his departure in 1840, had been drawn into public orbit, just when China was being pushed into the Western type of treaty relations.

8 ◆ The Caleb Cushing Interlude

Peter Parker's suggestion in early 1841 that an American diplomatic mission be sent to China was communicated by him before his own return to China to three presidents, one ex-president, two secretaries of state, and miscellaneous dignitaries and bystanders.[1] It was taken up by various public figures, among them Caleb Cushing, a Massachusetts lawyer, who expounded it to his friend President Tyler in December 1842, just after news of the Treaty of Nanking had reached Washington. At the urging of Webster, President Tyler asked Congress for funds to send a commissioner to China, citing optimistic prospects for trade.[2] Cushing was nominated for the position and then, with the Senate out of session, given a recess appointment.[3]

During his long career the new envoy served in Congress and Cabinet, undertook many special diplomatic assignments, and accumulated an unusual number of political enemies. Once given the China assignment, he prepared with devastating thoroughness. At his disposal was placed an expeditionary force of four vessels, one of which burned and sank on the way out. Having been offered support by the American Board,[4] he wrote ahead to Parker, asking for his services as an assistant. Cushing's subsequent arrival caused Parker some unexpected trouble, as one of the missionaries tattled to the home office of the American Board that the doctor violated the Sabbath. Parker was in Macao on a health break when Cushing arrived on Saturday evening, February 27, 1844, his ships short of supplies and the envoy himself eager to get in touch with the doctor. The latter, indisposed, decided not to go out to the anchorage that evening. He did agree to see Cushing "*after church*," and under the circumstances did not feel that he was doing wrong.[5]

It is clear that Parker was exhausted early in 1844 and had had several severe health problems in the year just past: prostration, neuralgic pains in his hands sufficiently acute to prevent him from sleeping, and a return of his lung trouble.[6] Depressed by the recurrent symptoms of tuberculosis, he was overcome with grief at the news of the severe illness of his beloved sister Catherine, which left no hope that she could still be alive.[7] It was similarly miserable, first to be separated from J. R. Morrison ("Never have I enjoyed Christian fellowship more than with this dear brother during the past two months.")[8] and then to learn of his unexpected death.

To grant Cushing's request for help meant that Parker would have to leave his hospital for some months, following a period when health problems had already reduced his work there. Although there was no available foreign surgeon who could take over, Dr. Parker did have a very gifted senior pupil, Kwan A-to, who in the previous year had successfully performed more than a score of cataract operations and had skillfully removed a large tumor. Kwan, who had studied with Dr. Parker since 1836 and was a nephew of the artist Lamqua, could keep the hospital open on a limited basis during Dr. Parker's leave. The latter, having had a tangy taste of diplomacy when he served as interpreter for Commodore Lawrence Kearny[9] of the East India Squadron, was eager to assist Cushing, particularly since Cushing told Parker that he wanted him not only as Chinese Secretary but as a confidential adviser, from whom he would have no secrets.[10]

Parker saw it as an opportunity of doing more in a few months than in all the rest of his life.[11] Duty called in the direction he ardently wanted to go, and he almost outraced his own shadow in getting to Macao. He and Bridgman were to be Joint Chinese Secretaries of the American Legation; Bridgman, in addition, would serve as chaplain. S. Wells Williams was rather tart about the whole arrangement, feeling that Peter Parker wheeled and

Peter Parker, seated, as Kwan A-to, his ablest pupil, attends an unidentified patient; oil by Lamqua, Dr. Kwan's uncle. *Courtesy of Peter Parker III.*

dealed to get into the Caleb Cushing mission. Williams may have coveted for himself the position which Parker secured; or he may have wished to be part of a twosome with Bridgman. He did help, informally, and it is likely that he was better as translator than Parker.

The purpose of the Caleb Cushing mission to China was "to secure the entry of American ships and cargoes into these ports, on terms as favorable as those which are enjoyed by English merchants." [12] The aim was to be achieved through "prudence and address" on Cushing's part. The American envoy was instructed to manifest a proper respect for Chinese institutions and manners but should make it clear that he bore no tribute, would not perform the deep obeisance of the kowtow, nor do anything that implied the inferiority of the United States. Although it was desirable that he should reach the emperor, the letter he bore to the latter could be sent, if it was not practicable to deliver it. Much was left to the envoy's discretion. Fletcher Webster, son of Daniel, was the mission's second in command and the principal executive officer. He thought of Hattie Parker as his cousin.

Cushing's first, and probably hardest, task was to cultivate that most contemptible of all virtues — patience. The Manchu official, Ch'i-ying, recently recalled to Peking and then reassigned to the South, could not reach Macao before early June, so Cushing who had been in Macao since the end of February had an appreciable wait. Characteristically resorting to study, he borrowed books locally and worked at the written forms of both Chinese and Manchu.

During this trying interval, Peter Parker having temporarily overcome the health problems which had beset him early in the year, worked at trivia. He tried to find a Manchu tutor for Cushing. He was sought out several times by a representative of the acting governor-general of Kwangtung in an attempt to ferret out Cushing's instructions. He also translated "Portuguese articles of commerce" for Cushing,[13] worked at the Chinese text of the Treaty of Nanking, translated some provincial communications which had been directed to Caleb Cushing,[14] and was back and forth between Canton and Macao as these events were going on. By May 2,

1844,[15] he and Mrs. Parker were both established in Macao, as everyone sat out the last weeks of the diplomatic vigil.

Finally came the vivifying news of Ch'i-ying's arrival on May 31, 1844, in Canton. A note from him promised an early appearance in Macao, but a side-trip to Pottinger at Whampoa once again postponed his approach and was the source of a testy interview between Parker and the chief Chinese magistrate of Macao. To the latter Parker reported Cushing as being "exceedingly dissatisfied" over Ch'i-ying's unending delays. Parker was angry that the Manchu negotiator should take time to see Pottinger, when Caleb Cushing by virtue of having waited since February had clear priority. The American doctor blustered a good deal, pointing out that the United States had three men-of-war in Chinese waters and might soon have three more.[16] Two did shortly arrive to toughen the threat of a trip to the north.[17]

Ch'i-ying left Canton only after a sojourn of ten days, arriving in Macao on June 16, nor was he ready to begin even the social preliminaries to the diplomatic prelude until his courtesy call two days later. Despite the cumulative frustrations on the American side, the meeting at Cushing's rented residence on the Praya Grande proved to be a very friendly affair, as was the American envoy's return visit which took him to a sumptuously furnished apartment at the rear of the Buddhist Temple to the Goddess of Mercy in the village of Wang-hsia, "within the barrier, but without the walls, of Macao." [18] It must have been a relief to the American to find such evident cordiality in Ch'i-ying as the negotiations with this experienced Manchu bureaucrat got underway. In the light of that friendliness it is startling to see in the published Chinese sources how contemptuous the latter was of Cushing and the other Americans in his memorials to Peking. This two-faced mode may well have been the most politically effective way out of an awkward situation, where he was in a position to give the Americans a treaty, but for his own survival not only had to head off Cushing's proposed trip to the north but had to display orthodox, lofty condescension toward foreign barbarians.

Ch'i-ying was accompanied by several assistants of middling distinction, of whom two were rather important in the subsequent encounter: Huang En-t'ung, provincial treasurer and a veteran of the Nanking negotiations in 1842,[19] and P'an Shih-ch'eng, assistant in naval construction to Ch'i-ying and descendant of one of the original hong merchants. P'an was a connoisseur, collector, and pioneer Westernizer.[20] These men had each had some kind of friendly connection with Dr. Parker: Ch'i-ying and P'an Shih-ch'eng's parents had been his patients; both P'an and Huang En-t'ung had been "personal and familiar" friends of his.[21] Parker felt these ties proved to be quite important as diplomatic lubricants.

At the second formal meeting, Ch'i-ying finally thrust a wedge of business into the social preliminaries by asking the American envoy to present a *projet* of the treaty he sought. The two men agreed that the three top subordinates from each side should meet and work up a joint draft.[22] Two days later a draft treaty was delivered by the American threesome, Webster, Bridgman, and Parker, to their Chinese counterparts at the Buddhist Temple of the Mountain Lily near the Barrier. The American document followed the substance of the Sino-British agreements of 1842–43. Refreshments were served and the negotiations, thus happily begun, seemed destined to move along briskly, although they were also jeopardized by news just arriving from Canton of a waterfront fracas between Americans and Chinese in which one Hsü A-man had been shot to death. This unfortunate case dragged along through the summer, embarrassing both sides in the negotiations.

On Monday afternoon, June 24, when the commissioners and their assistants reconvened at the Legation, Ch'i-ying utilized the occasion to present his own counterproposals, asking for trust and utmost frankness in the negotiations. Having agreed on a negotiating schedule for reconciling their differences concerning the contents of the treaty, they at once brought Cushing's major points into the open. The most important of these concerned the proposed trip by the American envoy to Peking for the purpose of delivering President Tyler's letter to the emperor; the lack of security in the Canton factory area; and the death of an American citizen in 1842. As Parker recorded in his minutes, "A *breathless silence prevailed* during the statement of these topics." [23]

Concerning the question of the need for protecting foreigners in Canton, Caleb Cushing proposed that it be handled by an officer from each side. Ch'i-ying at once agreed, smiling and saying "I appoint Huang and Parker to settle it." [24] Regarding the threatened trip north to deliver the president's letter, Ch'i-ying, after remaining some minutes grave and silent, erupted with a passionate and lengthy stream of eloquence. He pointed out that the trip was unnecessary, since he could transmit the letter for the Americans; that, the established ceremonials of the two countries being dissimilar, Peking had no way of receiving them; that, if the envoy was not received, an awkward situation would arise, leading to loss of face; that, the United States and China being friendly, wasn't it better to avoid jeopardizing that condition? and so on. Although the persuasiveness would have been diluted in translation, his speech must have had an appreciable effect, particularly when he added that he was not authorized either to obstruct or facilitate Cushing's trip to the court. He stated that, if the American insisted on going there at that time, he as Manchu commissioner had no power to continue negotiations for the treaty.[25] They agreed to postpone discussion and went into a dinner to which the ladies, by special dispensation, had been invited. The Chinese were gloomy, the meal was soon ended, and the envoys withdrew for further talk, at which time Ch'i-ying inquired of Parker the general nature of the president's letter. Although the matter was held in abeyance, before the end of June Cushing indicated to Ch'i-ying that he did not intend to press further the trip to Peking.

On June 27 at the Legation Webster, Parker, and Bridgman met the Chinese negotiators for an article-by-article scrutiny of the Chinese treaty text. General agreement prevailed until their discussion of Article 19, relating to attacks on foreigners by Chinese and indemnification for the attacks. "Upon this a spirited discussion of some length ensued," as recorded in Parker's minutes. This was the problem upon which he and Huang had acted as a subcommittee. Although they achieved a general agreement on such points as protection of the merchants and punishment of attacking mobs, a detailed agreement on Canton regulations was not worked out until later, after the treaty had been signed (see below). Dinner followed the productive evening, and the Chinese left at ten o'clock in a very good humor.

The top subordinates from each side met in this way for a number of days in succession, sometimes at Cushing's residence, sometimes in the temple at Wang-hsia. This was the essential, inner process that produced the treaty. Thus the agreement was the product of five or six workhorses, Peter Parker included, who, despite prior inexperience in the matters at hand, were remarkably successful in pulling together. Their success was virtually guaranteed by Cushing's decision concerning the trip to Peking. By July 2, Ch'i-ying jubilantly wrote to Cushing, gushing over the success they had had and inviting him to "a repast of fruits & tea." [26] He asked the American envoy to bring President Tyler's letter for the emperor, along with the treaty texts so they could be sent together to Peking.

The treaty was signed on July 3, 1844, at a round stone table in the temple garden in Wang-hsia. The chief negotiators with their principal subordinates, Parker among them, were present, as were several gentlemen from the Legation and Commodore Foxhall A. Parker, commanding the United States naval forces in the Far East. An off-center line divided the table into two unequal parts. Tradition has it that Ch'i-ying managed the ploy of sitting next to the larger part. The following day Ch'i-ying departed, and by the fifth of July Cushing had dispatched copies of the treaty homeward.

The pivot of the negotiations had been the successful clarification by Ch'i-ying on June 24 of his position regarding the proposed American trip to Peking, coupled with Cushing's intelligent decision not to insist on pocketing a brick from the Great Wall. Persistence by the American plenipotentiary would have meant no treaty. From the Chinese point of view, the more or less routine granting or withholding of the treaty was directly related to the American plan to go to the north. When the American envoy ceased threatening to go, he got his treaty, all the while thinking his "Yankee shrewdness very successful." [27] Even though the Americans had been alerted by way of London as early as March 1844 of the good chance they had of securing the treaty they sought,[28]

Parker had repeatedly urged Caleb Cushing in the March–May waiting period to maintain the threat. Superficially, this makes Parker look foolish. Actually, although a mistaken policy, it has only in retrospect become clear that it *was* mistaken. Neither Parker nor any of the other foreigners could have been sure at the time that the threat was invalid. Once it had been made, they appropriately maintained it until Ch'i-ying's arrival permitted meaningful negotiations. Thus, although Parker's advice was useless within the China context, it was also harmless. On the American scene it had a more positive function, because his prolonged insistence during the prenegotiation period protected Caleb Cushing's rear from a yelping congressional wolf-pack at home.

As to the presidential letter, we do not know what member of the State Department drafted President Tyler's communication to the emperor of China, and it is lucky for its author that we do not, since the letter has the distinction of being so fatuous as to be virtually a vaudeville performance.[29] Nevertheless, Ch'i-ying played it straight. His acknowledgement of the letter found its sentiments "superlatively beautiful . . . full of thought and elegant expressions."[30]

One of Dr. Parker's brightest moments came during the session when the deputies were discussing the points which ultimately comprised Article 17, that is, residence, construction of dwellings, storehouses, cemeteries, and so on. His presence, as well as his pioneering medical achievements, accounted for the inclusion of hospitals within this list of permissible foreign ownership and activities in the new treaty ports. Moreover, P'an Shih-ch'eng, knowing the gratification it would afford him, suggested the additional provision — Temples of Worship.[31] Dr. Parker believed that this addition served as a stepping-stone for Théodose de Lagrené, the French envoy, to ask subsequently for toleration of Christianity throughout the empire.

Parker became involved in miscellaneous rivulets of business relating to the mainstream diplomacy of the summer. Ch'i-ying's presence in Canton in July permitted him to carry on with Parker several subordinate negotiations concerning unresolved legal prob-

lems.[32] Parker played merely a routine role in all except one.
Cushing wanted more specificity than was contained in Article 19
where the treaty offered protection by the local authorities against
insult or injury.[33] Accordingly Parker and his friend Huang began
on July 12 their deliberations regarding an up-dated wording of the
Canton regulations. By August 5 they had completed this work,[34]
and Parker sent on to Cushing a translation of the new agreement:
the foreigners were to be permitted to build firewalls; an old
wooden fence was to be replaced by a stone or brick wall to
prevent Chinese from slipping into the factory area; the streets
were to have strong gates which could be closed when a fire or
quarrel broke out; sentry posts were to be set up at the ends of the
streets; peddlers, fortune tellers, and idlers were not permitted "in
front and on the right and left of the Factories"; an able military
officer was to be at an official station at the head of Old China
Street; the street in front of the factories was "not to be a
thoroughfare" and could be closed at sunset and on the Sabbath;
no more spirits were to be sold to foreigners in the shops; and no
trash was to be thrown onto the streets.[35] Parker had tried to get
sites for additional foreign residences on Honam Island south of
the city. Unsuccessful in that, he did secure agreement regarding
renting buildings wherever safe and convenient.

Dr. Parker's role as translator for Caleb Cushing can never be
entirely clear, because we cannot determine the precise extent to
which he may have been helped by Bridgman, Williams, and
Chinese secretaries. Judging from the translations in the Cushing
papers at the Library of Congress and from the handwriting,
Parker and Bridgman appear to have done about equal amounts.
For a later period Commissioner Humphrey Marshall described
Parker's method of producing a formal communication in Classical
Chinese. The doctor first translated a Marshall dispatch orally to
his Chinese assistant, whereupon the latter, "catching an idea of the
original," put it into the correct written form.[36] His competence
would not have been greater in the earlier period. Confirming that
point, Ch'i-ying reported to the capital that Parker and Bridgman,
not knowing many Chinese characters, had to rely on their spoken
Cantonese[37] — which Ch'i-ying himself did not know. To add to

the difficulty of assessment there is at least *some* evidence that Peter Parker's command of Cantonese remained poor.[38] Regarding that, it is likely that he was an energetic, uninhibited, and often inaccurate speaker, better by far than the overwhelming majority of resident foreign businessmen and diplomats of either the nineteenth or twentieth centuries, but persistently imperfect. Judged by the perfectionism of Chinese literati, Parker's linguistic skills were poor and probably laughable. Judged against the appalling Western ignorance and with regard for both the difficulty of the language work before the development of adequate teaching aids and the general competence of a job fairly well done, he was quite impressive.

After Cushing departed for Washington, Bridgman and S. W. Williams returned to their mission work. Parker, having received appointment as "Chinese Secretary to the Mission, with a compensation at the rate of 1500 dollars per annum," [39] entered a new phase in his work. As a symbol of a different trend in his career, he embarked August 28, the day after Cushing's departure, on the *St. Louis* for a trip up the coast to visit the newly accessible treaty ports.[40] One of his reasons for going was to consider whether there was now a better "northern" field for his mission labors than Canton, which had become so frustratingly xenophobic since the thirties.[41] Unfavorable winds blocked the voyage and Parker finally returned to Canton. Long absent from his medical labors, he was impatient to return to them, although the Canton locale was even gloomier than usual with the Danish, Spanish, and French Hongs still in ruins from their having been gutted by fire a year earlier.

Cushing's departure was studded with many compliments on the job he had done. Dr. Parker, for one, was effusive, his name heading the list of two dozen Canton residents (among them Paul S. Forbes, Warren Delano, and his brother Edward) who sent formal congratulations to Cushing.[42] By the time of Cushing's arrival in Washington, his treaty had been received in the Senate, where it was unanimously approved on January 16, 1845. Its processing was even swifter at the Eastern end, where the emperor had already ratified it in August of 1844.

After Ch'i-ying and Caleb Cushing, Parker was the most

important figure in the 1844 negotiations; and Cushing was openhanded in the compliments which he paid privately and publicly to Parker for his help.[43] Dr. Parker felt of his own performance that the result more than realized his expectations.

Nearly everything that America could ask, or China consistently concede, has been secured. Among the important objects gained is the article which provides for the erection of Hospitals and temples of worship at each of the ports of Canton, Amoy, Foochow, Ningpo & Shanghai. In a political point of view, the channel of direct communication between . . . Washington . . . and . . . Peking . . . is a desideratum of great moment . . . important commercial advantages [have been] obtained over & above those secured by the English Treaty. . . . I am convinced that a *real* bond of friendship now binds these two great nations of the East & the West.[44]

In dealing with these and other compliments and self-appraisals, one must avoid overloading the circuit. Even admitting all of them, it is nevertheless unassailable that the chief influences on the treaty were not American but British and Chinese. To be sure, the text of the American treaty went beyond that of the British by supporting the Chinese prohibition of the opium trade, but the United States failed to follow this up effectively, and it remained a dead letter.[45] The fault lay with Congress rather than the Treaty of Wanghsia. Cushing could negotiate a good text, as he certainly had done, but he could not remedy congressional failure to vote funds in support of his work. Despite the sense of letdown consequent upon this, Parker was immensely impressed by the swirl of events in China. Recent changes had been so swift — the hospital breakthrough of the thirties, the treaties, the newly opened ports, and the arrival of several dozen missionaries — that he felt "the conclusion is irresistable that God has some new designs regarding this realm of idolatry, & that from this day forth new & great things are to be expected and attempted in China." [46]

9 ◆ Schism in the MMS and Severance from the ABC

For the Medical Missionary Society the most important of the altered circumstances after 1842 was undoubtedly the newly won control by Britain of the beautiful, malarial island of Hong Kong. Unfrequented by foreigners and virtually uninhabited by Chinese before the war, it was, in the postwar period, quickly becoming a significant warehousing and residential port. To Hong Kong went Dr. Hobson in 1843 to open and conduct a Medical Missionary Society hospital; to it had gone from Macao a number of the men who were participants in the MMS; and to it now came new arrivals from England who might be recruited as supporters of the Society. When the Medical Missionary Society in 1843–44 quickly took advantage of the possibilities for expansion, the spreading of its work along the coast tended to attenuate the earlier centrality of Canton in medical missions and to encourage a shift of interest, greatly deplored by Dr. Parker, toward Hong Kong. By 1844 some of the MMS officers who lived in Hong Kong were urging the Society to hold its meetings there instead of Canton or Macao. After meeting in January 1845, the Hong Kong officers sent Parker a requisition for him as senior vice-president and executive head to call a general meeting of the Medical Missionary Society in Hong Kong.

Superficially innocent, the suggestion was calculated to set in motion a whole set of Dr. Parker's primary responses. To begin with, Parker was deeply hostile to the idea of identifying the

Society, through its meetings, with such an un-Chinese community as Hong Kong — in his words "a handful of outlaws and emigrants in a bordering usurped territory." [1] To him, Hong Kong, no longer even Chinese after its cession "in perpetuity" to Britain by the Treaty of Nanking, was too deeply identified with the opium trade, the foreigner, and non-Chinese ways of life. Moreover, its Chinese population consisted of but a few scattered villages, while on the mainland were numerous cities with enormous populations. He was also uneasy about the endowment of the Medical Missionary Society — specifically, the $6,702.64 which he had laboriously raised during his home leave. After certain expenses had been defrayed, about $6,000 of this sum had been deposited to the account of the MMS in Canton. To Dr. Parker a shift of meetings to Hong Kong foreshadowed future control by the Hong Kong vote, since too few Canton backers would bother to attend meetings down there; and such future control suggested the probable expenditure of an unsuitable proportion of the funds in Hong Kong itself. Dr. Parker quickly fired back his objections, supported in them by some of the interested merchants of Canton.

The Hong Kong officers then reconvened, this time in Macao in mid-February 1845, and this time with Dr. Parker present to trumpet his dissent. Over his objections, they passed a resolution which laid the basis for Hong Kong meetings and control.[2] The *China Mail* account, written by Dr. Alexander Anderson, held that six of the seven present approved the resolution; moreover that six constituted a majority of the members of the committee of management who were in China. Dr. Parker, soon back in Canton, claimed there had been only five supporters, a majority of those present but not a majority of the committeemen in China.[3] He then spiced the controversy with the following public announcement:

A General Meeting of the "Medical Missionary Society in China," will be held at CANTON, at No. 1, American Hong, on Wed., 26th of March, at 11 o'clock, A.M. for the election of officers, and the transaction of any general business of the Society.

Peter Parker
Senior Vice President [4]

The Hong Kong group, meeting again in Macao on March 8, 1845, angrily resolved that Parker's meeting would be illegal,[5] ordered the senior vice-president to change the announcement, and threatened — should he not do so — to convene a general meeting of its own. When Parker ignored this remonstrance, the group announced a general meeting for April 19 in Hong Kong, declaring that the meeting summoned for March 26 in Canton had "no claim to be considered a meeting of the Medical Missionary Society in China." [6]

A close reading of the "Regulations of the Medical Missionary Society" [7] reveals that the original requisition for a special meeting of the Medical Missionary Society was legally correct. The signatures of five officers, or a majority, were required. The matter of an absolute majority was in dispute, but not the number five. The regulations specified that the president (Colledge) or in his absence (he was permanently absent in England) the senior vice-president (Parker) was "empowered" to call the meeting. The regulations implied that the president or vice-president was required to call it, if properly requisitioned, but did not commit him with regard to the location. Parker's act of specifying Canton may have been irritating, tactless, or obstinate, perhaps all three, but it was coolly and clearly legal. On the other hand, the Hong Kong men, by now calling a meeting in their own city, were themselves without the requisite legal authority for such a summons—a latter-day finding which they would have indignantly denied.

In any case, Parker duly chaired the Canton meeting, attended by seventeen men, some of them probably newcomers. After a spritely discussion the meeting adopted a resolution requiring a vote in Canton on the subject of transferring the MMS to any place under another jurisdiction.[8] Meanwhile there should be no disbursement of funds. A date was set — April 23rd — for such a vote, but this procedure was set aside in favor of a peace meeting in Hong Kong.

The Hong Kong gathering on April 19, 1845, presented itself as a fully legal general meeting and proved to be a very animated affair. No one attended from the recent Canton meeting except Dr. Parker, who opened the discussion in his lively manner by saying that he had "an unpleasant duty to perform in repaying to the present meeting the compliment that had been paid to their last meeting in Canton," [9] and by then reading a letter of protest from the Canton group against the legality of the Hong Kong meeting.

The meeting, whether legal or not, was well attended by businessmen and missionaries alike and went briskly to work on a series of resolutions. One of the latter specified that general meetings not be held twice successively at one place, another designated Hong Kong as the next site.[10] Although the meeting bravely insisted that all reasonable ground of division had been removed, it in fact did not emerge with a healing prescription.

Parker, widely supported in Canton, was as widely blamed in Hong Kong, where one looks in vain for vindication of his conduct. One of the fullest documents on him in this period was produced by Benjamin Hobson, then in charge of the Society's hospital in Hong Kong. Publicly Hobson grounded the lightning of his vexation in order to avoid complicating a tense situation, but privately he discharged bright, angry flashes in a long letter to the home office of the London Missionary Society.[11] Careful reading of Hobson's letters reveals several things: the general implication that Parker was chiefly to blame; the specific charge that by his manner, obstinacy, and opposition he provoked disunion; and the absence of any thoughtful critique of Parker's general mission strategy.

It is by no means certain that Peter Parker was so deeply at fault. He shared in the responsibility for the quarrel, but the largely British group in Hong Kong bristled with nationalist sentiment and was jumpily defensive about the recent grab of Hong Kong from the Chinese. Its members appear unreasonable in their attempts to wangle the territorial shift of the Society through manipulation instead of waiting for discussion and a vote at the next general meeting of the Society in Canton. By going up to Canton the Hong Kong men would have met the requirements of legality and of the man who was at once senior vice-president, the chief figure in the Medical Missionary Society up to that time, and its star money-raiser. They could thereby have avoided the dubiously legal summoning of the April 19 meeting in Hong Kong.

As to the tactlessness and faulty leadership on Parker's part,

Hobson was doubtless correct. Parker, although generally good-humored, had an undernourished sense of humor. His obvious unpopularity with the Hong Kong group implies considerable provocation on his part, particularly since it is known that he had run-ins with many other people. He was far from unique in this respect, quarrels and feuds being common in those weird, waterfront communities so riddled with illness, sparked by sharp mercantile and national rivalries, and isolated both from Chinese culture and their own. For all of them, it was a very feisty coast. In his strategic preference of Canton over Hong Kong, Parker showed good appreciation of the long view. Hong Kong *was* a poor mission field, whereas major mission assignments beckoned nearby. Hobson himself was increasingly aware of the soundness of Parker's leadership on this matter, and indeed had recently written to this effect to his own Board.[12]

The Canton group met on April 23, 1845, at Dr. Parker's to hear him describe the Hong Kong meeting of the 19th. The participants received his account of apparent harmony "with much gratification" and adjourned to May 21.[13] At one or the other of these two meetings they appear to have established a committee of correspondence to remain in touch with the "gentlemen of Macao & Hong Kong." Such a connection was maintained during the summer, but to no avail, and the tentative separation of the spring, born of pique and tactlessness, hardened into the schism of two, hostile general meetings, each claiming at separate September meetings to be the real Society.

By the end of that summer of 1845 the controversy seems to have lost whatever charm it may once have had and to have greatly reduced interest in the Medical Missionary Society. Only about a dozen members armed with proxies convened in Hong Kong on September 21, with Alexander Matheson, prominent opium trader, in the chair. Not more than six of those present had been among the more than three dozen attending the April 19 meeting in Hong Kong. To this little band of repeaters there were added a few others. Hobson was not present, having recently left for England with his wife.

The meeting chose officers for the coming year, re-electing Dr.

Colledge president, eliminating Dr. Parker from — and elevating Dr. Alexander Anderson to — the senior vice-presidency, dropping six other vice-presidents, adding eight new ones, and placing new faces in the five remaining offices.[14] The islanders thus carried through their springtime threat to effect a separation from Canton's domination of the MMS. The certainty of their own rectitude and of their constituting the true MMS is reflected even some fifteen years later in Dr. Lockhart's account of the schism.[15]

A dismal side effect of the schism was the estrangement which continued between Parker and Hobson, two of the top exponents of the art of medical missions. Hobson resigned his connection with the MMS when he moved from Hong Kong to Canton, probably to avoid the embarrassment of attending MMS meetings in Canton. He remained critical of Parker's handling of the problem of MMS separatism.[16] Although they both lived for some months in the foreign part of the waterfront, they probably saw little of one another. Later Hobson moved to Kum-li-fu, a western suburb of Canton, to divest his work of the unfortunate connection at the factory area with opium traders and the atmosphere of aggressive foreignism. This move added effective physical separation to his earlier estrangement from Parker. Although Kum-li-fu was at no great distance, it was just far enough away, beyond a tough red-light section of the city, to expose a foreign pedestrian to all manner of insults.[17]

The Hong Kong Medical Missionary Society, in spite of the sympathetic support of both Hobson and Lockhart, did not long survive. An annual meeting was held in October 1846,[18] but no slate of officers was proposed for 1846–47, and apparently those in office continued for another year. There is no evidence of another annual meeting after 1847, and in 1848 only a printed Committee Report appeared, apparently published as a substitute for a full annual report. The end of the Hong Kong MMS, although obscure, is likely to have taken place within a few years. James Legge of the London Missionary Society wrote to his home office in late 1852 that the Hong Kong Medical Missionary Society was extinct.[19] Thus, the Hong Kong half of the Society had a brief and spotty history after 1845.

The Canton group, on the other hand, managed a moderately vigorous existence. They convened in Annual Meeting on September 25, 1845, calling Dr. Parker to the chair.[20] There were eleven present and seven proxies. Voting to help open a window on negotiations with their Hong Kong brethren, they balloted for "office-bearers for the ensuing year," 1845–46. Thomas R. Colledge was elected president, thus becoming president in absentia of both the MMS organizations. They retained Peter Parker as senior vice-president and corresponding secretary, and then filled out a list of fourteen other vice-presidents, all of whom — except Bridgman, who was also vice-president of the Hong Kong group — were new and most of whom were Americans. Despite the possible absence of a Canton meeting of the Medical Missionary Society in 1846, it met in 1847 and in many later years. Subsequent glimpses into its operations suggest that it continued with a certain vigor and effectiveness, as a small organization chiefly confined to Canton and with fluctuating contributions. In 1851, for example, the Society was obviously in good hands and in viable fiscal shape.[21] The reports for 1854, 1855, and 1856 show only five or six men attending the annual meetings, and reflect some of the difficulties of those years — conflict in Canton during the Taiping Rebellion and poor health for Dr. Parker.

The failure of such conciliatory overtures as were made by either Canton or Hong Kong men meant that the schism of 1845 had overthrown as fine an experiment in internationalism as the period produced. There were other manifestations — as in the Morrison Education Society; the short-lived China Medico-Chirurgical Society, founded in the summer of 1845 for professional meetings and interchange;[22] and Anglo-American cooperation within the Protestant missionary community in 1843 concerning a new revision of the Chinese translation of the Bible.[23] In none of these cases, however, was the internationalism as dynamic and impressive as in the pre-explosion MMS. The Hong Kong "branch" of the MMS did remain bi-national, but as an institution it soon faded away. The Canton MMS subsided into a basically American operation, British Consul Dr. John Bowring's membership in the Society representing a welcome exception.

One of the liveliest passages of arms between the Canton and
Hong Kong groups in 1845–46 concerned the disposal of the $6,000
which Dr. Parker had raised at home and in England. This matter,
and indeed all of Parker's maneuvers during this period, was made
more difficult by Parker's worsening relations with the American
Board, which at this time was threatening withdrawal of its
financial support from his work. Faced with that, he viewed with
consternation the additional removal of the $6,000. Although an
appeal to scattered contributors was not feasible, he luckily had
one consolidated bloc of contributors who together had raised
$5,286.32. Parker, therefore, wrote to this group of eminent
Bostonians and asked for a clarification of their purposes with
respect to the money. Their reply declared their wish to place the
fund at Parker's disposal, to be used as he thought best.[24] Parker
thus won his battle against the Hong Kong forces of darkness, but
at the cost of a medium-bad mission quarrel.

Probably much of Parker's prickly tactlessness in dealing with
the schism in the MMS arose from the pressures of his deteriorat-
ing relations with the American Board. At the basis of the
ever-widening split between them lay their different conceptions of
the nature of mission activity. Parker, exposed in China to
overwhelming human suffering, felt that he had to respond
primarily as a doctor to these immediate problems. The need was
so obvious, the pressure so relentless, that there could be no
evasion or withdrawal for someone of his training and compassion.
"Alas!" he wrote to Rufus Anderson in the home office of the
American Board, "for me I fear the die is cast. I have now a cable
about me that human strength can never sunder, and it is to be
feared, neither divine grace, nor divine providence ever will." [25]
This new type of mission activity, tailored to certain exact and
pressing needs, did not square with either the earlier ABC practice
or the letter of Parker's instructions. The Prudential Committee of
the ABC expected its appointees to be active evangelists and also,
in their capacity as doctors, to shield their fellow missionaries as
best they could from the stupefying number of diseases which
menaced them. In the mid-1830's priority was ordained, without

challenge, in favor of evangelism. It seemed clearly improper for Peter Parker to put Jesus as healer on an equal footing with Jesus as preacher. It is not surprising, then, that Parker had begun very early to be troubled by the problem of where his duty lay, and his concern is repeatedly evident in his letters and journals.[26] It is equally clear that he was persuaded of the essential Christian correctness of his course. The justification which he evolved emphasized especially the alleviation of suffering and how that offered the best means of access for missionary evangelism.[27]

What was painfully obvious in Canton as to the validity of a new type of Christian witness was substantially less persuasive in Boston, where Rufus Anderson coolly manipulated the machinery of the Board. This exponent of crispness and efficiency had initially tolerated Parker's ardor for medical missions. He apparently acceded to the early requests from Canton for more ABC doctors and was involved in (perhaps even responsible for) their appointment and dispatch. In the first decade (1835–1844) of medical missions to the Chinese, eight out of the total of fourteen medical missionaries were ABC appointees.[28] Such a record of the American Board was clearly one of notable receptivity to this new creation. What reservations existed were as characteristic of men in the field as of those in the home office.

When Parker, troubled by the diversion of his time and energy from preaching to medical work, had asked Anderson for advice, Anderson's response conveyed approval, cautioning only against a serious encroachment upon time for language study.[29] Anderson's wording, to be sure, was neither effusive nor explicit, and he may have had reservations pending the arrival of further evidence, but in the early years he did respond favorably both to Bridgman's urgings and Parker's activities.

As time wore on and by steps which are not fully clear, he withdrew his initial support of medical missions. The health record of missionaries may have influenced him, since all but Parker among the eight ABC doctors had disabling illnesses. Expense may have played a role. Although Parker was partly self-supporting, the others were costly to maintain. Possibly there were signficant pressures from the Prudential Committee because it believed too few converts were emerging from the large numbers of patients. Perhaps the chief factor was merely the passage of time, which allowed Anderson to recast his appraisal of the subject.

Although one is reduced to speculating about *why* he shifted, there is quite explicit information on what he shifted to. The structure of his mature "science of missions" is expounded in many of his writings, most concentratedly in a series of ten lectures, first given by Anderson at Andover, repeated at five prominent seminaries and finally published as *Foreign Missions: Their Relations and Claims* in 1869. He saw the world as a "great . . . and terrible wilderness of heathenism" [30] in which the American Board sought *"to save the souls of men, by the use of the most direct means. . . . Keeping this object constantly in view, it is easier to resist the powerful tendencies, on every hand, to a complex, expensive, cumbrous, and impracticable system of operations — in the form of missionary hospitals and dispensaries, manual-labor schools, schools for mere human science . . . all of which are well in certain circumstances . . . but are of questionable utility as a part of the system of means to be used by missionary societies for the conversion of the heathen world." [31] Experience had brought him to the conclusion that "the apostolic missions ought to be regarded as substantially the model for Christian missions to the heathen," [32] especially like that of Paul, clearly the topmost practitioner of the art. Again and again Anderson hammered at his central thesis: "We should give the people the Scripture, and organize our converts into churches — native throughout, self-governed, self-supported, self-propagating." [33] In each case, when a church had been fully organized, the missionary should boldly leave. He "is emphatically, in the essential principle of his calling, a sojourner, pilgrim, stranger, having no continuing city." [34]

Anderson travelled to numerous mission stations, one of the objects being to re-evaluate constantly the devices and usefulness of a given mission enterprise, with an eye to a Pauline handing-over and withdrawal. It must have been an unnerving experience at any mission to receive such a visit. Back of him stood Section 5, Articles 4–5, of the *Constitution, Laws and Regulations of the ABCFM*: "Whenever any missionary . . . , in the judgment of the

Prudential Committee, violated the instructions given him . . . , or has failed to perform any duty reasonably required of him, they are authorized to dismiss him." Though an appeal to the Annual Meeting was possible, this authorization in practice gave great power to the Prudential Committee, which Anderson came to dominate. Convinced that weapons were spiritual, missionaries were warriors, and the leadership had to study and plan like Napoleon, Anderson was a formidable leader, a kind of global planner overseeing all the Board's mission stations, a prototype of the empire-building industrialists and businessmen of the twentieth century.

Anderson's books convey the impression that he was not much taken by China as a mission field, and even less by the upsweep of the medical adjunct to missions. Although Anderson for some years, despite his obvious emphasis on preaching, had raised no objection to medical missions in his correspondence with Canton, Parker's success, by its very existence, represented a powerful challenge to the corresponding secretary's stark, Pauline conception of mission work. In October 1844, Anderson finally asked of the Canton brethren "what is the *religious* influence resulting from this [medical] practice? How far is it advisable for the Board to be concerned in the medical practice of Hospitals?" [35] Answering his own question long before a reply could be received, he divulged to them an urgent concern that the newly authorized Amoy mission should have "very little to do, if anything, with the Hospital system of missionary operations." [36] What the recipients of the letter in Canton did not realize was that the secretary had apparently decided to make a major move toward confirming and consolidating the Pauline policy of missions and that he viewed Parker as an obstacle to be met and overcome. Anderson's January intimations crossed with a Parker letter betraying not the slightest suspicion of what was in store for him.

Anderson's power base lay in the Boston office's Prudential Committee, the nerve center of the operation. This body, acting on behalf of the Congregational, Presbyterian, and Dutch Reformed churches, consisted of about a dozen men, usually eminent and devoted to missions, who met weekly. Despite the fact that as an executive officer Anderson had no vote, he became the decisive figure in the overall operation. In Bridgman's wild jangle of images, Anderson was not only "the connecting link in the Chain which binds pagan lands to those of Christendom" but also "the fulcrum in the machinery that is to overturn Satan's kingdom in the world." [37]

One of the key technical steps for Anderson's purpose was the creation by the Prudential Committee of a subcommittee on March 4, 1845, to deal with the Canton mission.[38] It consisted of Anderson and two others: John Tappan, merchant and evangelical layman, who had served on the parent committee only since the preceding year; and Daniel Noyes, who had been a member for three years. Neither Tappan nor Noyes is likely to have been a match for Anderson in terms of experience or clarity of missionary purpose.

The Prudential Committee itself had recently dealt with a problem involving Parker. The latter, having seen too many destitute widows of missionaries when he was in England, having become worried about putting aside some money for Harriet as a hedge against his own demise — a never distant menace in his hospital work — and having been paid for his 1844 services to Caleb Cushing, found himself in disagreement with his "*Batchelor* brethren" of the mission over his retention of the money.[39] In a prompt and good-humored letter he had referred the matter for settlement to Boston, where the Prudential Committee ruled against him.

That was all handled by the committee in December, giving Noyes and Tappan some small exposure to Parker-as-a-problem. For the following March there is no topical evidence on the role of these men in the discussions of their subcommittee, but a report emerged which was pure Anderson. It was presented at a full meeting of the Prudential Committee, March 11, 1845, with a fistful of resolutions. Among other things, the subcommittee defined the grand object for which the Board sustained missions in China as being "the oral publication of the gospel to the Chinese people." Another resolution declared that the Committee had increasing doubts as to the "propriety and ultimate utility" of Parker's devoting so much of his time to hospital practice, "unless he shall derive his support from an institution that is professedly medical in its object; and that, should he continue to have the same views as heretofore in regard to the course of his duty in respect to his medical and surgical labors, and if the doubts of the Committee are not removed, he be advised to make arrangement for his support, if possible with the Medical Missionary Society at Canton, and thus be at liberty to act more freely on the views he entertains as a missionary physician." [40]

The resolutions were adopted. There were seven others for the Canton missioners to digest, but none relating so directly to Dr. Parker. The heart of Anderson's case was doctrinal in the sense that fundamental aims and basic techniques were at stake. A clarification of purpose and a reaffirmation of the simple design of evangelism were being called for. He was not explicitly building a "case" against Parker at this time, although much use may have been made backstage of Parker's admitted deviation from his instructions. Anderson was, on paper at least, relying on the clarification of the central purpose of missions, and the suggestion (a fatuous one in Canton eyes) that Parker secure a new financial base from the Medical Missionary Society. Anderson had a copy of the brief MMS constitution and by-laws and was supposed to be aware that the MMS was not set up to undertake a major financial commitment. Soon a letter [41] from Anderson incorporating the nine resolutions began its slow trajectory to the Orient.

Received in Canton in the summer of 1845, the letter exploded in Parker's face. Basically, he was being fired. He sensed this sooner than the others, despite the fact that the process of dismissal was going to drag along for another two and a half years. Distraught over the outrageous lack of recognition of what he had done for China missions, aghast at the foolishness of the committee's suggestion that he secure a salary from the MMS, he asked them "to conceive of my feelings for I cannot and shall not attempt to describe them. Suddenly and unexpectedly deprived of a foundation for support as permanent, I supposed, as anything earthly could be." [42] The emotional devastation wrought by this communication was still evident months later. Bridgman's Christmas Day letter to Anderson reported that the doctor had allowed it to affect his mind in a manner and to a degree that the corresponding secretary had not intended. "He looks to the Board as to a venerable parent, and to be required to leave it, — would be like being disinherited." [43] Bridgman reminded Anderson of the excellence of the hospital for mission purposes and described to the secretary once again how he went there daily to distribute tracts at the door and to talk with its inmates. S. Wells Williams, having embarked for home, was not in China in the summer when the March 14, 1845, missive arrived, but soon visited Boston where he set the secretary straight on the fundamentals of the MMS.

If Bridgman had felt any smug superiority over Parker in the summer of 1845 when the March 14 dispatch detonated in Canton, he was shortly disabused by the receipt (jointly with his colleague, Dr. Dyer Ball) of a home office letter. Anderson, after reaffirming his line regarding medical work, reported the Committee as unanimous in voting that Bridgman devote himself to preaching the gospel and cease editing the *Chinese Repository*.[44] The doctor was clearly not Anderson's only target. Anderson, writing to Parker at this time, hoped that even if the latter decided to form another connection in consequence of the Committee's resolution he would favor the Committee with his views on the "whole subject of Chinese missions." [45] To Parker, hungry for something resembling appreciation from the Boston office, the tone of this note seemed kinder and was more welcome.[46]

One of Parker's chief responses to the March 1845 letter from Boston was to postpone repeatedly the task of writing his own rejoinder. Although "in such a deformed silence, witches whisper their charmes," [47] he resisted them and argued his case with dignity and restraint.[48] He stated that his desire was and always had been to render the highest possible service to China. If at the same time he could render a service to his own country, he would rejoice. He informed them, therefore, that owing to his several years' residence in China, his knowledge of the language, customs, prejudices, and policies of the empire, the friendship and confidence of the people and officers of the government, he had been appointed Secretary and Chinese Interpreter to the United States Legation. This unsought position would enable him, he pointed out, to support himself financially. Since he had been assured his labors would be comparatively light, he indicated how he longed to continue his medical work and his connections with the Board. "I love my brethren," he wrote, "and though disinherited will never cease to cherish a so warm affection for the Society with which are most tenderly associated in my mind the dearest names on earth." [49] His own view of the case was that he should be treated like Dr. Morrison, who, while he served as interpreter to the East India Company, still retained his old connection with the London Missionary Society. Parker wanted financial separation "but in all other respects to be to the Board the same as heretofore, harmoniously cooperating with my brethren by mutual counsel and untiring labor for the perishing millions around us." The records of the Prudential Committee merely report that Parker's letter was read to them and that "the Secretaries were instructed what reply to make." [50]

For Anderson the loss on the MMS salary issue as a device for easing Parker out of the ABC was compensated by the news of the doctor's acceptance of a part-time appointment with the American government. Such an undertaking broke an important rule of the American Board, although Anderson could not invoke this infraction at once, because a *temporary* government job was not a decisive point. Anderson had himself proposed the temporary assignment of Parker to Caleb Cushing. A *permanent* appointment, on the other hand, would be a clear violation of perfectly defensible Board procedures. But what constituted "permanence" in the flux of the China coast? And, from Dr. Parker's viewpoint, how would he piece out adequate support for his beloved young wife and hospital, if he gave up the government salary at a time when he sensed Anderson was trying to fire him anyway? Bridgman chimed in with the view that the less they had to do with political matters the better, but that a temporary connection with the political mission was not objectionable.[51]

Parker's rejoinder to the March note continued with his more doctrinal letter of January 31, 1846 — to the writing of which he devoted the relatively free time of Chinese New Year's. In this long and passionate exposition he argued the philosophy of medical missions and a view of missions much at variance with Anderson's.[52] He addressed himself particularly to two questions raised by Anderson: "How far is it advisable for the Board to be concerned in the Medical practice at Hospitals?" and "What is the *religious influence resulting from this practice*?" Regretful that he could not sit down and resolve the matter face-to-face with Anderson, he nevertheless rehearsed the points that seemed absolutely persuasive to him. Medical missions were not only sanctioned by the "repeated precepts and the living example of Christ"; they also confronted the special circumstance of the Chinese who were generally inaccessible to mission activity unless medical missionaries were used. "When the superstructure is braced, we may dispense with the scaffolding." But not until then. He went over the facts concerning the crowds of patients, the type of marginal evangelism that was practiced, and how the hospital was spared the generally insulting behavior of the Cantonese toward the foreigner in the postwar period.

Somewhere between the Parker and the Anderson mission views a new working compromise might possibly have been found. Anderson himself suggested that Dr. Parker, in order to create for his hospital a more obvious connection with *preaching* the gospel, attach the Reverend S. W. Bonney regularly to that institution as preacher.[53] Doctor and corresponding secretary remained unable to agree on this matter. To Dr. Parker it was evident that what Boston was requesting was already being done: there were services at the hospital, weekly and daily, attended in the course of a year by many patients. This point had been made repeatedly in letters to the home office.[54] Besides, Bonney was unusually tactless. S. Wells Williams, although not in "doubt as to the propriety of [the Board's] dismissing" Parker, thought that there was no question whatsoever about the effectiveness of Parker's medical approach "as an auxiliary to the direct preaching of the Gospel." [55]

Although Anderson was just about unflappable,[56] his letters grew testy as the Canton rejoinders came in. He sharply called the Canton brethren to task for not reading earlier communications carefully and for failing to supply full answers to his questions.[57] The secretary increasingly confined the struggle with Dr. Parker to the issue of the government job. "If your connection with the government is designed and fully intended by you to be temporary, and is so in fact, we shall be happy to have you continue in our connection." [58] After further letters which changed no mind and which included a new twitting of Parker regarding observance of the Sabbath,[59] Anderson seems to have concluded that the government job was "permanent," that the doctor should ask for a release from the Board, and (in the absence of such a request) that the Prudential Committee could go ahead with a formal dismissal. Final committee action, heavy with implications of a Pauline direction of Board policy, was taken on August 17, 1847:

> The Secretaries having inquired of the Committee, whether it would be proper to insert Dr. Peter Parker's name in the Annual Report now in a course of preparation, he having become Secretary of Legation to the United States Embassy [sic] in China; it was, after deliberation,
> Resolved, — That the connection of Dr. Peter Parker with the Board terminated on his accepting the office of Secretary of Legation from the United States government, and that he can no longer be reckoned, with propriety, among the missionaries of the Board.[60]

Parker was informed of this step[61] after no one appealed it at the annual meeting of September 1847. As Rufus Anderson kicked the doctor out the back door, the dismissal was handled with the utmost suavity in the Annual Report: "Dr. Parker having regarded it as his duty to accept the appointment of Secretary of legation to the United States Embassy [sic], his connection with the Board of course ceases. He continues his labors much as heretofore." [62] The secretary's final formulation was crisp and authoritative: "It is to be regarded as a settled principle with the Board, that a missionary, going into civil or political life, ceases *de facto*, from his connection with the Board." [63] This letter of Anderson's also served as a belated reply to Parker's request eighteen months earlier that he be treated as a "Morrison exception." Parker's request was repeated in May 1847,[64] but it arrived in Boston after the Committee had dismissed him. Anderson, not accepting Parker's reasons, had never bothered to deal with them in a letter to the latter prior to dismissal.

In this act of the drama some stirring curtain lines were delivered by the central figure. "Dear Brother," he wrote,[65]

The general principle stated in your last admits no question, but it is the *exception* that establishes that principle, and under the peculiar circumstances I had hoped that my case might be regarded in that light. . . . The assurance that "you believe I love the missionary cause" has greatly assuaged my grief. May the remaining portion of my life but confirm that belief in all who shall know my manner of life and labors for the temporal and eternal good of the Chinese.

May God evermore watch over and abundantly bless the American Board, its Prudential Committee, its officers and patrons, its missionaries, and its converts to Christ from every section of the pagan world.

With affectionate salutations to those of your associates in office whom death has not removed . . . ac[c]ept dear Brother in Christ the *heartfelt* Adieu, of

Yours affectionately
Peter Parker

This letter, born of rivalry and anguish, managed to rise to beauty and dignity.

In comment on the whole unfortunate business, one sees that to some extent the Board had put itself in the position of having asked Parker to build a new economic connection and then, when he had done so, fired him for doing it. The chances were very slim for Parker to find an economic base which would be acceptable to the Board and at the same time viable without the Board's tangible support. Anderson's suggestion of an MMS salary for Parker was impossible. A private medical practice was ruled out by Anderson's restriction against a board member entering civil life. Part-time, permanent government work was rightly unacceptable to the Board. An increase in public contributions in support of Parker's work was unlikely because of the MMS schism and the reduction of Canton's importance as a center for foreign merchants. The only apparent way out was for Anderson to be willing to continue ABC support, and that was where his negative attitude toward medical missions was decisive.

Anderson stood on unassailable legal grounds, if one reads the letter of Parker's instructions and the rules of the ABC, but the secretary's inflexibility resulted in dismissing a figure who was probably the most effective and deeply influential missionary that the Board had in China in the entire nineteenth century. "They could not see that the Great Shepherd has many kinds of sheep, and calls for different kinds of shepherds." [66]

Peter Parker's conception of medical missions, although rejected by his own Board for a generation, had already been picked up by other mission boards and pursued with marked success. How different in its cordiality was the support which the doctors of the London Missionary Society received from their home office! ("The healing art is an indispensable adjunct to any efforts put forth with a view to the spiritual good of the [Cantonese] people.") [67] The narrow governance of Anderson meant that the conception of educational missions, another creative advance, was similarly rejected in favor of "Jesus as preacher." Thus the American Board under his leadership (which may still have been an authentically great leadership despite this particular dimension) lost opportunities during a whole generation to contribute creatively in the two most positive and dynamic areas of mission development in the nineteenth century.

10 ◆ Pioneer Physician, Teacher, and Surgeon

Western medicine in the early nineteenth century was still largely premodern, whereas one generation later its enormous icy congestion of clever metaphysics, folk wisdom, and accumulated quackeries had begun to thaw, shift, and grind its way downstream. The medical phase of Peter Parker's career, extending from 1831 (when he entered medical school) to 1855 (when he retired as a doctor) coincided roughly with this transitional interval between the antique and the modern. The award of his medical degree came twelve years before the introduction of anesthesia, and his retirement from medicine was about the same amount of time before Pasteur and Lister shook the earth with their advances in bacteriology and antisepsis. In short, Parker never shared the surgeon's post-Lister liberation into thoracic, abdominal, and brain surgery, but had to accept a narrow confinement and limited procedures.

He did have available at some point or other during his medical years the fruits of noteworthy contemporary developments: the scientific study of the action of drugs was underway, and pharmacology was passing from the hands of the empiricist to those of physician and physiologist; obstetrics was achieving independence from surgery, and gynaecology beginning to emerge; the improved compound microscope of the 1820's was opening the way to histology; and physiology had moved from metaphysical speculation to its new identity as a natural science based on physics and chemistry.[1] The French invention of the stethoscope was available to Parker as were British advances in descriptive physiology and anatomy dealing with the nervous system, the mechanism of reflex action, chronic disorders of the kidney, the adrenal glands, and appendix.

As a counterweight to these promising advances, there were dead-hand aspects of his medical inheritance, typified by the practice of bloodletting. This procedure had taproots so deep in Europe's medical past that nobody knew then, or now, how or why it started. Bloodletting[2] reached its peak as a cure-all, along with purgative medicines, in the first three decades of the nineteenth century, when Parker was growing up. At this time it could be seriously regarded as "not only the most powerful and important, but the most generally used, of all our remedies."[3] Of the three standard methods—leeches, cupping, and venesection—leeching was the most popular in Parker's time. It called for the use on a patient of some five to fifty leeches. We know that Dr. Parker used leeches at least some of the time. In treating his case number 7489, a man thirty-three years old with elephantiasis of the scrotum, his therapy involved leeches, bandaging, and internal use of corrosive sublimate. Three weeks witnessed a diminution of the swelling by half.[4]

The procedure of cupping, less frequently used than leeches, was performed by inverting a cup over a cut and burning within the cup a bit of cotton soaked in flammable liquid. The partial vacuum drew blood into the cup. We have no evidence that Dr. Parker resorted to it. Venesection, the major mode of taking blood, involved the opening of a vessel, usually in the arm, and the drawing off of amounts varying from several ounces to several pints, ending not uncommonly with the fainting of the patient. Parker used this technique, but moderately, even sparingly, thereby placing himself among the growing body of its questioners. Scientific opinion during the generation of his practice was drifting away from heavy reliance on it.

Indeed, medical opinion was beginning to criticize all bleeding techniques. The most pungent critique was made by the eminent French clinician, Dr. P. C. A. Louis, whom Parker met during his visit to Paris in 1841. Louis proclaimed the ineffectiveness and even the danger of bloodletting as a treatment in many cases. As a result of his persuasive influence and of the discovery of various new drugs, American doctors in the 1840's and 1850's tended to become more judicious in their use of bloodletting. By the 1860's and 1870's bleeding was generally deleted from medical textbooks as a recommended treatment.[5]

When Parker opened his hospital, he had planned to confine his treatment to disorders of the eye. Unable so to limit his practice, he nevertheless did succeed in retaining ophthalmology as his chief specialty. Its predominance was very marked for about three years, but thereafter was progressively eroded in the direction of a rough parity between eyes, on the one hand, and everything else, on the other.

He found certain special problems: "The oblique curvature of the upper eyelid peculiar to the Chinese"[6] meant that they commonly suffered from a folding under of that upper lid, "occasioning the loss of many eyes, and the opacity and vascularity of the cornea in a still greater number."[7] One of the first eye operations he performed, and one entirely typical of his subsequent career, was for entropion.[8] His procedure included making "perpendicular incisions through the tarsi at the lower angle of the eye, avoiding the puncta, and then, with a pair of forceps, invented by T. R. Colledge, Esq. for the purpose, to take up a fold of the integument over the upper lid, and with curved scissors cut it out, leaving the fifth of an inch of skin next to the cilia, as the hairs are more effectually everted than when a wider portion remains. The operation is completed, by uniting the edges of the wound with three sutures, and applying adhesive strap. The second day after, the sutures are split, and in four or five days the patient is relieved."[9] The fact that Parker had the large hands of a farmer does not seem to have interfered with his dexterity and delicacy of touch in such operations.

The chief surgical procedure in ophthalmology of that era was for cataracts, a disorder that gradually impairs vision and may, if untreated, eventually cause blindness. Today we still have no specific cure and rely upon surgical removal of the clouded lens. Removal, first done in the mid-eighteenth century, was allowed to fall into disuse until the late nineteenth. It requires a larger incision than Dr. Parker was willing to make, and he therefore relied upon the older, standard, European process of couching, first successfully used in 1708.[10] The couching technique sought to impale the lens within the eye and to dislocate it from the visual axis. The doctor inserted a needle through the cornea and pushed the cataract into the inside of the eye "where, hopefully, it lay out of harm's way." [11] The procedure requires only a puncture wound which heals quite readily. Still practiced in some parts of the world today, couching remains a crude method relying on a lengthy absorption process and often involving prolonged recuperative discomfort for patients, at the same time compensating with a big lift to their morale if nothing better is available. Once so treated, the eye does not seem unusually vulnerable to other troubles. For a man of Parker's skills, the procedure was essentially simple and carried little risk of failure. Within the first four months of his Canton practice he had couched some thirty cataracts with only two failures.[12]

Some eye diseases were so widespread as to constitute a massive problem of public health. Such was the case with trachoma, caused by a virus which was not identified specifically until 1958.[13] This highly contagious disease of the eye is transmitted by flies, water, or direct contact, and occurs commonly in windy deserts or warm coastal areas. A low standard of living, unsanitary conditions, ritual ablutions, and undernourishment help it to flourish in many parts of the world. Its signs involve inflammation of the conjunctiva (lining of the eyelids) and the spreading of pannus (network) of blood vessels over the cornea, where it forms an opaque covering and causes blindness. Described in ancient Chinese records and doubtless persistent in Chinese history, it must have afflicted enormous numbers of Chinese during the period of Parker's career there.

Parker, although never mentioning trachoma by name, appears to refer to it as "granulations of the lid," "pannus," and "chronic ophthalmia" (although this last could refer to conjunctivitis or general ophthalmia). In one recorded example he dealt with the symptoms of trachoma by prescribing: sixteen leeches applied to the temple, sulphate of copper to the granulations, collyrium of nitrate of silver used daily, calomel and rhubarb at night, syringing of the eyes, scarifying the lids, and once again applying sulphate of copper. The same treatment was continued for several months, lunar caustic also being used on the conjunctiva, and the doctor reported complete recovery.[14] Copper sulphate as a wash for the conjunctiva remained the standard treatment for trachoma well into the twentieth century, and Parker's use of it conformed to competent medical practice of his day. Other eye diseases were widespread, and he commonly was presented with conjunctivitis, keratitis, trichiasis, ulcers of the cornea with perforation or staphyloma, and pterygium. Glaucoma appears to have been infrequent, Dr. Parker reporting only ten to twenty cases a year.

In general, Parker does not discuss his eye cases at all fully, nor give much detail regarding treatments employed, despite the fact that he regarded himself chiefly as an ophthalmologist. He does mention the frequent use of belladonna, similar to atropine and still commonly used. He records treating the blistered surface of an eye with strychnine, the dosage starting with one-eighth grain and increasing to one grain, accompanied by internal use of one-eighth to one-quarter grain as a stimulant and tonic.[15] He also refers to several other drugs in eye treatment.

We know also that, with the intent of improving the general health of a patient as a resource in ultimately correcting a specific eye disorder, Dr. Parker routinely gave his patients one or more of his usuals: blue pill, colocynth, or calomel. Blue pill, a common nineteenth century remedy in the West, was a purgative compound of mercury, confection of roses, and liquorice, a dose being 250–500 mg. Colocynth, also a purgative and similar in dosage, was known as bitter apple and came from the cucumber family, the dried white pulp being used. Calomel was subchloride of mercury.

The century after Parker's retirement has witnessed such special advances as x-ray therapy to control the growth of tumors in the eye; lasers for delicate welds on the retina; and radioactive isotopes to treat corneal disease. Compared with these methods, Parker's treatment of eye patients was medically and surgically primitive.

Nevertheless, considering the resources of his day, he compares satisfactorily with his ophthalmological peers.

In addition to eyes, there was a sector of miscellaneous cases, where Parker dealt with everything from leprosy and elephantiasis to strangulated hernias and gangrenous bound feet. He removed tonsils in 1836[16] and performed — as he thought, and so far as we know — the first voluntary amputation of a limb in China (Parker's case number 2152).[17] The miscellany of cases received a colorful diversity of treatments. He mentions frequent use of nitrate of silver on rough ulcerated skin; to neutralize its action he applied milk. For cases of both acute and chronic inflammation Parker frequently applied blisters, a procedure widely used, in varying ways, both in Western and in traditional Chinese medicine. Treating High Commissioner Ch'i-ying's cutaneous disease of twenty years' standing (it is not diagnosed more precisely), Parker prescribed extract of colocynth, warm baths, and ointment of oxyde of zinc.[18] He was usually moderate in prescribing drugs, probably because his supplies were limited. As a standard means of building up a patient's strength, he used food, rest, and the inevitable blue pill on alternate nights.

Edward Delano has left a patient's view of treatment by Parker. Suffering from chills and earache, Delano had summoned the doctor, who first "recommended care . . . and abstinence from exciting drinks." The next day Parker "prescribed poultices of Bombay onions; I have had them applied several times during the day, and also had my ear syringed by the Doctor's assistant (a Chinaman). The onions are disagreeable." [19] The following day Parker stopped the poultices and Delano reported himself "much better."

In the midst of his diverse medical activities, Parker also pioneered in pedagogy by becoming the first foreign doctor to train Chinese medical students. The beginnings as well as the results during his lifetime were modest indeed, his total students at any one time never exceeding six. He had begun the process within just a few years of the opening of his hospital and, by 1838, was reporting three "young men of good promise," with one "already able to perform easy operations."[20] After the 1840–1842 hiatus, Dr. Parker resumed his training of Kwan A-to, his chief pupil. And one year later reported: "My senior pupil has successfully operated for cataract in more than a score of instances, and has removed with skill and success a tumor of three pounds weight." [21] Pleased with Dr. Kwan's progress in both medicine and surgery, Parker handed over to him the running of the Canton hospital from April to September 1844, when he was himself assisting the Caleb Cushing mission. Apparently no abatement of the flow of patients to the hospital took place.

In the autumn of 1844 when Parker returned to his own medical duties in Canton, he resumed his medical school, this time with a student body of four, one of whom was a relative of a hong merchant.[22] Parker continued to display pride not only over Dr. Kwan's practical and theoretical knowledge but also over his "talents, address, correct moral character, and success as an oculist and surgeon."[23] Skilled in a wide range of procedures, he performed many tumor operations.

Parker continued with his medical pupils in 1845. Four were continually under his care; six, part of the time. They were usually present at family devotions, where three who read English well enough took turns reading Scripture in it. They worked mornings and evenings at English and geography; afternoons they were at the hospital with Parker.[24] In 1848 Parker still had four pupils but by 1851 only two. A few were also trained by the English missionaries, Doctors Hobson and Lockhart. The former took pride in the competence of one Assam, whom he had trained in medicine. Assam underwent "a rigid examination in the presence of Dr. [Alexander] Anderson and other medical gentlemen," demonstrating that he was competent to take charge of an ophthalmic hospital.[25] Lockhart trained some young Chinese, but they disappointed him by cutting short their medical studies.

Although Dr. Parker had made a strategic thrust into the training of Chinese doctors in Western medicine, he never witnessed much of an expansion of his initial beachhead. The first modern medical school was not established in China until Dr. John Kenneth Mackenzie did so in Tientsin in 1880, when Parker was an old man, long retired. Good medical schools soon followed in Canton, Shanghai, Nanking, Anking, Foochow, and Peking.

The Chinese continued to go first to practitioners of traditional Chinese medicine. If patients did elect to try Western medicine, they thought themselves better off consulting a foreign doctor, rather than one of the foreigner's pupils. The slowness in training Chinese physicians in Western methods also derived from the essentially hopeless set of circumstances for the Western doctor-teacher, who carried too heavy a practice to have adequate time for his students.

As Dr. Parker was pulled by importunate patients into treating an ever-increasing number of different maladies, he was drawn in the direction of tumor surgery. His first operations to excise tumors took place in 1836. On January 14 he successfully removed from a seventeen-year-old boy a fleshy excrescence which extended around the eye and had attained such a size as completely to close the eye and block its vision.[26] On January 18 he ventured into much more daring surgery. This case had come to his attention several weeks earlier when a Chinese parent appeared at the infirmary with his little daughter. As Parker wrote, "tho at first sight it might be supposed that she had two [heads] — I found on examination a sarcomatous (fatty) tumor projecting from her right temple — Completely covering her right eye & extending down to the cheek. This was about 16 inches in circumference at its base — its diameter three inches in one direction & from four to five in another." Left alone, the tumor might have ended the child's life before very long. Dr. Parker thought from the first that he could remove it, although he knew the operation had its dangers (case number 446).

The possibility of an unfortunate termination interrupting the Institution—rendered the undertaking more hazardous — Having often in secret prayer as well as in social [prayer] commended the Child to the Great Physician — & with the precaution of taking a written Instrument of the Parents stating the case of the child — their desire that the operation be performed — & exculpating me from censure, if after doing what I could, the child should die —

(Even the burial of the corpse was a subject of forethought — & agreement with the father.) — I resolved upon the undertaking, & with the signal blessing of God it has been this day performed. . . . The kind assistance of several physicians — Drs. Coxe & Jardine of Canton — Dr. Cullen surgeon to the *Lord Lowther* — Dr. Palmer of the *Vincennes* — presence of friends — the fortitude of a heroine with which the little girl submitted to & endured the operation — the ready removal of the tumor & the pleasing manner in which the little sufferer has rallied from the shock of the operation bespeak the faithfulness of God & excite the *gratitude* of the *heart* & call for ascriptions of praise to the source of all Mercies —

The extirpation was effected in 8 minutes — with the loss as was judged of about 10 or 12 ounces of blood — (the child vomited but did not faint —) The tumor weighs one pound & one quarter — On opening it found portions of it becoming black & two or three drachms of mucous fluid of dark chockolate color — which shews that it had already taken on a diseased action & is a confirmation of the propriety of its removal — even if it now terminate fatally — which may God in mercy prevent.[27]

Again on the following Friday:

To day have dressed the Child's head from which the tumor was removed on Monday — & to my great delight found that the healing process has advanced kindly — The wound which is 8 or 10 inches long from the cheek to top of the head has entirely healed in space of an inch or more. The child has uniformly said that she has no pain, & from her cheerfulness & the appearance of the wound I should draw the same conclusion. O! the goodness of the Divine physician.[28]

The ordeal of the child, her parents, and her physician was not yet over. On the following Sunday an extensive fire broke out near the factories between four and five o'clock in the morning. Some new buildings adjoining the hongs became wrapt in flames and were reduced to ashes. Dr. Parker, upon receiving the alarm, hastened to the hospital and found it largely deserted. The child and her mother were just about to depart. The doctor's medicines were hastily packed in chests for removal, when mercifully the fire was brought under control. "Such have been the excessive labors of the week that I have been but with effort able to perform Divine worship in the Chapel" [29]—one of the great understatements of 1836.

At Parker's next meeting with the little girl, he found her perfectly well & very happy. "I spoke to her of the recent goodness of God, made known to her for the first time the name of the Savior who died for her. When I spoke to her of his taking little children in his arms & blessing them, when on earth, she appeared as much delighted as children usually are at the rehersal of an interesting tale. On asking her if she would like to see Jesus she replied with much animation in the affirmative. This may God in mercy grant & I can ask for her nothing more." [30] Subsequently Parker operated on similar cases, and this new sphere became a famous specialty. His reports imply that he was able to differentiate between benign, locally growing tumors and malignant, or metastasizing, tumors for which local surgery would have failed.

In connection with the new specialty there remains spectacular documentation in the form of 110 oil portraits, nearly life-size, of individual patients of Dr. Parker. Eighty-six of these paintings are now housed in the Yale Medical Library; twenty-three, in the Gordon Museum at Guy's Hospital, London; and one, in the Countway Library, Boston.[31] They were all painted, so far as is known, in the Canton studio of Lamqua, a Chinese artist who had worked with George Chinnery and become a competent portraitist in the Western manner. Lamqua had an active business in Canton catering to both Chinese and foreigners.[32] He employed eight to ten artisans and artists in a workshop over his store, and above that had his own studio. Uncle of Kwan A-to, he had been impressed by Dr. Parker's benevolent and unremunerated services to China and offered to Parker to paint for him, free of charge, as a way of expressing thanks. The canvasses, with their sparing use of white and their Rembrandtesque emphasis on flesh colors, tan backgrounds, and dark brown garments are clever in conveying facial individuality. They usually focus on documenting gross pathology, especially tumors of a maturity (commonly five to thirty years) only rarely witnessed by Western surgeons today. About half of the paintings are of special interest, because they can be matched to case descriptions in Dr. Parker's hospital reports. Such matching also enables one to date them quite accurately. Of the half so fitted together, over thirty deal with tumors, thereby supplying clues concerning the probable chief types which confronted Parker.

His descriptions are terse, but helpful, often giving very good insights into this most dramatic branch of his surgery. For example his case number 3790 was described thus:

Sarcomatous tumor. — June 19, 1837. Yang She, aged 20 of Hwayuen, had a tumor pendulous from the chin and larynx. It commenced ten years since. Centrally it measured 2 feet, 3 inches, and vertically 3 feet, 2 inches. It extended below the umbilicus, but not so as to rest in the lap. The patient had to sit constantly in a bracing posture, to prevent its drawing down her head. Being in her fifth month, her case was the more critical. The tumor was removed in twelve seconds, and the patient dressed and in bed in twenty-four minutes. Her first attempts to walk were awkward, having lost so much "ballast." December 17, she returned, in excellent health and spirits, bringing her robust little son, 2 months old. October 14, her grandfather returned to inform me of her health, bringing some trifling presents, . . .[33]

A recent diagnosis of this case has been given by Dr. G. A. K. Missen: "While I am by no means certain of the nature of this lesion, a giant pedunculated lipoma would appear most likely. The appearances do not suggest a goitre." [34]

Parker's case number 1675 related to a man of twenty-seven years with a ten-year-old tumor, eighteen and one-half inches in circumference and standing out four to five inches from the face. The doctor delayed therapy until cooler weather, the tumor becoming increasingly serious. Extirpated successfully in nine minutes, it had some wound complications but finally healed. Dr. Missen's diagnosis: "Right salivary gland tumour, or possibly a sarcoma of the jaw, with ulceration of overlying skin." [35]

Dr. Parker's description of his case number 5119 discloses the following items of interest:

Tumor of the skin. — May 5, 1838. Wang Waekee, of Kaouyaou, aged 45, a man of doubtful character, had numerous tumors of the skin of a light flesh color, and smooth shining surface, situated about the arms, breast, neck and head. In the latter position one

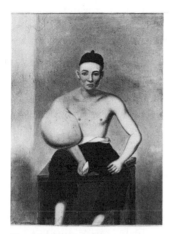

Case # 2152
(see p. 149 and n. 17)

Case # 446
(described on pp. 151–152)

Case # 3790
(described on p. 154)

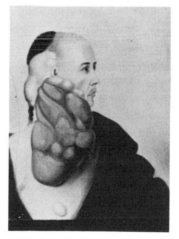

Case # 5119
(described on pp. 154 and 156)

Lamqua Portraits of Four of Dr. Parker's Most Celebrated Surgical Patients. *Courtesy of the Gordon Museum, Guy's Hospital, London.*

had attained great size, hanging pendulous from his left ear, to which it was attached by a peduncle of 2 inches' diameter to an almost immovable base formed by a similar disease of the skin, an inch thick, extending over the mastoid process and upward and backward over 5 or 6 square inches. Considering the age of the man, it seemed inexpedient to remove the firm base, but it was easy to excise the unsightly jewel that hung dangling on his breast, impeding his labor. It was more like cutting green hide, than flesh. The tumor weighed 4 pounds.

The singular appearance of this man excited strong suspicions, particularly with his countrymen, that he might belong to a band of ruffians. His eyes were usually fixed on the ground, his manners were most forbidding, and his answers to questions brief as possible. He bore with great impatience the necessary dressings on the tumor, and repeatedly removed them at his option, against the strictest injunctions, and was daily restless to be away, though he was provided with things necessary for his comfort. On the tenth day, the ligatures came away, and soon after the patient disappeared and has not been heard of since. There is no apprehension of danger from the wound, as it was small and fast healing. The manner of his absconding strengthens the suspicions that he was a bad man, and but little accustomed to the civilities he received and witnessed in the hospital.

Dr. Missen wrote: "While my originally hazarded suggestion ['left parotid tumour' and 'separate discoid tumour in or beneath the skin of the lower chest'] is not impossible, I think that a more likely answer to this remarkable appearance is that this man had neurofibromatosis (von Recklinghausen's disease) with a very large, partly plexiform and partly pedunculated neurofibroma behind the ear and an independent one beneath the skin of the chest." [36] A diagnosis of von Recklinghausen's disease might of itself account for the behavior of the patient, since those who have it are often grossly retarded and might act as described by Dr. Parker.

In all, Parker treated a considerable variety of tumors, among them:"congenital benign sacro-coccygeal teratoma";[37] "pleomorphic salivary adenoma";[38] " 'giant cell tumour' or osteo-clastoma";[39] and "turban tumour." [40] For these, as for many, the duration of the operation was carefully recorded, the first three of these extirpations requiring, respectively, two minutes fourteen seconds, about twenty minutes, and one minute. Other sample times, chosen at random but quite representative: four minutes, nine minutes, twelve seconds (!) and less than two minutes. The weight of the tumors was often extravagantly large: the first two of the above each being seven pounds. Many were substantially heavier, sometimes twice that weight.

Some of Parker's most remarkable tumor operations are not documented by paintings, none having been made, none having survived, or none having come to our attention. Such was the case with his first tumor operation, described above, and also with a noteworthy one in 1844 for which we have one of Dr. Parker's fullest descriptions. The latter was performed in October of that year with the assistance of Dr. Samuel Marjoribanks and Dr. Elisha Kent Kane. Kane had served as physician to the Caleb Cushing mission, and was at this time engaged in a temporary, pick-up practice in Macao. Later, in the 1850's, he was to carve out a spectacular career as Arctic explorer. One of the truly remarkable men of the mid-century period, his career was just beginning to unfold when he met Parker. The case in which he assisted Parker was described thus:

No. 15,000. October 16th, 1844. Glandular tumor. Yang Kang aged 35, of Sinhwai, latterly a beggar in Macao, had a tumor on the right side of his face, which commenced in the situation of the parotid gland, measuring two feet and six inches in circumference, weighing when extirpated 6½ catties, equal to 8⅔ lbs.. It commenced ten years since, and when its magnitude disabled him from acquiring a maintenance by labor he had no resource but begging. His burden, wearisome to bear for an hour, he could not put off for a moment, day or night, from year to year. He had been a lothsome and pitiable object to the foreign citizens for a long time, and sometimes on passing him in the street he presented, from unknown authors, written appeals to sympathy and a request that the poor man might be relieved of his burden. He was greatly delighted when informed of the feasibility of an operation and resigned if the result should be fatal, as he deemed death preferable to life of mendicity and suffering.

Oct. 26th, assisted by Drs. S. Marjoribanks and J. K. Kane, the tumor was extirpated. A gentleman present made the following note of the operations.

"First incision made at 18 minutes of 1 o'clock P.M.

"Tumor fell on the floor 14 minutes of 1 o'clock P.M.

"Wound sewed up 6 minutes past 1 o'clock.

"Wound bandaged and patient in bed 20 minutes past 1 o'clock."

Three arteries of moderate size required a ligature. The patient discovered great fortitude, cooly remarking on commencement of the first incision, "it hurts, doctor." The tumor was of a glandular structure, and being laid open was found to be discolored in parts, and containing small cavities filled with dark mucilaginous fluid, and others with yellowish or lympid. Portions of the tissue cut harder than the rest, and approached a cartilaginous or semi-osseous structure. The patient rallied very well from the operation, loss of blood, and shock to the nervous system, and all appeared right till 7 o'clock P.M., when secondary hemorrhage occurred. The wound was laid partially open, and coagulated blood removed, but no artery was discovered. Cold water and tincture of the muriate of iron was applied to the bleeding surface, and when the hemorrhage seemed arrested a few sutures were again inserted, and the wound dressed lightly, and cold effusions applied. A sleepless night was passed with the patient, meeting new symptoms as they occurred. Though there was no more external hemorrhage, there was considerable tumefaction on that side of hand and face, which gradually subsided under the use of chamomile flower fomentation applied next morning. The edge of the wound united by the first intention, for the most part, requiring to be partially opened subsequently, for the escape of the pus from supuration of parts beneath. With this exception and more or less paralysis from the division of the portio dura, nothing untoward occurred. It was remarked by a professional gentleman, immediately previous to the operation, that he "advised the man to make his will beforehand," yet the tumor was extirpated with complete success, and the man recovered in three weeks.

The magnitude of the operation, the elliptical incisions being about eighteen inches each, and the adhesion, at the base, over the parotid, being deep and strong, rendered it impossible, [that] it should be performed with ordinary solicitude. The mingling hope of success and fears of the worst possible consequences, excited devout and sincere intercessions at the throne of grace in his behalf, and an earnest use of means to prepare him for whatever might be the divine allotment. He was told that others fervently entreated the most high God to save him, but that it was desired that he himself should pray to Him who alone could succeed the means to be used. When laid upon the operation table, he was reminded, that after the most careful attention to his case, the conviction was strong that the operation was feasible and judicious, still it could not be denied that it was formidable, and again he was urged to lift his heart to the God of heaven and to the only Savior. Our prayers have been answered in respect to the means used for prolonging his life. Partly from a desire to have him where he can be instructed in the knowledge of the truth, and from the impression that his influence in the hospital might be salutary, he has been made its porter, in which capacity he acquits himself with great propriety, a living monument of gratitude, witnessed by thousands who come thither. Though mild and gentle, he possesses much natural energy of character, and commands attention when the dense crowd requires him to raise his voice. He quite spurned the idea of specifying any sum for remuneration of his services in the new situation. He had been rescued from mendicity, suffering, and the prospect of death at no distant day, and had little disposition to place a value upon the services he might render while his subsistance was provided him. The relatives, by whom he was scarcely recognized in his adversity, look up to him, and many have sought through him professional aid. The transition from the condition of a beggar in the streets of Macao, to that of a door-keeper in the Ophthalmic hospital, no doubt seems to him great, but the infinitely more desirable one, of conversion from an idolater to a trophy of redeeming love, can alone form the climax of our desires concerning him." [41]

Having consolidated the two specialities of eye and tumor in the 1830's, Parker added a third in the mid-1840's, when he began on lithotomies, operations for kidney or bladder stones. Although Parker had begun treating patients with urinary calculus as early as the summer of 1836, he waited until the waning months of 1844 to perform his first lithotomy. Of that occasion he wrote:

The first [was] upon a man belonging to the city of Canton, thirty five years old, who had been some time under notice. A year previous the stone had been grasped and broken into two pieces by means of Lithotrity, but was of too hard a character to be broken down, especially in the irritable state of the cyst. As a last resort Lithotomy was proposed and acceded to. For weeks previously he was as much under *moral* as physical preparation for the operation, being supplied with the Gospels and Christian books in Chinese, with a desire he would acquaint himself with their contents and become a worshiper of the God they reveal. When the hour for operation arrived he too was again reminded of the nature of his situation and the possible results. That the case had been one of long and diligent study and frequent prayer to God. He interrupted the conversation by saying he had been too long acquainted with the surgeon, had "seen too much in the hospital with his own eyes to require anything now to inspire his confidence." The operation was then performed. The stone in two pieces, originally measuring three and a half inches in the shortest, and five and a half inches in the largest, circumference, and weighing one ounce and a drachm, was extracted by the latteral operation.

Of the several available surgical modes to remove bladder stones, Parker had chosen the lateral perineal operation (evolved from a sixteenth-century procedure) which involved cutting the body of the prostate instead of "dilating" it, cutting the bladder neck and part of the bladder wall.

All was favorable. In a little time he was free from pain and enjoying a relief that could be purchased only at the cost of what he had suffered. Allusion was made to the constant gratitude that was ascending to God for his blessing on the part of the operator, and a desire expressed that that of the patient might ascend with it. With a sincerity more easily conceived than described, he took the surgeon by one hand and putting the other partially around his neck, as though he would embrace him, but timidly shrinking back and looking up to see if he might not be considered presuming, in reply to remarks that the books he had in possession would tell him more of Jesus who died for the world, and that . . . he would find in them the *true-doctrines,* he repeated with emphasis "*they are the true doctrines.* I will pour out my heart to know them and will circulate them among my relatives."

Not an unfavorable symptom followed. *In eighteen days he was perfectly well.* When about to return home he attempted to knock head at the surgeon's feet, but was prevented and the reasons for it explained. . . . This case has been extremely interesting, not only from the amiable character of the man, but as being in all probability, the first instance of Lithotomy either in antient or modern times, which has been performed upon a Chinese, and this too in the highest degree successful.[42]

A week after the first lithotomy operation, a second was performed. The patient was a man, twenty years old, "who for fourteen years had not, according to his statement, been able to sleep in a recumbent posture, and often in severe paroxisms he appeared, as his mother remarked, more like a delirious than a sane person." Two stones were removed: one, 2 by 2½ inches around, and the other, 3½ by 4½. This case was less successful, but Parker reported the patient as "able to be about again." No prior operations at the hospital had excited as much surprise and attention as these lithotomies and the giant tumor of October 1844.[43]

His records refer to two chemical types of calculus: lithic acid (today called "uric acid") and triple phosphate. For the latter there was a special variety, the mulberry calculus (for example, number 40,075 of May 26, 1851), the name referring to its shape and not chemical makeup. The dimensions of the stones were invariably given by Parker in the hospital reports. Some, illustrated in woodcut diagrams in the 1850–51 report, were as large as turkey eggs. Examples may be seen among the Parker materials at the Yale Medical Library.

Although there was no headlong rush into repetitive lithotomies, Parker did undertake a third in May 1845 and a fourth on his birthday in June. The third went well, and he wrote of the fourth: "God crowned the operation with success." [44] He did some in each subsequent year of his practice (nine in 1851 was the maximum), often assisted by Dr. Marjoribanks and almost invariably successful.[45] A failure was reported in case number 29,015 where the patient was lost after a December 1848 operation.[46] By 1850 the lithotomies were all being performed with chloroform.[47]

Before undertaking such a serious case as a lithotomy Parker asked for a legal release, an example of which he has supplied to us:

Agreement I, Chung Ping, thirty-three years of age, of the district of Tsingyuen, in the department of Kwangchau, being afflicted with stone, have several times sought aid, yet without avail. Now, fortunately I am under obligation to Dr. Parker of America, for employing his knife, and extracting it, and when cured, not merely I, one person, will be bedewed with his favor, but a united family will be grateful for his great kindness. Should the mountain from its height, and the water from its depth, be impassable (i.e. should the result be fatal), it shall not concern the Doctor; all will acquiesce in the will of heaven. Lest oral evidence be invalid, I make this written agreement, and deliver it to the Doctor to hold as evidence.[48]

From the hospital reports we get interesting, random glimpses into his supportive techniques: in a specific case of calculus, at the suggestion of the assisting physician, Dr. W. S. W. Ruschenberger, USN, he used matico (the leaves of *Piper angustifolium,* a shrub of South and Central America) to check bleeding; as a dressing he often employed simple cerate, a mixture of benzoinated lard and white wax, melted together; he occasionally applied a carrot poultice to a scirrhus breast (for example, number 5707).[49] The methods appear to have resulted in an astonishingly high percentage of successes. At the same time Parker seems to have been very aware of the dangers inherent in surgery. As a rule he undertook an operation only when the patient's life was at stake or unbearable; with tumors, only when clearly necessary and when the tumor was easily removable. He does record the occasional loss of a patient, as with number 11,700, a woman thirty-seven years old, operated upon for steatomatous tumor on the inside and front of her right thigh. The doctor, finding it mixed in with muscle tissue, took five minutes to get it out and lost the patient through hemorrhage and exhaustion during the operation, his first such setback.[50]

One of the puzzling aspects of examining Parker's medical performance is the unexplained absence of mention by him of "hospital disease." For his counterpart in the management of a European hospital in that era this was one of the most harassing and persistent difficulties. It appears in reality to have been a group of conditions: gangrene, septicemia, pyemia, and erysipelas. It was common with amputations and often fatal. A sensible surgeon tended to confine himself to "closed" surgery (for example the setting of simple fractures) and broke the skin only if it was absolutely necessary.[51] Wards were periodically closed to be fumigated with sulphur candles, given fresh whitewash, and had their floors scrubbed with lime.

It is evident that by initially trying to confine himself to the treatment of eyes, he had chosen a field which minimized the danger of infection. Moreover, a majority of those treated by him for eye disorders were probably out-patients, the eye treatments (even operations) being quick and involving general health to a less obvious extent than amputations or the removal of tumors. Possibly his failure to mention hospital disease may be partly accounted for by some combination of: superior nursing care (usually performed by the family rather than paid nurses); the spacing of beds to allow family members to camp around; or his attempts to get his patients into good health before operation, often spending a week or two building up their strength, thereby enabling them to resist more effectively postoperative infection. Parker turned away hopeless cases,[52] and we can tell from his hospital reports that he stuck close to a relatively few surgical procedures, just as wise European or English surgeons did in that period. Even if these insecure speculations are given maximum confidence, they do not satisfactorily explain how most of Dr. Parker's reported surgical wounds healed by the first intention, and why he should only occasionally mention suppuration or pus escaping from a wound. One wonders if, in some as yet undocumented way, Chinese patients had substantially more resistance than Europeans to hospital disease. The puzzle remains.

One of the most interesting surgical experiences for Parker in the period of the 1840's came with his first use of sulphuric ether in an operation. Using a supply from the United States with a Chinese-made apparatus, the ether was "administered [for three minutes] to a Chinese of about thirty-five years of age, who had a steatomatous tumor upon his right arm." The patient apparently felt no pain from either extirpation or sutures. His pulse quickened and then sank, "the blood from the wound was very dark," that afternoon he walked about the room, that night he slept well, and the wound soon healed.[53] The precise date of this operation is not clear, but it appears to have taken place not long before July 15, 1847. On that date the doctor's second use of ether was abortive: the patient, nauseated by the anesthesia, requested the doctor to proceed without it. He did so, and with successful results.

In Parker's report for the period of July 1, 1845–Dec. 31, 1847, he indicates that he had received both ether and an inhalation apparatus from Boston. He wrongly believed Dr. Charles Thomas Jackson, an eminent Boston chemist and geologist, to have been the originator of the new technique.

Having received the Jackson type of apparatus from Boston, Parker used it (he had earlier used a different type) on October 4, 1847, in his case number 25,870.

I selected for its first trial a Chinese, a robust farmer, forty-nine years old, of the district of Heo Shan, who had a steatomatous tumor, situated in the right axilla but distinct from the glands and nearly the size of his head. He was placed upon the operation table, in a sitting posture, ready to be laid down. He was then directed to inhale deliberately with full inspirations the Ether from Dr. Jackson's apparatus. I had hold of the right arm with one hand and the other behind him, ready to lay him gently down. In forty-three seconds, the muscles of his arm suddenly relaxed and he ceased simultaneously to inhale the ether, and in a state of insensibility he was laid back upon the table his head being still elevated. His pulse was quickened, and the eyes assumed a dull and vacant appearance.

The tumor was then extirpated by Kwan-Taou, my Senior pupil, and three arteries tied, in four minutes. There was not the slightest apparent consciousness during this part of the operation. As there was considerable oozing of blood, cold water was applied, and the wound exposed to the atmosphere for eight or ten minutes, before proceeding to apply sutures. By this time the effects of the ether upon the system had begun to subside, and the patient gave signs of sensibility to the prick of the needle, particularly in the parts nearest to the axilla, and after the wound was dressed and the patient placed in bed, he complained of the tightness of the sutures, but had no recollection of the incisions during the operation.[54]

Parker does not mention further resort to ether after this successful introduction of it in 1847, as he promptly switched over to a new anesthesia. On January 19, of this same momentous year (1847), Sir James Young Simpson, an Edinburgh obstetrician, had first used chloroform in surgery. Having received a supply of chloroform from H. M. Schiefflin of New York with a pamphlet by Dr. Simpson, Parker had soon decided upon his preference for this form of anesthetic, a choice which is reflected in his next hospital report (for 1848–49). Chloroform had a more pleasant fragrance than ether, required no special inhalator, and needed only a fraction of the amount which would have been necessary with the other. Parker may also have been impressed by the greater ease of using chloroform in a hot climate: ether, being flammable and much more volatile, is both harder to control and more dangerous to use after dark under conditions of illumination from an open flame lamp. Despite the obvious advantages of chloroform, Parker remained cautious in his use of it, and believed that it should never be employed with affections of head, lungs, or heart.

During Parker's medical career of two decades in China, over 53,000 patients were treated at his hospital in Canton—most of them by him, some by Dr. Kwan or one of the several visiting doctors. On the average Parker undertook about fifty new patients each week, this figure saying nothing about how often in the week he may have seen each new or old patient. He was a pioneer teacher, a practitioner who was in touch with the advances in his field, and a dynamic doctor of courage, decision, and resourcefulness. Primarily an ophthalmologist, he was forced by pressure from patients into many diverse medical fields. Owing to the way he chose to publicize some aspects of his surgery, we know more about his dramatic tumor excisions and lithotomies than we do about the eye specialty. The imbalance in our knowledge of his medical work is reinforced by the fact that his contributions as a pioneering doctor lay more in his transmission to China of Western techniques relating to his subspecialties — tumors, lithotomies, amputations, and anesthesias — than in relation to ophthalmology.

11 ◆ Chargé

The South China scene in the decade following Peter Parker's service with the Caleb Cushing mission was enlivened by the arrival of a number of the century's most famous sailing vessels — the new clipper ships. He was lucky enough to see some of the great ones. They raced to glory against each other, cutting fifty to sixty days off Parker's transit on the *Morrison* only ten years earlier. The passion that drew them to Chinese waters was the lure of the cup that cheers but not inebriates. Of thirteen American clippers launched in 1850–51, six went at once into the British tea trade, shattering the comfort of the established merchants. The British were wild with dismay.[1]

Within the circle of Dr. Parker's career the tea-and-clipper years of the mid- and late 1840's were the setting for the second great phase in his surgical work, when he moved into lithotomies and the use of anesthesia. His mission career had inevitably changed in important respects after the American Board dismissed him. His official standing as a missionary ceased and his other commitments increased. It is noteworthy that he continued his hospital, although with fewer patients, and maintained religious services there along with the distribution of tracts. Superficially the hospital scene of the late forties remained much the same as that of the thirties. On the other hand, severance of ties with the ABC may well have drained his ardor for the mission doctor's daily ordeals. If so, it is even more to his credit that he continued to give a substantial portion of his time to the hospital, much as a surgeon of note today might give a generous part of his week to charity patients.

This period also witnessed the diversion of an important part of his energies into his new official duties as a part-time employee of the American government. Parker's overall career as diplomat had three facets. He served (1) as translator, advisor, and negotiator assisting the Caleb Cushing mission (1844), as has been noted; (2) he was part-time member, often chargé, or acting commissioner of the new American Legation, as will be described in the present chapter; and finally (3) he became commissioner (1855–1857), to be covered in the next. His positive contributions in the first of these phases launched his diplomatic career with a satisfying splash, giving him optimistic and very misleading ideas about the desirability of remodelling his own career to include diplomacy. The longer second phase enabled him to proceed with that plan, under conditions which fluctuated between nearly complete independence and periodic subordination to a miscellany of diplomatic superiors.

Once the Senate had created the post of Commissioner to China, problems seemed to emerge from nowhere. Since that position was frustrating, hazardous, and without great distinction, it proved to be difficult to fill and keep filled. Alexander H. Everett of Massachusetts, a former member of the diplomatic service, exeditor of the *North American Review*, and recent college president, initially went only as far as Rio en route to China before problems of health intervened. He delegated to Commodore James Biddle, commanding the United States squadron in the Far East, the authority to exchange ratifications for the Treaty of Wanghsia. Biddle performed that job in December 1845, with Peter Parker present, two miles upriver from Canton at the home of a friend of Ch'i-ying. Everett started again for China when his health was better, but his arrival in the Orient was shortly followed by his death.

Three other incumbents — Davis, Marshall, and McLane — held the post before 1855 and functioned intermittently as Parker's chief. John Wesley Davis, former doctor and Indiana stalwart of the Democratic party, Speaker of the House in 1845, and later presiding officer of the Democratic National Convention that nominated Pierce, went out as commissioner in 1848, returning in 1850. Humphrey Marshall sailed to fill the post but only after two intervening appointees resigned. Marshall was himself both West Point graduate and Kentucky lawyer. A member of Congress from 1849 and then commissioner to China under President Fillmore, he remained one year only (1853). Yet another politician refused the job before it was accepted by Robert M. McLane, a West Pointer and lawyer who had also served in Congress. McLane was a close, trusted friend of President Polk and an organizer of the election victory of President Pierce. The latter sent him to China, his single discouraging year (1854) coinciding with Commodore Perry's flaming success in Japan. Despite his feeling of failure, that year was probably the most successful one for American commissioners between 1845 and 1857 by virtue of its including the productive negotiations with the Manchu official I-liang.

With these appointees, despite the frustrations and minimal success, a new American framework for a Western type of international relationship with China had been set up, funded, and launched. The relationship, a novel experience for the Chinese, suffered from periodic insubstantiality. Nevertheless, despite its tendency to fade and reappear like the ghost of Hamlet's father, there was a set of sporadic functions and routines associated with the new office, and it was with these that Peter Parker, in his capacity as Secretary of Legation was concerned. He served variously as advisor, interpreter, and chargé in the decade under question. His time as chargé was concentrated chiefly in 1846–1848 and 1850–1852, that is, in the appreciable gaps immediately before and after Commissioner Davis' tenure of office. For some six years he was "Acting Commissioner" *in fact,* although he never held that title.[2]

Before Davis' appointment, Everett's illness had meant that Parker had to handle many of the official duties himself. Although Everett's authority had been delegated to Commodore Biddle, the latter was either literally or figuratively at sea, with decisions devolving on Parker. Everett's presence was accompanied by illness; his death meant the usual time-lag before the arrival of a successor. Under these circumstances Parker was very useful to his government as a knowledgeable, on-the-spot, adequately healthy functionary who could be counted on to fill in for the usually arriving, departing, or absent (and ignorant) commissioner.

Among the fragments of evidence which document the relations between Parker and his sequential commissioner-bosses, one finds such items as the following. Marshall had intercepted a letter from the Secretary of State to Parker, broken the seal, and told others of the contents. When Parker finally saw the despatch himself, he acknowledged it with: "I have the honor, if such it may be considered, to be in receipt of . . ."[3] Marshall, according to John K. Fairbank, possessed "a fervid sense of the importance of his position; and had soon antagonized nearly all the other foreign officials in China, beginning with Commodore Perry and his American colleagues."[4] Nevertheless, in reporting to Washington on Parker, he was reasonably gentle.[5]

Everett's death meant that Parker had to handle a case concerning robbery in May 1847, at Reverend Issachar J. Roberts' mission. An international commission, as called for in the Treaty of Wanghsia, set the loss at $1400, which Parker then demanded the Chinese government pay, basing his claim on Article 19 of the Treaty of Wanghsia. Ch'i-ying offered to help search for the criminals and try to recover the stolen property as Parker continued to insist that the Chinese government was responsible for Roberts' loss. By the article in question, Chinese officials were responsible for protection of foreigners and were liable to punishment for negligence, but the Chinese government was not responsible for repaying losses. Given the wording of Article 19 and the lengthy debate over its implications when it was first agreed upon, Parker's manners and actions were high-handed and mistaken.[6] This pattern persisted in the case of a Chinese merchant who owed the American firm of Nye Parkin and Co. 9000 taels of silver and would not pay. Parker complained to Ch'i-ying, who had the man arrested. When investigation showed him to be bankrupt, Parker held the Chinese government responsible for his debt. Ch'i-ying appealed to Parker as a friend, asking that he re-examine the case and be a bit more sympathetic to the man's plight. Without either official realizing it, cultural patterns were in conflict here—the Chinese traditionally treating an unforeseen disaster with compromise; the Westerner with stringent and unrelenting legalisms.

Parker had a lot more to worry about than either such cases or his transient and sometimes disagreeable American superiors. His diplomatic career in Canton coincided with the presence there of one of the most strident xenophobes in the Sino-Manchu hierarchy — Yeh Ming-ch'en. Canton had witnessed his arrival in 1847 in the role of provincial treasurer, seen his elevation to governor the following year and finally to governor-general in 1852. The period of Yeh's last two appointments gave him a decade in which to place his special stamp of heightened, outraged intransigeance on the conduct of foreign affairs in a very crucial city, the chief place for the handling of China's foreign relations with the West. In those years there was still no foreign office. For all that one can point out in sympathetic understanding of Chinese victimization by blundering foreigners, Yeh Min-ch'en remains a man so narrow in attitude and so cruel toward large numbers of his countrymen as to caricature mankind. According to his own claim, he had been responsible for the execution of more than 100,000 people—several times the number of victims of the French Revolution.[7] It is not surprising to discover that Parker was unable to secure an interview with Yeh or to transact any normal flow of business with the latter's office.

One of the seismic forces which opened the rift between Governor-General Yeh and the foreign missionaries was the Taiping Rebellion. Originally based on South China, led by Hung Hsiu-ch'üan, a partly Westernized scholar who had studied with Issachar Roberts in Canton, the rebellion had sufficient Christian content to encourage many in the mission community to feel at first that it showed God's powerful reshaping of China. Bridgman visited the Taiping capital of Nanking, as did Roberts. In the end, both were utterly disenchanted, the latter leaving after bad scenes with his former pupil, whom he described as "a crazy man, entirely unfit to rule . . . with his coolie Kings." [8] Parker, by sharing the early mission enthusiasm for the Taipings, had made himself utterly unacceptable to an orthodox Chinese like Yeh Ming-ch'en.

One of the doctor's duties was to assist the commissioner. In this capacity he accompanied McLane in 1854 on a frustrating trip to the north, in belated fulfillment of the threat by Caleb Cushing ten years earlier.[9] This venture concerned treaty revision and initially involved the representatives of Britain and France in addition to the American commissioner. When the French withdrew, the expedition to the mouth of the Pei-ho, downriver from Tientsin, became Anglo-American in nature, with two missionary translators, Medhurst and Parker, serving Bowring and McLane. Having arrived there in mid-October, the translators shortly established contact with Chinese officialdom, and the envoys began their wrangling negotiations in search of treaty provisions granting free trade in China. Problems arose over procedure and protocol. The traditional way of receiving foreigners at Tientsin was in tents in front of the Taku forts. Medhurst asked that because of the rank, age, and poor health of Bowring and McLane they be allowed to go to Tientsin instead of staying in tents by the river. When the Chinese refused, Medhurst asked for living quarters at Taku. Upon further refusal, he settled for the usual mode of reception. In the course of two formal meetings the Chinese repudiated most of the Anglo-American proposals, allowing negotiation on only a few lesser items. After about a month of inactivity off the Pei-ho, with the menace of a northern winter at hand, the joint expedition left for Shanghai. Nothing of any importance had been accomplished. McLane's attitude had toughened, and his recommendations to Washington included the suggested use of a three-power blockade of key spots on Chinese rivers. Fortunately Washington rejected the advice, but Parker may well have been influenced by the hard line toward which McLane had moved.

Never lacking problems, Parker was confronted with a rich harvest of them in another sector of his official duties—his involvement with the gaggle of newly appointed American consuls. By the Treaty of Wanghsia the United States could have consuls in all the treaty ports. If the port was active, the position was sought after. Paul S. Forbes shows in a letter how desirable the Canton office of consul was; he held it, but thought the elections at home, especially if Polk got in, might lead to his being turned out in favor of a commercial rival. He was convinced that Wetmore and Co. would do all they could to get it.[10]

In the post-1842 dispensation, the consuls theoretically could communicate orally or in writing with Chinese officials on a basis of equality and respect. Although the position was a part-time one, it involved multiple duties, such as the appointment of assistants; the handling of records, reports, invoices, accounts, passports and bills; protection of local United States citizens; quasi-diplomatic functions, especially with the consuls of other nations; and some judicial functions, coupled with the care of prisons. Their sphere of operations was the treaty port environment with its weird pidgin culture, neither authentically Chinese nor Western; its foreign clumsiness, mercantile dynamism, and vitriolic feuds; its gross displays of alien wealth, arrogance, and racism; its ill-health, poverty, and waterfront rackets. Given this setting, the problems of the new treaty ports were often acute. In Canton they were exacerbated, and to some extent special, because it was not only an area of older contacts but the site of recent depredations by the British invaders.

In that context Parker was occasionally caught by the absence of both consul and commissioner and forced to assume the role of presiding judge in legal snarls, for example, in unsavory cases relating to the coolie trade.[11] Chinese emigration to California had been the immediate predecessor of this trade. So far as one knows, those emigrants had gone voluntarily, and American authorities had scant reason to be disturbed over it. However, when West Indian and South American needs for labor — especially in Cuba, Peru, and Brazil — created a new demand, a variation on that trade sprang up in the 1850's.

Firms contracted with Latin American governments to supply a certain number of laborers. A whole system of recruitment was built up in Amoy, Swatow (not one of the treaty ports), Hong Kong, Canton, and Shanghai, whereby Chinese were persuaded, cajoled, bought, or often kidnapped. They were stuffed into barracoons and receiving ships at the waterfront and then into vessels for transport to the Philippines or Latin America. Food, confinement, water, and health conditions were usually wretched, and great vulnerability to dysentery and other problems prevailed. In many instances the ill were dumped overboard with the dead. In Amoy those jammed in the barracoons were stripped, and C (for Cuba), P (Peru), or S (Sandwich Islands) painted on their breasts. Such emigrants, outraged by the trickery and cruelty visited upon them, often resorted to violence, numerous cases of which were brought before consular authorities in the China ports. During one of Parker's stints as chargé, in the interval between Commissioners Davis and Marshall, he was exposed to the complexities of the coolie trade in one of these cases.

The *Robert Bowne*, an American ship, Captain Lesley Bryson, had left Amoy March 21, 1852, with 400–500 coolies for San Francisco. Mutiny occurred on March 30, the fatalities including Captain Bryson, two officers, four crew, and ten Chinese. A group of the coolie passengers went ashore in the Liu-ch'iu Islands, others at Amoy, some of this latter group being apprehended and taken to Canton where they came before "Judge" Parker. He and the local Chinese authorities appear to have been left to act largely on their own, as neither Washington nor Peking wished to become involved. The former was too far away; the latter, having forbidden Chinese emigration, could not discuss the coolie trade with foreigners without appearing to recognize de facto the right to emigrate. This reluctance hampered all attempts at regulation for over a decade. It appears that Dr. Parker accepted the version of the surviving officers and crew of the ship and took a stringent view of the Chinese mutineers. Acknowledging that the crew had used cane brooms and cold water to scrub the Chinese before cutting off their queues, he nevertheless found seventeen of the coolies guilty of "aggravated piracy" and recommended to the Chinese authorities a penalty of execution. The latter, unable to report the case to their capital, investigated it to some extent and carried on an exchange with Parker. The case dragged along for a couple of years, with one execution, one death in prison, and fifteen acquittals.

Appearing ill-informed, gullible and harsh, Dr. Parker shows up badly in his handling of this case. His earlier experience had been with Chinese emigration to California, and he seems to have confused the character of the new, ruthless coolie trade with its relatively innocent antecedent. On the other hand, his exposure to such cases soon revealed to him the inequities and iniquities of the coolie trade itself and converted him into a crusader for its regulation or abolition. When back in the United States in 1855, he was able to discuss it with the State Department and to alert the government with ample detail concerning what was going on. Having emerged as an ardent opponent of this dreadful traffic, his first official act upon his return to China as commissioner was directed against it. He was, however, severely hampered by lack of adequate legislation, as Congress did nothing. His lobbying against the "pig stealers," in the ugly lingo of the trade, continued after he left the diplomatic service and retired to Lafayette Square in Washington.

Problems of jurisdiction routinely cropped up, for example, in the case of William Taylor, an English deserter from an American ship who was accused at Canton of stabbing an English deserter from another American ship. The seamen would normally have been subject in a Chinese port to the law of their ships' country—in this case the United States. Taylor was accordingly sent by the British consulate to the American authorities. Parker, having considered the issues, held that, in deserting, Taylor had forfeited protection by the United States, and should be returned to the jurisdiction of his own nation.[12]

In Parker's official duties his tie was primarily to the incumbent commissioner at the American Legation. This loyalty often set him against the consuls, since the diplomatic officer represented the interests of the nation, whereas the consul was much involved with the special problems of the business community, usually frankly representing the latter. This was the common American separation of duties. Sometimes contact between diplomat and consul went relatively well. Often it did not. One of the basic problems was the endless coming and going, the average length of appointment for consular officers being less than two years.[13] Ill-health caused many of the interruptions. The fluidity of this scene had its own special problems, among them the difficulty of finding good substitutes. We know that when Parker disapproved of Consul Bradley's nomination of a substitute at Amoy in 1851 the nomination was dropped.[14] Later the consul at Amoy for a rather long term was T. Hart Hyatt. Parker disapproved of Hyatt's choice of substitutes. In one case the latter left a Britisher in charge. That Parker should have been nettled over this seems entirely reasonable on the surface, although one cannot recapture the overtones of the controversy. Hyatt would not accept Parker's authority and gave him hot rebuffs. They wrangled over other matters as well.[15]

In retrospect it does seem acceptable for the Legation to have exercised quite a bit of control over the consuls: the fifty appointments varied in quality, the system was weak in continuity, the consuls poor in language skills and placed in difficult situations up against a puzzling China. On the other hand it is unclear whether the Department of State sought to assert such Legation control over the consuls. The need in the field was evident enough to Parker, who wanted to straighten out the juridical role of consular officers and give the commissioner appellate jurisdiction.[16] In this, he failed to win sufficient support among the consuls. Special anti-Parker activity emanated from Hyatt, who carried on a vigorous correspondence with the chargé, raising legal objections to Parker's expansion of the Legation's powers. Quite possibly the latter was grossly tactless, but there does seem to be a case for his attempt to assert the power of the office of the commissioner over the very miscellaneous performances of the consuls.

Parker's fracases with assorted consuls were interrupted, and nearly terminated, by his embarking on the *Larriston* on April 30, 1853, Captain Baylis, bound for Hong Kong. While getting under way at Woosung, near Shanghai, the *Larriston* came in contact with the United States sloop *Plymouth*, part of Perry's fleet, the latter vessel having swung with the tide before the steamer passed clear of her. Although the *Plymouth* suffered some small injury, the *Larriston* lost mizzenmast, main-topmast, and foreyard. It had its longboat crippled but escaped injury to hull or machinery.[17] After a delay of a few hours Parker's vessel departed on its coastal voyage. Two days out of Shanghai with the ship proceeding at ten knots through thick weather, Dr. Parker went on deck at about 11:00 P.M., when to his consternation he saw land close at hand.

Immediately giving the alarm, he was nevertheless too late: the ship smashed onto rocks, the force of the shock stoving in her bow. Despite the hole, the coal next to it formed a kind of temporary bulkhead, holding back the water. When the captain tried to rig pumps to keep the stern free of water, it was found that the waste water pipes had been broken by the shock, and were useless. The crew managed to launch the lifeboat and to get most of the foreign passengers into it. With them went the second and third mates and some crew. After landing these passengers on the nearest island, the boat tried to return to the ship but was forced to desist. The longboat which had been damaged in Shanghai came crashing onto the island with the passengers' servants, all scrambling out safely except Dr. Parker's aged teacher who was swept away. The captain's account reports two others lost.

For the many left on the vessel the nightmare had only begun. When the tide went down, they built a raft from spars, the chicken coop, and other items, but then decided not to use it. By cutting away the foremast around 3:00 A.M., they eased the strain on the vessel and all joined Captain Baylis on the forecastle deck. At dawn a heavy sea was breaking over them, the decks were disintegrating, and wreckage was breaking away. They saw a Chinese boat coming out, but it was forced back. With Captain Baylis urging the group to stay *on* the wreck as their best chance, quite a few of the crew tried in the wildness of their desperation to float ashore on wreckage, but were lost. Several boats tried to reach the vessel and turned back. Another batch of Lascars took to the sea and were lost. The remainder crowded on the bowsprit and the night-heads. About 10:00 A.M. a Chinese boat came out; two men swam to it and were picked up before it had to withdraw. The ship's lifeboat struggled out and managed to take all but Captain Baylis and four others. An hour and a half later the lifeboat was back. Of the five who remained, one was by then dead and another so close to death that he had to be left. The other three were saved. In another hour and a half, the vessel had slipped underwater except for the top of the mainmast.

The island had some huts and six fishermen, who made available dried potatoes and salt fish to Parker and his fellow survivors. The fishermen conveyed the ship's carpenter, a Chinese, to the main-land for help. Tuesday night was miserable: they were cold, wet, and without shelter. Wednesday morning the crews of three boats appeared, "the leader of whom was a villainous cut-throat looking fellow with a long knife." [18] The captain thought that numbers (there were seventy survivors) and a few cutlasses saved them. The carpenter returned with word that a junk was being sent for them. It arrived at 3:00 P.M. and took the seventy survivors to the mainland, where they were received by mandarins, given a temple to sleep in, and victualled with six eggs—for seventy half-starved people.

In the bay was the Macao *Lorcha No. 30*, whose captain was very kind: Señor José Francisco Salaio provided clothing, tea, coffee, sugar, rice, and biscuit. After a difficult night in which Parker and the others felt half dead from the cold, fleas, and mosquitoes, they struck a bargain with the owner of the lorcha, who agreed to convey them to some shipping, gave them some money for the purchase of further food, and took them aboard at 10:00 A.M., May 5. At night they anchored at the mouth of the Min River after a dangerous cruise close to shoals in half a gale. Parker and his companions were subsequently transferred to the *Mahamoodee* and later yet to the *Zephyr* and *Audax* for the completion of their trip to Hong Kong.

Having survived the shipwreck, probably to the dismay of his consular ill-wishers, Parker was soon ready to return to battle with them. An example of the antagonism which he inspired among this group may be seen in his relations with Consul Robert C. Murphy over the problem of the Shanghai duties.[19] Their controversy began late in 1854 when Commissioner McLane suddenly departed, dropping that financial hornets' nest into Parker's lap. Part of Shanghai was then in the hands of the Triad insurrection (not the Taiping rebels but collateral insurrectionists), that part being in turn under siege from the Manchu Imperialists, who sought to reassert their lost authority in one of their chief ports. The established commercial norms, as evolved in 1842–1844 and elaborated since, had begun to dissolve. With no Manchu authority in Shanghai to collect customs dues and attend to the myriad formalities of arrivals and departures, shippers had variously paid customs duties into the safekeeping of their own consuls, or given bond for future payment, or — in increasing numbers — simply evaded payment. Those that paid were naturally resentful of those who did not, and were eager to have an agreed-upon, enforceable arrangement, or get their money back. The disagreement between Parker and Murphy found the former attempting to carry out an order from the Department of State to release the dammed-up funds to the merchants, whereas Murphy thought the order unjust and incorrect. It violated, he believed, the government's own recent agreement to turn the money over to the Chinese.

Murphy was the first American *political* consul at Shanghai — in contradistinction to a merchant consul like a member of Russell and Co. Although a political appointee, he inherited a situation of unusual independence which had been shaped by the tradition of merchant consuls.[20] He thus held a rather strong position. On the other hand, the post of commissioner, even more so that of acting commissioner, was a weak one. The department had no way to back Parker up quickly, and his perch was in many respects awkward and unenviable. Moreover Parker, combative just as Murphy was, had no flare for diplomacy. Their lingering quarrel quite possibly contributed to the ill-health of both men. The most acrid period of their relationship came in the spring of 1855, when Parker was himself a wreck, eager to take permanent leave of the China coast and its problems.

In Parker's relations with official China, the year just past was one of the periods during which he achieved repeated mention in government documents. Other such periods came during the Cushing mission and Parker's incumbency as commissioner. He was mentioned both in memorials to, and edicts emanating from, the emperor.[21] These documents treated him variously: from one pleasant mention ("seemed rather trustworthy") through seven neutral references (for example, "the American chief Parker") to twelve of routine superiority (the "American barbarian Parker" and his "barbarian woman") and eight derogatory ("Parker will sow his trickery among the others"; "his mentality is inscrutable"). Of the eight abusive references, all but one emanated from superheated Governor Yeh (1856, and another eruption in 1858 after Parker's retirement) and the Hsien-feng Emperor (1856, echoing Yeh's July memorial). Given the vocabulary of condescension and contempt which was customary bureaucratese in the official Chinese documents until 1860, Dr. Parker came off quite well. Aside from the derogatory items accounted for (and in retrospect who would not prefer *dis*approval from two such dubious characters?), there were no other mentions in this category in all the remaining documents dealing with him.

There were copious reasons for Parker to contemplate leaving China. Although mission opportunities were still rapidly increasing and were optimistically assumed to be capable of boundless further expansion, Dr. Parker's own pioneering contributions had all been made some years earlier, and his role in missionary expansion had necessarily dwindled. The press of government duties had caused him to be absent a good deal from the hospital in 1852–53, the work devolving on his Chinese assistants.[22] Then, in 1854 the hospital was closed for some time, owing to the disturbed state of the city, which was beseiged by an army of Triads, the potent, anti-Manchu secret society of the South. He had gotten himself into a series of unpleasant difficulties as chargé and had failed as a repeated aspirant for the post of commissioner.

Moreover, the unspeakably dismal conditions in Canton had been hard on Mrs. Parker. When the Parkers attended balls despite the remonstrances of the local missionaries, the latter would no longer hold their meetings in the Parkers' living quarters.[23] Balls cannot have occurred very often, and to have had attendance at them become a moral issue in a small, tight community seems grotesquely unjust. The doctor's release from that Canton waterfront to the Legation activities of the other treaty ports and his further release from the overwhelming and exhausting commitment to the hospital opened the way for Harriet to freer and pleasanter routines.

The seventeenth Annual Meeting of the MMS was held at the Parkers', and served as an opportunity to wind up the doctor's mission career. Its report recorded a high-flown, but moving summation by Parker in which he touched on the years of toil, the wide range of both patients and diseases, the wearisome days and sleepless nights, the doctrines which had been declared and expounded, and his evangelical hopes.[24] In March and April 1855, while suffering from kidney and back trouble accompanied by "great mental prostration," he was in a very retrospective frame of mind, rereading his early sermons and journals. "How different the laying aside the armor—from buckling it on!" he wrote. "I remember my first visit to this place [Macao] — then with me all was vigor—and *hope* was buoyant; now I am like a bow too long bent . . . and unless a change of climate, & *rest* for a time, shall restore my wonted energy, my work, I fear, is nearly done." [25]

The list of lost friends and associates was particularly depressing: Stevens, J. R. Morrison, Wisner, Olyphant, Jardine, his mother and sister, Gutzlaff, Wang Asui (for twelve years the chief dispenser at Dr. Parker's hospital, d. 1854),[26] and Liang A-fa, just lost in April 1855.

The hospital, which had been turned over to Dr. John Kerr, an enormously energetic man at the beginning of a fabulously productive mission career, had to be closed in October 1856 during a period of great tension. Meanwhile, on May 10, 1855, the Parkers had sailed for home. The doctor, sick and despondent at age fifty, did not expect to return to China.

12 ◆ Commissioner

The trip home in 1855 took the Parkers by way of Singapore and Southampton. There is no record of the voyage beyond their departure from Hong Kong on May 10, 1855,[1] nor of possible visits to friends in England. Evidence places the Parkers in Washington on or about August 10, suggesting that their fast transit of ninety-two days may have been the result of taking passage on one or more of the speediest clippers of that era. Their best chance to save time lay in taking one vessel to the Suez isthmus and crossing the latter overland for a sailing connection on the other side.

Arrival in the United States, aside from reunions with relatives and friends, meant official encounters in Washington, which led to discussions with Secretary of State William L. Marcy concerning the vacant position of commissioner to China, most recently filled by Robert McLane. Some years earlier Parker had been one of the apparently few men who really wanted the post, but had been passed over repeatedly in the processes of political patronage. In 1849 Mrs. Parker had sought help of Mrs. A. H. Everett, who had then asked her well-known brother-in-law, Edward Everett, to write to Washington on Parker's behalf. Everett cheerfully complied, emphasizing Parker's language skill and his good relations with many Chinese through his hospital work. He added that his brother had "entertained the highest opinion of Dr. Parker's talents, and general practical ability."[2] There had been other attempts, equally unrewarded. Now in late 1855, when insecure health and dulled enthusiasm were upon Parker, and after having abandoned the scene of his professional career, he was persuaded to come about and return to China under the cherished appointment. It is not hard to imagine why he should have accepted: the prestige, the salary, the flattery of a request by the secretary of state and the president, the return of a combative man to his favorite coastal conflicts — this time armed with bigger guns, and the opportunity of making a glittering name for himself as the successful refurbisher of the Treaty of Wanghsia, by its own terms scheduled for revision in 1856. There were even more potent reasons for *not* accepting: dubious health, his unsuitability for a diplomatic post, and the general hopelessness in that period of dealing constructively with the Chinese authorities—but he apparently turned a blind eye to them.

The appointment, accepted in August 1855, meant that Parker served chiefly under Secretary Marcy and President Pierce, but briefly in 1857 under President Buchanan and Secretary of State Lewis Cass, who had taken Parker to his 1841 court interview in Paris.

This first appointment of an American diplomatic officer who had already had substantial direct experience in Asia was received with the heterogeneous reactions one would have expected. Dr. Hobson, now indefatigably critical of Peter Parker, thought a worse appointment could hardly have been made. He had become, in Hobson's view, so political and secular as to set a bad example for younger missionaries and thereby to inflict positive injury on the cause of missions in China. Hobson was alarmed by the printing and circulating of a placard "by the Chinese (professedly the *people* of Canton) denouncing the character and conduct of Dr. Parker, whom they charge with having favored the rebels, and warn him not to show himself in this city." [3] The *China Mail*, editorially friendly to Parker, suggested that the defamatory placard "looks much more like a pasquinade, which someone has been hired to write, than the expression of the united opinion of a respectable body of men." [4] There had been an anti-Parker placard in Canton a decade earlier, declaring that he had become "a *proud* man . . . a mandarin . . . building a large house and chooses to make a grand flourish." [5] The *China Mail* praised Dr. Parker's policy statement which had been contained in his letter to a group of fifty-two Boston merchants who had invited him to a public dinner at the Revere House before his departure from the United States.[6] That invitation had been one of the most cordial affirmations of President Pierce's new appointment. To be sure, one should not attach undue importance to the rhetoric of an invitation where polite civilities may be no more reliable than epitaphs, but the likelihood in this case is that there was indeed abundant support for Parker in the Boston area, where his record as evangelist and doctor was known and admired. In Parker's letter to them there was a suggestion of hard-line policy toward China that would have pleased a merchant group.

Parker's instructions from Secretary Marcy enjoined him to carry through the treaty revision and cited as the primary objectives the establishment of a United States diplomatic resident in Peking, the free extension of foreign trade throughout China, and the removal of restrictions to the personal liberty of United States citizens.[7] Interviews with Secretary Marcy had allowed Parker to discuss with him the tactical options which lay open, the two men agreeing that the commissioner should try for joint, concerted, tripartite action with the envoys of British and France.

The new envoy, traveling without Mrs. Parker, left Boston October 10, 1855, on the *America.* His first stop was London where he saw Lord Clarendon, foreign secretary in the Palmerston cabinet. Parker was aiming at a "triple alliance," that is, group action to the extent of a joint naval force being assembled in North China waters when treaty revision was being discussed with the Chinese. Despite a distracting British involvement with the Crimean War, Parker emerged optimistic from the interview. A trip to Paris allowed him to consult with Count Alexandre Walewski, the French minister for foreign affairs. Once again, in an atmosphere of cordiality tempered only by routine caution, he found a heartening response.[8]

Their preoccupation with their own war on Russian soil may have made more attractive to both the British and French foreign secretaries the prospect of projecting their united activity in the

Crimea outward to the Orient and simultaneously enhancing their bargaining power in treaty revision by adding to it the force of American participation. Since each power had most-favored-nation clauses in its prior treaty arrangements with China, all three would automatically and uniformly benefit by renegotiation of their treaties. This deduction reinforced the logic and cogency of the American's proposition that they could maximize their pressures by joint action and thereby secure for each a better form of treaty revision.

Arriving in Hong Kong on the last day of the old year, Commissioner Parker was received with widespread and flattering cordiality. His old friend, John Bowring, recently knighted and appointed governor of the Crown Colony, invited him to reside at Government House and entertained him with baronial receptions. Parker's good relations with the British are noteworthy because the latter often had abrasive contacts with Americans in a variety of matters. Moreover, given the propensity of Hong Kong's foreign residents to fight among themselves, it was refreshing for Parker to be on good terms with so many.

During his weeks in Washington at the end of the preceding summer he had conferred with Marcy, Cushing, and McLane about the coolie trade, their meeting being specifically connected with the abandonment of coolie traffic by the firm of Sampson and Tappan. Now upon his return to China in the role of commissioner, he issued as his first official act a "Public Notification" [9] against the coolie trade. He called upon all United States citizens "to desist from this irregular and immoral traffic," and withdrew United States support from such dealers. It was a bold and appropriate action, although crippled by the absence of sanctions for enforcing it upon a ruthless adversary. Nevertheless some American in public life had to do something about it, and Parker was one of the prominent, early ones. He continued for some years to lobby for the termination of the trade.

The year had been for him one of physical decline followed by some recuperation during nearly six months of sea travel, to and fro. The next year, 1856, was devoted to a variety of contacts with his British and French counterparts and a series of attempts at regularizing diplomatic contacts with the Chinese. He had no luck in this terminal phase of his public career. We can see in retrospect that Chinese policy between 1839 and 1860 went through repetitive cycles in its accommodation to the West.[10] Each of these two cycles began with a hard-line; moved through confrontation, defeat, and the signing of a treaty; and ended with conciliation and appeasement. One's success in dealing with the Chinese establishment was largely a function of timing: Caleb Cushing arrived on the Chinese scene during an appeasement phase and therefore painlessly secured benefits which the Chinese had in an important sense conceded even before he came ashore; Parker entered during the hard-line phase of the second cycle, having been badly prepared for it by recently experiencing the appeasement phase of the first.

After a pleasant visit in Hong Kong he departed rather early in 1856 for Macao where he "temporarily" located the Legation, hoping to establish it later on a permanent basis in Peking. An interesting sidelight to this Macao interlude was Parker's employing as secretary for three rather idle months the remarkable Yung Wing, Yale '54, the first Chinese student to have attended an American university. The embers of Parker's old conflict with Consul Murphy were soon glowing again. Parker's return as commissioner took place shortly before Murphy had to go on sick leave himself. Before his departure, they conferred in Hong Kong and were able to agree on the disposal of a further part of the unsettled Shanghai claims. Murphy later felt that Parker took advantage of his absence and that Parker moreover was indiscreet in living, as commissioner, at the firm of Russell and Company at a time when a Chinese subject had a claim against that firm for $50,000.[11] The consul still believed that Parker was sympathetic to the self-serving pleas of the merchants and unreceptive to the legitimate arguments of the Chinese. It was a case of consul and commissioner reversing their customary roles. As to Murphy's conviction that Parker was a captive of the mercantile establishment, it is noteworthy that the Forbeses themselves did not think so.[12]

Murphy's return to Shanghai in August, after his leave, brought with it fresh difficulties between the two men, as they disagreed over new instructions from the department of state. Once again Murphy sought clarification from the department. It was not until after Christmas that he was able to report a final settlement with the Chinese on the basis of part of the McLane award. Under the new agreement the United States paid about one-third of the sum Americans owed, which was about one-tenth of the promised Anglo-American total. Great Britain welshed on all of her's in spite of everything Bowring could do. He was unable to compete effectively with the lobbying at home by Governor George Bonham of Hong Kong and merchant spokesmen.[13] The quarrel between Parker and Murphy appears to have simmered down.

Parker, confronted with Commissioner Yeh's refusal to have anything to do with him, asked the American consul at Shanghai early in 1856 to notify the governor-general of Liang-Kiang of a projected American trip north for the purpose of treaty revision. On March 24, the emperor noted the situation by issuing an edict ordering Yeh Ming-ch'en to receive Parker in Canton and stop him from coming north. Yeh ignored the order, probably feeling able to do so because Taiping control of central China virtually isolated him from the capital. Parker planned to wait for the arrival of Commodore James Armstrong on the warship *San Jacinto*, and then carry out with the French and English a prearranged, joint, armed expedition to the Pei-ho to secure negotiations for treaty revision. When he sent inquiries to the French and British envoys in May 1856, to see if they had instructions from their home governments to cooperate with him, he learned that the British were prepared for only very limited cooperation and that the French representative had received no relevant instructions. Moreover, although Commodore Armstrong arrived in Hong Kong in June, he was under strict orders to proceed immediately to Japan. He did assign a sloop of war, the *Levant*, to Parker, who took off east along the coast expecting to visit Amoy, Foochow, and Ningpo on his way to Shanghai.

While Parker was on this trip, Yeh submitted a lengthy memorial to the emperor in which he rehearsed the details of Parker's life and diplomatic involvements at Canton and indicated that the American was "generally regarded as crafty." Two years earlier, Yeh reported, Parker had expected Taiping victory at Canton and had established some connections with the rebels. When the imperial forces had put down the rebellion there, Parker had lost so much face from that event that, even after becoming the United States Commissioner to China, he sought "to silence people's ridicule." [14]

In Foochow in mid-July, Parker was cordially received by Governor-General Wang I-te. Parker requested Wang to forward to Peking a letter from the president of the United States. When asked why he did not send it through the usual Canton channels Parker said he preferred Foochow and did not tell Wang that Yeh Ming-ch'en had refused to see him. The letter was later returned with its seal broken and with instructions for it to be sent through the Canton mechanism. This letter, never received by the court, was a substantial improvement over the fatuous document which Caleb Cushing had taken to China a dozen years earlier.

From Shanghai in August Parker wrote again to the British and French envoys on behalf of joint action, receiving a negative from Bowring and learning in the same month that the *San Jacinto* had been disabled. With his own transport temporarily unavailable, the commissioner nevertheless nourished optimism for a bit longer concerning the possibility of Peking either granting him residence in the capital or sending an envoy to Shanghai or Ningpo to renegotiate the American treaty. He was encouraged by word from Bowring that the British government was sending a fleet to China in support of treaty revision.

On October 8, 1856, the *Arrow* incident occurred, out of which developed a local war between the British and Chinese. In the incident itself the Chinese initially attacked a British-registered lorcha, the *Arrow*, and then failed to satisfy the British with the proffered apology. Dr. Parker, at first "surprised and delighted" by the spunky, ill-advised Chinese action in the incident, felt that it put Americans in an advantageous position by briefly reviving the possibility for a triple alliance.[15] When that still failed to materialize, Parker abandoned the plan for sailing to the Pei-ho. He left Shanghai on the *San Jacinto*, and from Hong Kong went back to Macao, November 11, 1856.

In this tag end of the year as relations began to collapse once again between foreigners and the Chinese, Parker himself came under increasing pressure to refuse to be insulted by the Chinese government and to be more aggressive.[16] One of the episodes which generated these pressures arose out of the actions of James Keenan, American consul at Hong Kong, who was reported to the commissioner as having joined the British attack of October 29 on Canton, carrying the American flag. Harry Parkes, British consul in Canton, spread the report of this evidence of American support. Keenan, a superpatriotic type, disliked both Parker and the interference of the Legation, and now denied that he had carried the American flag in the British assault. He was in all likelihood lying, but when Peter Parker thought Keenan should be dropped from the service, the consul fought like a wildcat and wrote at length to the state department regarding his innocence.[17]

In this same period, when the Chinese authorities in the south understandably thought that Americans were actively supporting the British in their desultory hostilities, overzealous Chinese guards fired on an American warship travelling from Macao up toward Canton, whence it was to escort the Americans who were withdrawing from Canton at Yeh's request. When a boat was sent from the *San Jacinto* to investigate the shooting, the Chinese compounded their error by killing one of its occupants. Whereupon Commodore Armstrong sent vessels to shell the forts on both sides of the Pearl River. At this point the commissioner made himself horribly unpopular with bellicose Americans in Canton by interrupting the retaliation on the Chinese. "That day [wrote a red-neck who signed himself "Honesty"] . . . arrived the mighty Doctor Peter Parker (that extraordinary compound, as a worthy member of our community [Canton] dubbed him — *semi-clerico, semi-politico, semi-medico, semi-* ---. . . . It was only want of firewood that saved *his effigy* last night from throwing more light on this community than the *original* ever succeeded in doing) on board the *San Jacinto*, and . . . *stops all proceedings at a point where the Chinese are sure they have whipped the Americans* . . . and writes a despatch calling on Yeh to beg pardon in 24 hours!" [18] In this instance the commissioner played the role of pacifier,[19] but not for long. Having demanded an explanation of the attack from the imperial commissioner within twenty-four hours, the Americans found the account unsatisfactory when it arrived. Without further delay, Armstrong renewed his own attack on the river forts, and by November 22 had captured several of them. The Americans lost 5 men; the Chinese, 160. Parker's report to Washington declared, "This is the first blow that has ever been struck by our navy in China, and it has been done in a manner calculated to secure for it an important prestige in the mind of this haughty government." [20] After his multiple frustrations in trying to deal with the Chinese, Parker had found a kind of catharsis in the resort to force.

Parker's major claim to notoriety in this period is based on his aggressive recommendation that United States forces land on Formosa and hold it as a hostage for acceptable Chinese behavior during treaty revision. This proposal evolved out of his failure to secure treaty revision in 1856 and constituted the next step in his escalating ideas about how to deal with official China. It was related to the toughness of Commissioner McLane's policies at the end of his tour of duty in the Far East. In a despatch of December 12, 1856, to Washington, Parker proposed that the representatives of the United States, England, and France should act in concert and present themselves together at the Pei-ho; that, if not welcomed to Peking, as a "last resort" the French should occupy Korea, the British should take Chusan, and the United States seize Formosa; that when the Chinese gave in to all Western demands for a favorable treaty revision, the territories should be relinquished. This formulation marks the beginning of the last phase of his period as commissioner. Henceforth, Parker worked toward closer cooperation with Britain and France, even if it threatened to involve the United States in war with China, and toward American seizure of Formosa.[21]

Some weeks earlier Sir John Bowring had finally come forward with a proposal that a joint Anglo-American communication be sent to Tientsin. Parker, surprisingly cool to the suggestion, had refused participation. One may surmise that the reason for his refusal was that Bowring was offering a too bland suggestion, and that Parker sought a bigger, tougher policy. By the end of December, the commissioner was writing again to Washington, this time requesting extensive naval support, "not less efficient and imposing than the Japan expedition of 1853–'54." But the Pierce administration would have none of it. Despite other pressures as well, the president and secretary of state sensibly withheld any American cooperation which could lead to war no matter how limited; they knew Congress would refuse support. They were also able to convince Buchanan and Cass of the incoming administration that their policy of restraint should be continued.[22] Secretary Marcy, without having received either of the commissioner's December letters urging escalated action, wrote Parker that the United States should not be drawn along with Britain; that the November sending of a warship past the Pearl River forts had been indiscreet; and that the Legation should investigate the Keenan incident.

The administration found Parker's Formosan elaboration objectionable. The island province had for some years interested various Canton merchants.[23] In 1854 Commodore Perry sent a well-arranged exploratory expedition to collect information. The following year two American adventurers, Gideon Nye, Jr., and his friend and associate W. M. Robinet, sent another expedition and by order of Parker made a study of political and economic conditions. In February 1857, Nye wrote Parker that parts of eastern and southern Formosa should be under American protection, and added that Nye and others would colonize the island if they could be sure of American protection. Parker forwarded the Nye letter to the state department. At the end of February he and Commodore Armstrong met at Macao to discuss Formosa, agreeing that Formosa was desirable and legally obtainable, but that a bigger naval force would be necessary to assure protection. When Robinet sent Parker a detailed report on American trade at Formosa, urging prompt American action to colonize, Parker forwarded the report to Washington.

The commissioner, understandably out of touch with the political mood of the country he represented (he had not resided there since 1842 and then only for a year), and unaware of how unacceptable his brand of incipient imperialism was to the generality of Americans in that era, continued to elaborate and ornament his selected project. His December conception of temporarily holding a part of Formosa as a way of twisting the tiger's tail, grew within a few months to implied support — as he forwarded Nye's letters — of American colonization of southeast Formosa, then to fears over the rumor that Great Britain might herself take the island as she had done with Hong Kong, and finally to his attempt to forestall such a taking. In a solemn March dispatch to Sir John Bowring he wrote: "In the event of the island of Formosa being severed politically from the Empire of China, I trust to be able to substantiate a priority of Claim to it on the part of the Government of the United States: first, by contracts already entered into with the Imperial Authorities of the island, by Citizens of the United States, and secondly, by their actual settlement upon it with the consent of the Chinese, over which the United States flag had been hoisted for more than one year." [24]

Despite Parker's growing uneasiness over what he assumed might be Bowring's policy, they conferred with apparent amiability early in April. Without the commissioner's knowing it, instructions were on the way and would arrive in a few weeks, telling him to avoid any aggressive policy of joint action with England. As Parker's luck would have it, Bowring was at long last prepared to adopt a variation of the American's tail-twisting suggestion of the previous year — in this case a proposal for "common cooperation of the military and naval force of the treaty powers for the reduction of Canton." [25] Conferring also with M. de Bourboulon, minister plenipotentiary at the French Legation, the American indicated, with his hopes revived, that he expected full support from his home government for close cooperation with France and Britain, that he was merely waiting for sanction from Washington.

One of the often agitated aspects of the mission movement is its interlocking to an undefined extent with Western imperialism. Missionaries were pioneers; as pioneers they could not be sure what was coming after them; when imperialism often came after them, they became stereotyped as its forerunners; and as the latter, they have been especially suspect in the anticolonial atmosphere of the mid-twentieth century. It can be demonstrated that there is no organic or necessary connection between missionaries and imperialism — witness the Jesuits who went to China in the seventeenth century, and the Buddhist missionaries to Japan from T'ang China. In neither case was there an imperialist accompaniment. On the other hand, the absence of an organic connection between the two does not mean that they cannot or have not accompanied each other. They sometimes have, as is shown by their coincidence in nineteenth-century China or by the urging of David Livingstone that Britain take colonies in southeast Africa as a means of ending the abomination of the slave trade in that area. Much of the explanation may lie in the fact that imperialism needed weak areas and also needed forerunners to demonstrate imbalance, reveal possibilities, show weakness, and amass information. In many cases the missionaries fulfilled that role. And one should add that in many cases they did not — businessmen did, secular explorers did, sailors and others. Often missionaries were ardent and potent critics of the foreign activities of business, of government, and of military enterprises. Although missionaries, unlike conventional expansionists, did not need weak areas, they could often flourish in them, given endurable conditions of climate and public health. Despite the fact that the mission movement was eminently diverse in its make-up and contained many stout opponents of imperialism and defenders of Asian independence, there were many others who indeed served imperialism in one way or another, Peter Parker included.

His Formosan plan, a policy suggestion born out of frustration, was sufficiently ill-advised to have supplied numerous critics of Parker with a handy bludgeon. He never saw his plan as a step toward an American empire. To him it was chiefly useful as a device for maximizing pressure on a haughty Chinese officialdom while minimizing the dangers of bloodshed. His foolish Formosa suggestion did point toward the general thesis ultimately adopted and elaborated by his country: that the United States should participate in the power politics of the Far East, should not only flex its muscles, but on occasion intervene (Samoa, Philippines, Japan, the Trust Territories, Korea, and Vietnam). A more appropriate proposal would have been for a neutral, conciliatory, waiting type of long-term inaction, quite the reverse of Parker's idiom.

The logistics of the period led to weird chronological overlaps. On April 22, 1857, William B. Reed was appointed to replace Parker. To the latter a dispatch was sent with notice of his recall.[26] Shortly thereafter Parker (now technically out of office) received the February 2 instructions of Secretary Marcy, also out of office by the time Parker received them. The instructions must have been humiliating to Parker, since he had to reveal to the British and French envoys that he could not go through with the "last resort" plan which he had personally urged on them for nearly half a year. Without knowing yet about his having been replaced, he promptly answered Marcy's admonitions by writing the new secretary of state, Lewis Cass, trying to win support for a policy of pressure on the Chinese. Meanwhile, although hoping for an acceptance of his policy by Cass and President Buchanan, which he never got, he was of course under orders to abstain from cooperation with the British. He was bitterly disappointed, and his withdrawal symptoms were embarrassing. Having overdone the original ardor, he now overemphasized his aloofness, becoming uncooperative to the point of discourtesy.[27]

Earlier in the year a diversion from his official duties appeared in the form of the nineteenth Annual Meeting of the Medical Missionary Society, held February 21 at the American Legation, Macao. For him the freshness of the missionary morning was gone. His report on the MMS [28] brought together troubling details on the factory area for late 1856. Most of the medicines of the Canton Hospital had been destroyed by a dispensary fire[29] near the end of October, during the aftermath of the *Arrow* incident. Then on December 14 a mysterious fire gutted the factories, the British claiming the Cantonese had set it. For years that remained the usually accepted explanation. It is quite possible that British set it, as a ploy to secure active support from the other foreigners.[30] Whatever the origins, the destruction really ended an era for foreign merchants in Canton. The numerous fires of the past had always witnessed a restoration of the "Canton system"; this time no such restoration took place. When Hunter returned to the factory area a few years later, he sadly recorded it as utterly desolate.[31]

The destruction of the factories and hospital served also as a symbol of the end of Dr. Parker's career in the Orient. By June he received a letter from Marcy rejecting an aggressive policy toward Formosa.[32] Notice of his official recall, dated April 24, 1857, finally reached him in early August, and he and Mrs. Parker left China within a few weeks, this time for good. He was the last American commissioner to China. His successor assumed the higher rank of envoy-extraordinary and minister-plenipotentiary, which had first been held by Caleb Cushing.[33] The man who succeeded Parker — William Reed, a cultivated and able lawyer, a political appointee garnering a reward for his support of Buchanan in the 1856 presidential election — knew little about China nor was he temperamentally well suited to the task. Nevertheless, the wheel of destiny had turned just enough so that he assumed office during a phase in China's foreign relations which made treaty revision feasible. Luck gave him what it had denied to Parker.

In sum, Parker's career as a diplomat began auspiciously but became progressively less impressive. With Cushing he was helpful, effective, and influential, his medical contacts enabling him to make the most of good luck in dealing with Chinese officials during their manic phase in the diplomatic cycle. This was his diplomatic peak. In the Legation as a subordinate serving Everett, Davis, Marshall, and McLane, he repeatedly acted as chargé during their absences and in the rather long intervals between the departure of one and the arrival of the next. Standing for some consolidation of the jumbled consular scene and for its subordination to the Legation, he was unafraid to quarrel with the consuls who resented those changes. His legal talents were minimal, but he tried hard to perform adequately the juridical aspect of the job; he was unpleasant in some of his dealings with the conciliatory, and slippery, Ch'i-ying. Overall, it was not a notable performance, but he supplied expertise, continuity, willingness, adequate health (a very important item), and an insistence (unpopular) on coordination. It was a period when all those attributes and contributions were needed. Many of his years as a subordinate at the Legation came within the depressive phase of the Chinese cycle, and the job had both its difficult and hopeless aspects. Finally, as commissioner, he had the bad luck to be there in the high period of Yeh's intransigeance. No commissioner — no matter how able, tactful, or experienced — could have altered the basic structure of failure of that immediate period. He might have attempted less than Parker and avoided the latter's mistakes, but he would inevitably have been as unsuccessful as Parker in securing treaty revision itself.

The price Parker paid for these efforts was not only a second-rate reputation among historians for his work as diplomat, but the tarnishing of his notable work as medical missionary.

13 ◆ Retirement and Epitaph

The Parkers arrived home from China late in 1857 and decided to reside in Washington, where they would be near Harriet's connections and could savor the excitement of the political main tent. Here began the long anticlimax of Peter Parker's declining years. Retirement from medicine had really taken place earlier, when he had handed over to Dr. John Kerr the direction of the Canton Hospital. Even before that he had been phasing himself out of medical and surgical involvements, and by the time his Washington years began there seems to have been no desire on his part to open a private practice in the nation's capital. In this connection one recalls the Yale "legend" of Parker's having promised, when awarded his medical degree, not to practice medicine in the United States. The great distinction of his medical contributions might have been presumed to have released him from such a promise, if indeed it had ever been extracted. His health, so shaken in 1855, seems never to have become robust again, although he lived another full generation.[1]

He had a good head and a tight fist for family finance, saving substantial sums from the combined income of his government salary and the medical fees of private practice among the foreign community after his discharge by the American Board. Dr. Hobson estimated that Parker's income from these sources was "probably not less than £2000 a year; and Mr. Olyphant . . . said he had saved already $30,000 . . . from being pennyless or poor he has become comparatively rich." [2] Modest affluence is corroborated by evidence on Parker's investments through his friend John M. Forbes,[3] younger brother of Robert Bennet Forbes. While prudent in management and development, Forbes did invest risk capital in American railroads, and became thereby the agent for the introduction of Chinese capital into the financing of railway expansion in the American midwest.[4] His investments on behalf of Dr. Parker probably did very well. To date, although there is no information concerning what Harriet may have inherited as a supplement to family funds, it can be shown that Parker's will of 1877 contemplated special bequests totalling $30,000 (later reduced to $25,000) over and above the (presumed) lion's share, which was to go to Harriet Parker.[5]

His income enabled the Parkers to settle comfortably at 388 C Street North, relatively near the Capitol. In this location they were also close to the Harvey Lindsly home at number 370. Mrs. Lindsly was Harriet's sister Emelyn, in whose parlor the Parkers had been married in 1841. That Washington provided more congenial surroundings for Harriet is suggested by her having a baby—Peter Parker, Jr., born June 13, 1859—after eighteen childless years of marriage. The father, fifty-five and already retired, was moved to record one of his rare journal entries in that period:[6]

The happiest birthday of my life. Pen cannot record, nor language express, all the emotions of this day. I never celebrated it as a father before. Now I know that "praying breath shall not be spent in vain"; that in God's own time, a long time, yet the best time, it will be answered. It has been with tearful emotions that I have perused the reflections of my thirty-ninth birthday, and the prayer then recorded; but now, on my fifty-fifth, it has been answered.

The most remarkable fact about Peter Parker's Washington years was his change of residence in the early 1860's to the spacious red brick home at the southwest corner of Lafayette Square.[7] Catercorner to the White House, it backed onto Blair House, from the windows of which in 1814 Dolly Madison had seen her belongings in the White House burned by the British. The front windows looked out onto Lafayette Square, the center of much of the city's life in the nineteenth century. The Square, a blend of the formal and informal, its air heavy with the lemon scent of magnolias, had already acquired the bronze statue of Andrew Jackson, cast from cannon captured in the war of 1812. On the other side, where the Metropolitan Club is located today, stood a building which was used during the Civil War by General McClellan as headquarters of the Army of the Potomac, while soldiers were encamped in the Square itself to guard the White House. In the 1870's the Georgetown and Navy Yard Horse Railroad was built along Pennsylvania Avenue on the south side of the Parker residence, between the latter and the White House, while the Metropolitan Horse Railroad passed just one block to the north. As is clear from contemporary representations of Washington, the general scene was abundantly supplied with trees and fields and was astonishingly rural.[8]

Given this location, Dr. Parker came to know as personal friends a long sequence of political notables, among them numerous senators, representatives, members of the Supreme Court, and his neighbor President Lincoln. The Parkers were not far from the Winder Building, still standing today just west across the street from the executive offices. A plaque indicates that when it was the War Office in the Civil War, Mr. Lincoln used to walk over there to read the latest messages from the front. According to family tradition Lincoln called from time to time at the Parker home, sitting in a particular chair in the parlor and holding young Peter on his knee.

Dr. Parker's main diary-keeping days were over. Aside from sporadic entries which were supposed to reactivate his writing habits and which never did, there are very few records of what he observed at close-hand of the Washington scene during those critical and interesting decades. On the other hand, he had rarely been a Pepysian recorder of everyday details and never a chronicler of the political context around him. Had he kept a diary as he descended into old age, it might merely have been warmed-over Presbyterian platitudes, dully interlarded with the familiar self-excoriations.

To escape Washington's summer heat, the family usually went

north to Parker Villa in Framingham, Massachusetts, where Peter had grown up. The farm having come into his hands with the house weakened by dry rot, Parker had the structure torn down and in 1868 replaced by the present home on the old foundation.[9] The land, much of which had been with the family since 1683, was augmented by several adjacent purchases, which are mentioned in Dr. Parker's will and were ultimately left to his son. During one of these family summers in Framingham he participated in the reception and entertainment in Boston of the official Chinese embassy which was touring the Occident under the guidance of Anson Burlingame. One gets another tiny glimpse of him in his mid-seventies. President Noah Porter of Yale reported to Wells Williams that he had found Parker "looking in very good health." They had met at "ceremonies" at Wellesley College related to the completion of its new Music Building.[10]

The bulk of the year was spent in Washington, where Parker invested his time in nonprofessional enterprises. As a member of the Scientific Club of about fourteen members he participated in meetings held at the members' homes. "Peter Parker, Citizen of Washington," is listed as a regent of the Smithsonian Institution in 1870 and thereafter.[11] He attended the New York Avenue Presbyterian Church, lobbied against the coolie trade, and corresponded with friends in the mission field who were hungry for news of the Civil War. They in turn kept him informed of the parallel agony of China where the Manchu establishment, having reached its nadir in the Second Opium War and attendant treaties, had begun to pick itself up with the termination in 1864 of the Taiping Rebellion and the reforms of the T'ung-chih Restoration.

The periodic and affectionate letters of Wells Williams from Macao and Peking (after moving there with the Legation) reported an interesting miscellany: that Dr. Parker's former house on the Praya Grande in Macao had been painted sky blue; that they mourned Bridgman, "departed in the peace of Jesus"; that the French had appropriated Imperial Commissioner Yeh's Canton yamen for some of their missionaries, and were constructing a church inside it; that John Kerr was doing a good job as Parker's successor in Canton, but that Hobson's hospital had been closed.[12]

Early 1862, Parker was told, had produced a frightening abnormality of weather: "Ice has been seen even in Macao; many trees . . . frost bitten, and at Canton some killed. The ice clogged the river at Shanghai, where the snow lay 12 to 15 inches on a level."[13] Quite astonishing to a former resident. Williams reported of Peking fewer visitors compared with the numbers at Canton; and life, more monotonous though busy enough. He preferred the "moisture, heat and bustle" of Canton to the "dust and quiet" of Peking. Nevertheless, it had been exciting when Nanking was recaptured from the Taiping rebels.[14] Later, in 1875, he relayed rumors about the emperor's weakness from smallpox, speculating about the succession probably going to Prince Kung. He also reported the fascinating odd bit of information that he had unexpectedly come into possession of President Polk's letter to the emperor of China, which had been delivered by Commissioner Davis to Governor-General Sen at Howqua's garden house in December 1848, probably with Dr. Parker present.[15] The letter, excellently preserved, had recently been given by some Chinese Catholics to three American Board missionaries when the latter were visiting the Nestorian monument near Sian. It seemed unlikely that the missive had ever reached Peking.

Dr. Parker was involved in various ways with the presence in Washington of the official Japanese embassy of 1860, and again in 1872, when he entertained at his home a similar, but more imposing, embassy from the same country. With his flair for bluntness and his reputation as one of the town's "characters," he probably had some choice words to say to the Japanese visitors about their cannonade during his attempted visit to their homeland a generation earlier.

In 1871 Parker was appointed by the Evangelical Alliance as a delegate to Russia to memorialize Tsar Alexander II on behalf of religious liberty in the Baltic Provinces, but ill-health prevented him from going. In the same year he became a Corporate Member of the American Board and attended in October its sixty-second Annual Meeting in Mechanics Hall, Salem, Massachusetts. This act of the Board healed the long-standing and ridiculous breach with its greatest living missionary. The Corporate Members, of which there were then about 200, were the members that had the vote. Elected by ballot at annual meetings, one third at least were — and are — laymen. They are bound to attend the meetings of the Board, and their travel expenses are paid.[16] (Dr. Parker, probably for reasons of health, did not get to the meetings in 1877–1879, although he did continue as a Corporate Member.) As a body they still make up the Board of the corporation, and the Prudential Committee is selected from among them.

Another appropriate honor came his way when, upon the death of his English friend Thomas Colledge, the Medical Missionary Society elected Parker president. The office of the president had been treated as an honorary one ever since it had been bestowed on Dr. Colledge in 1838. Departing from China in that year and never returning to the Orient, Colledge held the presidency down to 1879 in absentia. Parker's election continued this tradition for the better part of another decade.

Old age held for him its share of physical disabilities, as documented by a letter when he was eighty-one to one of his successors in Canton: "The condition of my health for several years has been such as to render it very difficult to express myself in writing. I daily experience the infirmities of age, having completed my fourscore years and over, — cerebral hyperaemia, daily pains in my head, with vertigo, confusion, and loss of memory, and other grave symptoms." [17] Death, which came on January 10, 1888, must have been a blessed release. He was buried in Oak Hill Cemetery in Washington.

It is difficult to evaluate with fairness Peter Parker's career and the movement of which it was a significant part. For one thing, the range of views about him spreads all the way from the adulation of many of his patients on the one hand to Commissioner Yeh's hatred and contempt on the other; from Dr. Cadbury's pronouncement: "a great man with a great vision," [18] to the Marquis de Courcy's verdict of "tricky and subtle." [19] Dr. Parker felt that his own career had been most successful when he utilized diplomacy to prepare the way for religion, whereas others — among them his friend and investment counselor, John M. Forbes — thought that the two should never be mixed. Also, intellectual fashions have changed: nineteenth-century readers had an appetite for sentimental, canonizing biographies of missionaries; in our own era, that has given way to suspicion and nausea.

In Peter Parker the American Board, despite its subsequent decision to fire him, had found an individual unusually well suited to its needs. From farm boy eating peas with his knife, through various cosmopolitan exposures in the Canton merchant ghetto, to excommissioner in diplomatic regalia entertaining the Japanese mission in Washington, Parker remained temperamentally a dynamic individual, serious and dignified, possessing normal amiability, with a blending of bluntness, toughness, idealism, and gullibility. Although his tongue could speak its own kind of rough poetry, he had little sophistication in the sense of a cultivated taste in the arts. He did have abundant dedication, tenacity, and courage.

His decision to become a missionary had required all three. A career of high mortality, it represented a controversial choice at the time when he made it. Only later during his active career, and partly as a result of it, did American society come generally to romanticize the missionary's career and to lionize the missionary, his rough edges smoothed or overlooked. The missionary image filled some new, transient need of Americans, roughly comparable to the way astronauts came to symbolize the aspirations of many in the 1960's.

Parker saw his own life as one of struggle — "no cross no crown." [20] As it unfolded, it proved to be one of fierce and tenacious commitments rather than of passionately abandoned positions. Mainly oriented toward religion, attempting great things for God and expecting great things of God, he was at the same time significantly different in mode from his missionary peers. His vocabulary of evangelism was primarily medical and activist, whereas for his colleagues and other missionaries it was more often a sedentary pronouncement, extravagant in tone, hysterical, millenarian, and apocalyptic.

Dr. Parker was broad and narrow in an interesting jumble of ways — broad enough to get off the farm, to get an education, go to the other side of the earth and consolidate a new profession, but very sharply focused in the central motivation of his work, the passion to save souls. Cosmopolitan in his array of friends and in combining several careers in one lifetime, he nevertheless disclosed strata of intense conventionality and sometimes epitomized truculent American orthodoxy.

His mission career encapsulated the range of routine problems which typically confronted missionaries, running from loneliness and health hazards to the difficulties of defining the role of the mission doctor. There in the muggy heat of Canton, he had to evolve a workable strategy and technique of missions, maintain relations with the home office, disentangle finances, cope with language problems, and figure out not only how a provincial, nongentry American should fit into the Chinese social scheme but whether or not the individual missionary might work for his own government at the same time.

His career penetrated diverse social and intellectual contexts, coinciding with important medical developments, crucial historical trends, and notable events. This concatenation of roles and episodes intersected with the lives of such a large number of celebrated contemporaries as to be almost eerie; among Protestant missionaries: the Morrison family, Bridgman, Williams, Legge, Gutzlaff, Lockhart, Kerr, Hobson, Anderson, Tidman, and Medhurst; among businessmen: R. B. Forbes, Jardine, Matheson, Wetmore, Dent, Nye, and the fabulous Howqua; among scientists: Silliman, Willard Gibbs, and Kane; among statesmen: expresident John Quincy Adams, and presidents Van Buren, Harrison, Tyler, Pierce, Buchanan, and Lincoln; secretaries of state Forsyth, Webster, Marcy, and Cass; various members of the Supreme Court, miscellaneous politicians, and commissioners Lin, Cushing, Ch'i-ying, and Yeh; and in addition Louis-Phillippe of France, Bowring and Clarendon of England. He met, and in some cases knew well, the distinguished doctors of London, Paris, New York, Philadelphia, Boston, Canton, and Shanghai.

Dr. Parker's career illustrates also that the mission movement itself was in his century a major form of "international relations," that phrase including not only policy but all the significant interconnections and transmissions among states, cultures, and peoples. Not all times and places are marked by the movement of major cultural influences, but nineteenth-century China certainly was. In that context Parker was a major figure, more significant than many a well-known diplomat, despite the paradox that he was not very important in the strictly diplomatic sphere. There, although his role in the Cushing mission indeed had a moderate importance, the longer second and third phases of his career as diplomat were second-rate in performance, unspectacular in achievements, and anticlimactic in denouement. Scrutiny of his governmental career is edifying more for the glimpse it gives into the essential futility of his job at that particular time.

His special accomplishments were, of course, not diplomatic but missionary and medical. At his waterfront hospital he effected a very significant breakthrough in international communication by bringing Protestant missionaries for the first time into touch with large numbers of Chinese drawn from all social strata. Although he was not the first medical missionary, he was within the earliest group of pioneers in that field, was the most important of them, and served as their decisive publicist. Chiefly through his work, medicine came into its own as a distinctive missionary method ultimately recognized as "truly interpretive of the Christian Evangel." [21]

Going to mighty China from the culturally deprived background of rural New England, Parker was a kind of Albert Schweitzer in reverse. It was as though Schweitzer had grown up in French Equatorial Africa, been trained there as theologian, philosopher, and doctor, and had been sent as a missionary to the renowned, ancient city of Strasbourg in the Rhineland. Given the limitations of Parker's background, he had a surprisingly large impact on the mission movement and, through it, on China. One of the important effects of his work was to render less naïve the general missionary endeavor by diversifying and lifting it above its early level of scriptural literalism and camp meeting revivalism. With him an enormous stride was taken toward ultimate sophistication of missionary activity and mutuality of communication with the Chinese.

In his unhesitating use of these new medical opportunities for evangelization Parker had seized a more dubious weapon than he realized. A sensitive observer may well feel that medical service rendered in love is fine; the spoken word by a hospital doctor may be appropriate; but "use of medical . . . service, as a direct means of making converts . . . is subtly coercive, and improper."[22] To gain the central benefits of religious, medical, or other transmissions, particularly when missionaries worked under conditions of difficulty and danger, the recipients had to expect side effects, some of which may have been much resented.

Indeed, whatever their accomplishments, missionaries were regarded by many Chinese as dogmatic, complacent, odiously condescending, and unacceptable in the first place. (Just as war is too important to be left to the generals, transmitted religion may be too important to be left to missionaries and their sponsoring boards.) For some of these critics at least, the general interests of the religious life would have been better served if Christianity could have gone as a fresh and stimulating approach to man's deepest theological problems, not as finished dogma borne by an unbending foreign evangelist. To have denied Christian missions a sphere of action in China would have been to reject in principle the expansion of Christianity beyond the Holy Land, to cancel out the civilizing transmission of Buddhism to Mongolia, China, or Japan, and to withhold from Islam its great role in Africa, Asia, and Indonesia. But a Chinese could understandably have insisted that the process, to be fair, ought to have been reciprocal, with the Chinese exercising equal rights and opportunities in sending missionaries of their own to Europe and America in a kind of mutual interpenetration.

In the medical sphere Dr. Parker's contributions were numerous and impressive: the founding of a key hospital, treatment of 50,000 patients, performance of the most spectacular surgery of the day, significant cultural transmissions (the methodology of Western science, plus specific therapies connected with eye treatment, eye surgery, tumor surgery, lithotomies, ether, chloroform), the inspiration of a very remarkable pictorial documentation of gross pathology, the establishment in 1838 of a bi-national institution—the Medical Missionary Society—to publicize a new profession and to assist in securing new recruits for it. Dr. Parker's ophthalmic institution was *the* decisive step in the evolution of medical missions and therefore for Western medicine in China. Whereas before him medical westernization had been random and sporadic, once this hospital opened its doors, the momentum of alien medical influence led on irresistibly to modern hospitalization, medical schools, the legalization of autopsy and dissection, public health programs, midwifery training schools, and the creation of a national department of health.[23] In 1933, near the peak of mission involvement in China and close to the centennial of Dr. Parker's Canton Hospital, there were about 300 medical missionaries, serving approximately 235 mission hospitals of all sizes in China with more than 1,000,000 patients each year.[24] Western medicine was practiced at that time by an additional 4,000 Chinese doctors, most of them trained in about two dozen medical schools, led by the impressive, mission-derived Peking Union Medical College.

One should understand that, important as Western medicine has been in China, it also has remained a minority tradition right down to the present time. The numbers of Western or Western-trained physicians were toweringly overshadowed by an estimated 1,200,000 practitioners of traditional Chinese medicine,[25] serving a high proportion of the total population.

In his various roles, Dr. Parker was an agent of the overall process of Westernization, the outflow since the time of Columbus of multiple European and Europe-derived influences, ideas, techniques, and institutions, into non-European parts of the world. Among the numerous types that took part in the slow Westernization of China, four had especially noticeable impact: trader, missionary, diplomat, and warrior. They possessed approximately equal importance, although for quite different reasons. Two had major, indirect influence on the peasantry of substantially large regions—the trader through opium and the influence of silver scarcity on the inflation of the copper currency in the rural South, and the missionary through the accidental impact of the Reverend Issachar Roberts on Hung Hsiu-ch'uan, the Taiping leader. The other two (diplomat and warrior) had special influence from the top down. Three were linked together by economic motivation (trader, diplomat, and warrior); the missionary remained separate, seeking no monetary recompense and costing the Chinese little in a financial sense.

A limiting condition in the Westernizing of China, and incidentally a source of loneliness for the outsider, was the fact that the communities of foreigners and Chinese did not interpenetrate. In the coastal cities and many of the treaty ports, they were de facto segregated for a century after Dr. Parker. In the interior, in spite of the closeness of some Sino-Western friendships, there was no substantial integration, miscegenation, or genuine cultural mingling, never any ease or naturalness enabling a member of one community to fit into another. An Englishman who became a Buddhist entered a limbo between two cultural universes, deprived of his welcome in one and coolly received in the other. The relative isolation of Chinese communities in the West and indeed in many parts of Southeast Asia has been a standard characteristic of the Chinese diaspora. Usually unassimilated, alienated, and ghettoed in foreign lands by their own choice, they illustrate the tenacity of cultural pride and aloofness of which the Chinese are capable.

Under these conditions of isolation in China, the missionary nevertheless tended to have the closest ties to the Chinese of any of the foreign types here considered. The businessman (often too the warrior and diplomat), despite daily contacts with a few Westernized, pidgin-speaking Chinese, was apt to seal himself off socially at the club, the racetrack, in first-class cabins on the river steamer, and in grand homes which were alien in architecture, foreign in their routines, and devoid of spoken Chinese save a few ungrammatical instructions to the servants. These men as a group were for the most part cut off from Chinese culture, possessed too many servants and mistresses, were contemptuous of the China they exploited as its major opium dealers, were in their own way fanatics — about profits — and often urged aggressive policies toward China. The missionary, despite his alienation from many aspects of Chinese life, was an active participant in the language, in the daily problems of hospital, school, or congregation, and in the amelioration of China's press of difficulties. All of these points are well illustrated in Parker's life in China.

One of the awkward and interesting things about missionaries in China was how they, as foreigners, functioned as a free-floating gentry — not committed to study the Confucian classics in order to pass the qualifying imperial examinations as a passport to acceptance in major roles, and yet thrust by their own assertiveness and education into a higher Chinese rank than their provincial background would have given them at home. All very evident in Peter Parker's career. Their peculiar freedom enabled them to fit into a great variety of roles in Chinese society. The missionaries succeeding Parker in the nineteenth century moved in a milieu in which China was losing its position of oriental leadership. Voices of criticism rang out and rebellions beset the government. The West slowly imposed its pattern of international relations, as institutional and social changes were taking place in the Chinese pattern; as the governmental mode of the Chinese was being drawn away from its ecumenical, "papal" type of kingship toward the Western concept of a national monarchy; and as a semicolonial Chinese relationship to the West was emerging, symbolized and legalized by unequal treaties. In short, the traditional Confucian order was being buffeted in fundamental ways by an accumulation of inherent weaknesses, cyclical problems, and Western influences. Meanwhile, China's image of the world shifted, and her intellectuals groped in uncertainty and insecurity for realistic solutions.

While all this was going on, the Christian movement grew and spread in the interior, the missionaries rumbling their evangelical thunder. They bore a cultural message, compounded of attitudes toward religion, manual labor, diplomacy, warfare, the role of government, sex, education, and science, which was derived from the American scene and which fitted American society more logically than it ever could China's. What were reasonable, progressive, or innocent attitudes in America, were almost inevitably radical, heterodox, and disruptive in a society built on such different assumptions about the individual, the family, and the community. The missionaries were generally preanthropological in their outlook, viewed the breakdown of Chinese society with dismay, considered Confucian traditionalism as inadequate to deal with the breakdown, and offered — in their innocence, ignorance, arrogance, and love — a total message as a substitute way of life. It was, in its way, of incalculable value to the Chinese. Parker's vigorous missionary critique of China, bearing the stimulus of unintentional radicalism, radiated a concern that Chinese leadership abandon its outmoded world view of a Middle Kingdom surrounded by suppliant barbarians, and take practical steps to accommodate to the real world of nation states.

The Chinese and their overlords the Manchus expected outsiders to regard China as cultivated, relatively homogeneous, devoted to the Confucian way of life, and well-administered by carefully selected, public-spirited Confucian gentlemen. Although the simplicities of this myth have been of immense help in enabling Westerners to come to grips with the awesome vastness of Chinese history, the myth itself did not fit at all well the somber facts of China's nineteenth-century slide toward disintegration and political collapse. Neither Parker nor his mission colleagues were impressed by the myth. They had a direct look into many of the brutal, runaway problems of Chinese life—such as endemic famine, cataclysms in public health, and crumbling, often abominable, administration. It seemed evident to them that China, like so many of its temples, was in a state of decay, that its moral and spiritual powers had become static, and that what power remained was scarcely worth reviving save to a new order and ideal. The message of Christianity, they felt, could supply the ideal, the assurance, the new energies, the needed dynamism.[26]

It is right to reject this Christian grand strategy as unrealistic, outrageous, or impossible — or all three. At the same time one must realize that there remains unanswered the harrowing question concerning what type of general accommodation the Confucian order should have been making to its internal and external pressures. As the remainder of the century unfolded, many answers accumulated. Yeh Ming-ch'en stood for xenophobic reaction, rejecting the non-Chinese outer world; Hung Hsiu-ch'uan, for semi-Christian, theocratic peasant communes; Tseng Kuo-fan, for self-strengthening through selective adoption of Western techniques; Li Hung-chang, for acceptance of Western diplomatic norms; K'ang Yu-wei and Liang Ch'i-ch'ao, for sweeping internal reform moving toward the creation of a nation state under a constitutional monarchy; and Sun Yat-sen, for a revolutionary republicanism. None seemed for long to have the real answer. Each formula, no matter how authentically Chinese it may have been, appears to have been unrealistic, outrageous, or impossible. Often all three. The truth may indeed have been that "no part of this well-knit and remarkably stable society could be remade without an eventual pulling apart and remaking of the whole structure." [27] The unfitting, inapplicable strategy of Peter Parker and his fellow missionaries may have been correct, at the very least, in its love and its radicalism.

◆

Notes
Works by Peter Parker
Bibliography
Index

Abbreviations

ABC	American Board of Commissioners for Foreign Missions
Ch. Repos.	*Chinese Repository*
Harvard Journal	Peter Parker, Harvard Journals 1–8
Lockhart	William Lockhart, *The Medical Missionary in China*
LMS	London Missionary Society
MMS	Medical Missionary Society in China
Stevens	George B. Stevens and W. Fisher Markwick, *The Life, Letters, and Journals of the Rev. and Hon. Peter Parker, M.D.*
Wong and Wu	K. C. Wong and Wu Lien-teh, *History of Chinese Medicine*
Yale Journal	Peter Parker, Yale Journals 1–10

◆ Notes

1 ◆ The Rough Road to Commitment

1. For relevant genealogical data, see Theodore Parker, *Genealogy and Biographical Notes of John Parker of Lexington and his Descendants* (Worcester, 1893), pp. 164, 299, 300; William Richard Cutter, *New England Families, Genealogical and Memorial* (New York, 1914), II, 621; and James Savage, *A Genealogical Dictionary of the First Settlers of New England* (Boston, 1861), III, 356–357.

2. This tale of religious conversion is recounted in a harrowing and moving series of recollections in Parker, Amherst Memoir-Journal, pp. 6, 7–8, 11.

3. Kenneth Scott Latourette, "Peter Parker: Missionary and Diplomat," *Yale Journal of Biology and Medicine* 8:243 (1935–1936).

4. See the chronology which Parker drew up during the 1840 return voyage from China; Yale Journal 8, pp. 90–95.

5. George B. Stevens and W. Fisher Markwick, *The Life, Letters, and Journals of the Rev. and Hon. Peter Parker, M.D., Missionary, Physician, and Diplomatist* (Boston, 1896), p. 16.

6. Yale Journal 8, pp. 91–92; Latourette, "Peter Parker," p. 244.

7. On Amherst in the 1820's, see W. S. Tyler, *History of Amherst College during Its First Half Century, 1821–1871* (Springfield, Mass., 1873), pp. 34–35, 72, 160–164, 626; George R. Cutting, *Student Life at Amherst College* (Amherst, 1871), p. 60; Thomas LeDuc, *Piety and Intellect at Amherst College, 1865–1912* (New York, 1946), pp. 2–7.

8. An assist from the Registrar was indispensable in interpreting the grade scale; Robert F. Grose to the author, Amherst, Oct. 4, 1966.

9. Yale Journal 1, June 3, 1829, p. 35.

10. Thomas M. Howell to Professor Edward Hitchcock, Canandaigua,

N. Y., Feb. 18, 1879, in Amherst College Memorabilia Room; quoted by permission of the Trustees of Amherst College.

11. Yale Journal 1, Oct. 9, 1830, p. 44.

12. On New Haven, see Rollin Osterweis, *Three Centuries of New Haven, 1638–1938* (New Haven, 1953), and Oscar Edward Maurer, *A Puritan Church and Its Relation to Community, State, and Nation* (New Haven, 1938).

13. Yale Journal 2, Oct. 16, 17, pp. 1, 2.

14. Ibid., Jan. 11, 1831, p. 70; Yale Journal 3, May 17, 1831, p. 65.

15. Yale Journal 3, March 15, 1831, p. 20.

16. See, e.g., Yale Journal 2, entry for Friday, Dec. 31, 1830, pp. 62–63; and his other diaries, passim.

17. Stevens, pp. 15, 28–29.

18. Parker to ABC, Framingham, Oct. 12, 1831, in ABC 6, vol. XI (Candidates, M-P), under general item #30, p. 8.

19. Yale Journal 2, Dec. 26, 1830, pp. 58–59.

20. Yale Journal 3, March 23, 1831, pp. 23–24; April 16, 1831, p. 41.

21. Ibid., April 21, 1831, p. 44; April 22, 1831, pp. 44–45.

22. *Missionary Herald* 36:38 (January 1840); for the ensuing figures, see Fred F. Goodsell, *You Shall Be My Witnesses* (Boston, 1959), p. 293.

23. *Missionary Herald* 30:8 (January 1834).

24. *Constitution, Laws and Regulations of the American Board of Commissioners for Foreign Missions* (Boston, 1839), p. 3.

25. ABC, Sub-Committee Reports (1848–1866), I, 11.

26. ABC, "Statistical View of the Officers, Missions, and Missionaries of the Board," *Missionary Herald* 36:37 (January 1840).

27. Yale Journal 3, April 17, 1831, pp. 41–42. At this time he was particularly caught up in reading about the evangelical work of Henry Martyn, pioneer English missionary to India in the early nineteenth century. When he encountered Martyn's assertion that the prime need for a missionary to India was wisdom in regulating one's temper, Parker recorded in his journal: "If I am not mistaken, through Divine Grace, I do possess the mastery of my passions." Just then interrupted by someone trying to force the door into his room, Parker noticed how upset he became. (Ibid., April 29, 1831, p. 56.) Concerning Martyn's account of his own work, he wrote: "have seldom read one with more delight. Oh that his mantle might fall on me" (Yale Journal 3, May 25, 1831, pp. 67–68).

28. Yale Journal 3, April 22, 1831, p. 45; May 24, 1831, pp. 70, 80.

29. Ibid., May 15, 1831, pp. 63–64.

30. Yale Journal 4, June 30, 1831, p. 12; also July 7, 1831, p. 15.

31. Ibid., June 18, 1831, pp. 1–2.

32. Ibid., Aug. 31, 1831, pp. 57–58.

33. Ibid., Sept. 20, 1831, pp. 66–67.

34. Ibid., Oct. 5, 1831, pp. 68–69.

35. Parker to ABC, Framingham, Oct. 12, 1831, ABC 6, vol. XI (Candidates, M-P), #30, eleven pages long. The letter is largely a reproduction of one of his own journal entries for the preceding May, during the high period of his torment; see Yale Journal 3, May 24, 1831, pp. 70–80.

36. Parker to ABC, Framingham, Oct. 12, 1831, ABC 6, vol. XI, #30, pp. 5, 7.

37. On the subject of the mission impulse, O. W. Elsbree, *The Rise of the Missionary Spirit in America, 1790 1815* (Williamsport, Pa., 1928) remains the most helpful work; for Hopkins, see pp. 139–148.

38. Yale Journal 4, Oct. 20, 1831, p. 73; also 5, Dec. 25, 1831. Yale Journal 5 begins Christmas Day, 1831. The un-Parkerian handwriting of Yale Journal 5 is unexplained. The "copy-book" penmanship is much too regular and legible to be his, unless one can assume a massive effort on his part in reforming his handwriting. The content is authentically his own, suggesting that someone else later copied it.

39. On the early history of the Yale Divinity School, see R. H. Bainton, *Yale and the Ministry* (New York, 1957), excellent on the faculty and poor in its brief coverage of Parker; for sketches of the faculty: T. Dwight, *Memories of Yale Life and Men, 1845–1899* (New York, 1903); and *The Semi-Centennial Anniversary of the Divinity School of Yale College, May 15th and 16th, 1872* (New Haven, 1872).

40. Yale Journal 5, April 1, 1832, p. 28; Jan. 25 (misdated as Jan. 15), 1832, p. 11; Jan. 12, 1832, p. 4; Nov. 24, 1832, p. 46; Aug. 2, 1833, p. 82; Jan. 20, 1832, p. 10; Jan. 12, 1832, p. 5; Aug. 2, 1833, pp. 83–84.

41. Ibid., Jan. 25, 1834, p. 106.

42. See ibid. for July 3, 7, 14, Aug. 22, 29, Sept. 1, Nov. 28, 1832.

43. On the "United Band of Foreign Missionaries in Yale University," see Yale Journal 5, Dec. 25, 1831, p. 1; also Parker to Anderson, New Haven, March 4, 1832, ABC 6, vol. XI (Candidates M-P), under general item #30.

44. Day, Taylor, and Fitch to Benjamin Wisner, New Haven, corresponding secretary of the ABC; no date, but received in Boston, Oct. 30, 1833; ABC 6, vol. XI (Candidates, M-P), under general item #30.

45. Yale Journal 3, May 3, 1831.

46. Yale Journal 5, Feb. 29, 1832, p. 21.

47. Ibid., Feb. 8, 1832, p. 15; Jan. 5, 1832, p. 2; Aug. 2, 1833, p. 82.

48. Parker to Anderson, New Haven, March 4, 1832, ABC 6, vol. XI (Candidates, M-P), under general item #30.

49. He went to West Haven for rest and wrote up these events while there; Yale Journal 5, April 1, 1832, p. 27; see also Parker to Wisner, New Haven, Oct. 23, 1833, ABC 6, vol. XI (Candidates, M-P), under general item #30.

50. Samuel C. Harvey, "Peter Parker: Initiator of Modern Medicine in China," *Yale Journal of Biology and Medicine* 8:229 (1936).

51. Yale Journal 5, July 1, 1832, p. 31.

52. Ibid., March 5, 1833, p. 62.

53. Ibid., pp. 67–68.

54. Ibid., Aug. 2, 1833, p. 82; Aug. 7, 1833, p. 86; Sept. 16, 1833, p. 89; Sept. 27, 1833, pp. 92–93.

55. Parker to Wisner, New Haven, Oct. 23, 1833, ABC 6, vol. XI (Candidates, M-P), under general item #30. See also Yale Journal 5, Oct. 22, 1833.

56. Yale Journal 5, Jan. 8, 1834, p. 102; see also Parker to Anderson, New Haven, Jan. 9, 1834, ABC 6, vol. XI (Candidates, M-P), under general item #30.

57. Parker to Anderson, New Haven, March 20, 1834, ABC 6, vol. XI (Candidates, M-P), under general item #30; Yale Journal 5, March 29, 1834, p. 109.

58. Latourette, "Peter Parker," p. 244.

59. Yale Journal 5, passim.

60. Records of the Examining Committee . . . March 6, 1834; in Yale Medical Library.

61. Yale Journal 5, Jan. 8, 1834, p. 102; see also Parker to Anderson, New Haven, April 11, 1834, ABC 6, vol. XI (Candidates, M-P), under general item #30.

62. *Missionary Herald* 30:267–268 (July 1834).

63. Yale Journal 6, May 16 and 23, 1834, pp. 1–5.

64. Instructions of the Prudential Committee of the ABCFM to Peter Parker; Peter Parker collection, Yale Medical Library.

65. The text is in the Peter Parker collection, Yale Medical Library. On the service see "D. A. C." in the *New York Evangelist* 5 (June 7, 1834), no. 23.

66. James C. Richmond to Mrs. Parker, New York, June 9, 1834, in Stevens, p. 91.

67. Yale Journal 6, June 11, 1834, p. 11.

68. Text in ibid., pp. 12–13.

69. Ibid., May 23, 1834, p. 3.

70. P. Perit to Mrs. Parker, New York, June 4, 1834, in Stevens, p. 90.

71. Richmond to Mrs. Parker, New York, June 9, 1834, ibid., p. 91.

72. Yale Journal 6, June 4, 1834, p. 7; June 11, 1834, p. 15.

73. Ibid., June 11, 1834, pp. 14–15.

2 ◆ Arrival in China and the Singapore Internship

1. E. C. Bridgman, Journal, Aug. 2, 1830, ABC, So. China, 1831–37, #29.

2. Parker's account of the 1834 voyage can be followed in Yale Journal 6 or in Harvard Journal 1 (ABC, So. China, 1831–37, #177–180). The Harvard Journal consists of excerpts copied from the Yale Journal and forwarded to Anderson at the American Board office. The long Yale Journal is devoted largely to religious matters.

3. Harvard Journal 1, Oct. 27, 1834, ABC, So. China, 1831–37, #175.

4. For the interested reader today, W. C. Hunter, in *The "Fan Kwae" at Canton before Treaty Days, 1825–1844* (London, 1882), writing in sentimental retrospect after circumstances had transformed the Canton scene, has left an account which is at once the fullest, the most loving, and the most authoritative. Maurice Collis, *Foreign Mud* (London, 1947), reworked and expanded Hunter's information in a highly readable, up-to-date rendering.

5. S. Wells Williams, *The Middle Kingdom* (New York, 1848), I, 137.

6. Fitch W. Taylor, *A Voyage around the World in the United States Frigate Columbia* (New Haven and New York, 1847), II, 137–138.

7. Frederick Wells Williams, *The Life and Letters of Samuel Wells Williams, LLD, Missionary, Diplomatist, Sinologue* (New York, 1889), p. 62.

8. Bridgman to Anderson, Canton, March 26, 1835, ABC, So. China, 1831–37, #112, p. 28.

9. Williams, *Middle Kingdom*, I, 129–130.

10. Harvard Journal 2, Oct. 28, 1834, ABC, So. China, 1831–37, #181, p. 1.

11. Tyler, *Amherst College*, p. 206. Bishop Boone, obituary on Elijah C. Bridgman, *North China Herald*, Nov. 9, 1861; quoted in Eliza J. Gillett Bridgman, ed., *The Life and Labors of Elijah Coleman Bridgman* (New York, 1864), p. 274.

12. For a description of his activity, see his journal entries for March 28, 1831, ABC, So. China, 1831–37, #41.

13. Harvard Journal 2, Oct. 28, 1834, ABC, So. China, 1831–37, #181.

14. Bridgman, *Life and Labors*, p. 100.

15. Harvard Journal 2, Oct. 28, 1834, ABC, So. China, 1831–37, #181.

16. Ibid., Oct. 29, 1834.

17. Bridgman to Anderson, Canton, Oct. 31, 1834, ABC, So. China, 1831–37, #102; Williams to Anderson, Canton, Oct. 13, 1834, ibid., #225; Bridgman and Williams to Anderson, Canton, Jan. 20, 1835, ibid., #10, p. 6.

18. Bridgman, *Life and Labors*, p. 97.

19. Bridgman to Anderson, Canton, Feb. 14, 1832, ABC, So. China, 1831–37, #58.

20. Bridgman to Anderson, Canton, Jan. 25, 1837, ibid., #133.

21. Bridgman to Anderson, Canton, Jan. 17, 1832, ibid., #57; see also Williams to Anderson, Canton, April 26, 1834, ibid., #219.

22. In Concluding Remarks in ABC, 36th Annual Report (Boston, 1845), p. 207.

23. Bridgman to Anderson, Canton, March 26, 1835, ABC, So. China, 1831–37, #112, p. 21.

24. Harvard Journal 2, Nov. 15, 1834, ibid., #181.

25. Parker to Anderson, Canton, Feb. 10, 1845, ABC, Amoy, Siam, Borneo, 1820–46, #73, p. 2.

26. For a translated text, see J. L. Cranmer-Byng, ed., *An Embassy to China, Being the Journal Kept by Lord Macartney during His Embassy to the Emperor Ch'ien Lung, 1793–1794* (London, 1962), pp. 337–341.

27. See M. Frederick Nelson, *Korea and the Old Orders in Eastern Asia* (Baton Rouge, 1945), chapter on "Confucian Familism and the Inequality of Nations." Attention is called to John K. Fairbank, ed., *The Chinese World Order* (Cambridge, Mass., 1968). Although the ties between China and her tributaries are understood, no one has clarified the relationship among the tributaries themselves in the instances when they were in touch with each other.

28. Mouloud Mammeri, *The Sleep of the Just* (Boston, 1958), p. 84.

29. *Re-thinking Missions, A Layman's Inquiry after 100 Years*, William E. Hocking, ed. (New York, 1932), p. 85.

30. Bridgman to Anderson, Canton, July 14, 1834, ABC, So. China, 1831–37, #99.

31. Parker to Anderson, Canton, Oct. 30, 1834, ibid., #173.

32. Harvard Journal 2, Oct. 31, 1834, ibid., #181.

33. Ibid., Nov. 6, 1834.

34. Yale Journal 7, Dec. 23, 1834, pp. 5–6.

35. Harvard Journal 2, Nov. 15, 1834, ABC, So. China, 1831–37, #181.

36. Arthur Waley, *The Opium War through Chinese Eyes* (London, 1958), p. 234.

37. Harvard Journal 2, Nov. 25, 1834, ABC, So. China, 1831–37, #181. Parker to Anderson, Canton, Dec. 4, 1834, ibid., #174. Waley's estimate was more pungent: "a cross between parson and pirate, charlatan and genius, philanthropist and crook." Waley, p. 233.

38. Parker to Anderson, Canton, Dec. 4, 1835, ABC, So. China, 1831–37, #174; Bridgman to Anderson, Canton, March 26, 1835, ibid., #112, p. 1.

39. Harvard Journal 2, Nov. 27, 1834, ibid., #181; Parker to Anderson, Canton, Dec. 4, 1834, ibid., #174.

40. Information on Parker's sojourn in Singapore may be found in Yale Journal 7, which begins with the voyage to Singapore in December 1834, covers 1835, and ends with some entries for 1836. This journal he retained for his own use. His Singapore period is also covered in 200+ pp. of a series of journals which were sent to the ABC: see end of Harvard Journal 2; all of Harvard Journals 3, 4, 5; and nearly all of 6.

41. Yale Journal 7, Jan. 3, 1835, pp. 12–13.

42. Parker to Anderson, Sept. 12, 1835, ABC, So. China, 1831–37, #197.

43. For a sampling of references to his medical practice, see Harvard Journal 3: entries for Jan. 18, 24, Feb. 10, 1835; and Yale Journal 7: entries for Jan. 1, Aug. 16, 21 (for a jaw operation), 1835.

44. Yale Journal 7, Feb. 22, March 5, 1835.

45. For the Malacca trip, see his journal entries for late April, May, and early June, 1835.

46. Yale Journal 7, April 30, 1835, pp. 26–29.

47. Ibid., Aug. 17, 1835.

48. Parker to Anderson, Sept. 12, 1835, ABC, So. China, 1831–37, #197.

49. Harvard Journal 6, ibid., #187, p. 6.

50. Harvard Journal 7, ibid., #188, p. 7.

51. Details of the voyage are found in Harvard Journal 6, ibid., #187, pp. 6–18.

52. Ibid., 18a–19; see also Parker to Anderson, Canton, Sept. 12, 1835, ibid., #197.

53. Harvard Journal 8, April 5, 1836, ibid., #189.

3 ◆ A Hospital for Canton

1. For information on Chinese medicine and medical history, I have relied on: K. C. Wong (Wang Chi-min) and Wu Lien-teh, *History of Chinese Medicine*, 2nd ed. (Shanghai, 1936); Clara B. Whitmore, "An History of the Development of Western Medicine in China" (unpub. diss., Univ. of Calif. at Los Angeles, 1934); W. R. Morse, *Chinese Medicine* (New York, 1934); Georges Beau, *La Médecine chinoise* (Paris, 1965); Stephan Pálos, *Chinesische Heilkunst, Rückbesinning auf eine grosse Tradition* (trans. from the Hungarian by W. Kronfuss, Munich, 1966); Joseph Needham, "The Roles of Europe and China in the Evolution of Oecumenical Science," *Journal of Asian History* 1:3–32 (1967); Dr. Needham's zoological and medical volume for his *Science and Civilization in China* (Cambridge, Eng., 1954–   ) has not yet been published; William Lockhart, *The Medical Missionary in China: A Narrative of Twenty Years' Experience* (London, 1861); Edward H. Hume, *Doctors East, Doctors West: An American Physician's Life in China* (New York, 1946); same author, *The Chinese Way in Medicine* (Baltimore, 1940); A. Chamfrault and Ung Kang-Sam, *Traité de médecine chinoise; d'après les textes chinois anciens et modernes* (Angoulême, 1957–1964).

2. Lockhart, pp. 112–113.

3. Ibid., p. 114.

4. Wong and Wu, p. 59.

5. Ibid., p. 60.

6. Ibid., pp. 63–64.

7. Lockhart, p. 115.

8. Hobson, *Report of Chinese Hospital at Shanghai,* for 1857, pamphlet, Shanghai, 1858; quoted in Lockhart, p. 155.

9. Whitmore, "Western Medicine in China," p. 54; see also p. 57.

10. Quoted from Hobson's Hospital Report for 1854; Lockhart, pp. 184–185. Dr. Hobson also did a paper on this subject for the *Medical Times and Gazette* (June 2, 1860). On the Chinese *materia medica,* see Morse, *Chinese Medicine,* pp. 99–110.

11. Lockhart, pp. 58–59.

12. Ibid., p. 114. For a discussion of acupuncture, see Wong and Wu, pp. 44–45, 227–232; Morse, *Chinese Medicine,* pp. 137–161; Pálos, *Chinesische Heilkunst,* pp. 97–115; Hume, *Chinese Way,* pp. 165–167; and esp. Beau, *Médecine chinoise,* pp. 42–119.

13. Needham, "Europe and China," p. 21. For another interesting speculation, see William Y. Chen, "Medicine and Public Health," *China Quarterly,* no. 6 (April–June 1961), p. 162; cited by Edgar Snow, *The Other Side of the River* (New York, 1962), p. 310.

14. Lockhart, p. 113.

15. Hua T'o appears in the *Romance of the Three Kingdoms,* and is supposed to have employed some kind of an "effervescing powder" for anesthesia; see Wong and Wu, pp. 53–56, and *San Kuo or the Romance of the Three Kingdoms* (trans. by C. H. Brewitt-Taylor, Shanghai, 1929), II, 157–159, 188–190.

16. The successful and extraordinary use of acupuncture for anesthesia in major operations is a research development since the late 1950's and not a traditional aspect of acupuncture.

17. Lockhart, pp. 23–24, 37.

18. Wong and Wu, pp. 264–272.

19. D. G. Crawford, *Roll of the Indian Medical Service, 1615–1930* (London, 1930), p. 624.

20. Wong and Wu, pp. 82, 215–216, 269, 273–274.

21. Lockhart, pp. 120–121. See also Alexander Pearson, "Vaccination," *Ch. Repos.* 2:36–39 (May 1833). Later a Dr. G. X. Balmis claimed to have been the first to use Jennerian vaccination in China, but Dr. Pearson showed that it had been used quite extensively both by himself and by Portuguese practitioners prior to Balmis' arrival. Also, the tract on vaccination which he wrote and which Sir George Staunton translated into Chinese, had been published before Balmis arrived. In his own account Pearson did not claim priority over the Portuguese practitioners. He implies that his and their introductions of vaccination were simultaneous.

22. Crawford, *Roll of Indian Medical Service,* p. 624.

23. The chief source on this dispensary is J. C. Thomson, "Historical Landmarks of Macao," *Chinese Recorder* 18:392–393 (October 1887).

24. Wong and Wu, p. 307.

25. Crawford, *Roll of Indian Medical Service*, p. 624; Wong and Wu incorrectly have him leaving Macao in 1825.

26. Crawford, *Roll of Indian Medical Service*, p. 624; Wong and Wu, p. 308.

27. Crawford, *Roll of Indian Medical Service*, p. 624, gives 1830; Crawford, *A History of the Indian Medical Service, 1600–1913* (London, 1914), p. 91, gives 1831; S. W. Williams, *Middle Kingdom*, II, 344–345, supports 1831, since he has the dispensary opening in 1827 and operating for four years.

28. "A Brief Account of an Ophthalmic Institution . . . by a Philanthropist" [Anders Ljungstedt], Canton, 1834; quoted by Wong and Wu, p. 309. A terse reference in the archives of the Commonwealth Relations Office in London (India Office Records, China and Japan Factory Records, Abstracts of Factory Consultations, #277A, p. 25) indicates Colledge's ophthalmic infirmary at Macao received $500 annually from Howqua and $500, Jan. 13, 1832, from the East India Company. Unpublished Crown copyright material in the India Office Records reproduced in this book appears by permission of The Controller of Her Majesty's Stationery Office.

29. Williams, *Middle Kingdom*, II, 344–345; Dr. Parker thought the Macao dispensary had only "three years of continuance" (Peter Parker, *Statements Respecting Hospitals in China*, [Glasgow, 1842], p. 22). Many of the facts are unclear; for example, Colledge was absent from Macao during an appreciable part of those years and obviously unable to have attended to the dispensary. For further information on Colledge, see the chatterbox diary: (Harriet Low), *My Mother's Journal: A Young Lady's Diary of Five Years Spent in Manila, Macao, and the Cape of Good Hope from 1829–1834*, ed., Katharine Hillard (Boston, 1900), passim.

30. See John R. Latimer, testimony in "Report of the Chester County Medical Society: Biographical Notice of Dr. James H. Bradford," *Trans. Med. Soc. of the State of Pa.* 5:82 (1860); pp. 81–83 of this source contain the best account of Bradford and his work in Canton; references may also be found in *Ch. Repos.* 2:276; Harold Balme, *China and Modern Medicine: A Study in Medical Missionary Development* (London, 1921), pp. 38–39; Wong and Wu, pp. 331, 824; and Whitmore, "Western Medicine in China," p. 145 (where he is erroneously referred to as Bradley Bradford, instead of James H.). Harriet Low records being escorted in 1829 to theatricals by a Dr. Bradford, very probably the one in question; entry for Oct. 18, 1829, *My Mother's Journal*, p. 35.

31. R. H. Coxe (sometimes "Cox") eludes satisfactory identification. He had arrived on the East India Company ship *Mangles*, became "resident surgeon to the community in Canton" and was then appointed by the

Company as assistant surgeon in Canton during the absence of Dr. Pearson from China. (Consultations, transactions and correspondence of/to H. C. Plowden Esq., President . . . Season 1832–33, China and Japan Factory Records, vol. 249, Dec. 7, 1832; see also Cox to H. R. Alexander, undated, ibid.) He was to have the use of the surgeon's apartments when Dr. Colledge was not occupying them himself. (H. H. Lindsay to Cox, Dec. 7, 1832, ibid.) Bridgman relates that the ABC missionaries were given free medical attention by both Coxe and Bradford (Bridgman to Anderson, Canton, March 26, 1835, ABC, So. China, 1831–37, #112, pp. 22–23).

32. Wong and Wu (p. 311) felt, rather surprisingly, that the institution lasted until 1839.

33. On the origins of the Canton mission, see the useful account by Clifton J. Phillips, *Protestant American and the Pagan World: The First Half Century of the American Board of Commissioners for Foreign Missions*, Harvard East Asian Monograph #32 (Cambridge, 1969), pp. 173–174; ABC, *Thirty-eighth Annual Report* (Boston, 1847), pp. 160–161; and Bridgman, *Life and Labors*, p. 38.

34. ABC, Records of the Prudential Committee, II (1825–1831), 196.

35. Joint mission letter to Anderson, Canton, May 2, 1836, ABC, So. China, 1831–37, #12; and E. C. Bridgman to Anderson, Canton, Dec. 19, 1833, ibid., #81. Parker to David Green, Canton, August 1, 1844, ABC, Amoy, Siam, Borneo, 1820–46, #71, p. 2.

36. Bridgman to Anderson, Canton, March 26, 1835, ABC, So. China, 1831–37, #112, p. 13.

37. E. C. Bridgman, Journal, July 25, 1831, ibid., #48.

38. Circular, by R. Morrison, signed by him and by Bridgman, Canton, Sept. 4, 1832, ibid., #2.

39. Bridgman to Anderson, Canton, March 26, 1835, ibid., pp. 17, 20.

40. Williams to Anderson, Canton, Jan. 29, 1849, ABC, So. China, 1846–60, II, #291.

41. Bridgman to Anderson, Canton, Feb. 8, 1836, ABC, So. China, 1831–37, #125.

42. "Report on the Return of Missionaries, 1838": ABC, Sub-Committee Reports, #2, pp. 4–5.

43. In January 1835, ABC listed seven physicians under "Missionaries and Assistants: American": S.E. Africa, one; Ceylon, one; Siam, one; Sandwich Islands, two; East Cherokees, one; and Creeks, one. "Table of Stations, Missionaries, Churches, and Schools," *Missionary Herald* 31:31 (January 1835).

44. See, e.g., Bridgman to Anderson, Canton, Jan. 17, 1832, ABC, So. China, 1831–37, #57. See Bridgman, Journal, Sept. 5, 1831, ibid., #48, for his first request for a medical dimension in their mission work. For

Bridgman's subsequent harping on the need for a physician in Canton see Bridgman to Anderson, Canton, ibid., #77, #91, #97, and #99.

45. Parker's health had been especially bad in the summer, but was "comfortable" (Yale Journal 7, Oct. 18, 1835, p. 62) during the return from Singapore, only to deteriorate sharply for a time in the latter part of October. His Harvard Journal does not record this deterioration, perhaps because it was being written with an eye to publication by the Board, or because he wanted to avoid parading his own health before other members of the mission station (communications to the Board were read aloud to each other before mailing). In the more private Yale Journal 7, which was not intended for publication, he disclosed his conditions more frankly.

46. An undocumented letter apparently written in this same period; Stevens, p. 116.

47. Parker to Anderson, Canton, Nov. 28, 1835, ABC, So. China, 1831–37, #198; there is the usual mix-up on dates, and this letter to some extent contradicts Yale Journal 7, pp. 62–64.

48. Parker, "Ophthalmic Hospital at Canton; First Quarterly Report, from 4th November, 1835 to 4th February, 1836," *Ch. Repos.* 4:461 (February 1836). Another source, shakier but not negligible, declares that Colledge had suggested to Parker in 1834 that he establish a hospital in Canton. "Prospectus of the Medical Philanthropic Society for China & the East" (tiny pamphlet of 6 pp., London, 1840), p. 3; G. Tradescant Lay, British evangelist, naturalist, and consul, knew both Parker and Colledge, had been in China in the 1830's, and was on the Provisional Committee which issued this pamphlet. Thus the evidence has a certain circumstantial force.

Parker was certainly closely tied to Colledge, although we have no data on the precise connection between the two men in 1834–35. We do know that Parker was briefly in Macao in those years on his way to or from Canton; that the Ljungstedt article on Dr. Colledge's work appeared in the December 1834 issue of the *Chinese Repository*; that Bridgman reported in early 1835 having stayed at the Colledges' (Bridgman to Anderson, Canton, March 26, 1835, ABC, So. China, 1831–37, #112, pp. 5–6) in Macao; and that Colledge was someone Dr. Parker would naturally have sought out, because of the former's professional commitment, his sympathy toward the ABC work, and his attractiveness as a man. On these grounds it seems safe to assume that Dr. Colledge's Macao and Canton dispensaries, which emphasized the treatment of eye ailments, served as the chief inspiration of Parker's major decision in 1835.

49. Williams, *Middle Kingdom*, I, 138.

50. Parker, quoted in Lockhart, p. 174. Williams underplays the problems: "when the scheme was made known to How-qua, he readily fell in with it." *Middle Kingdom*, II, 346.

51. Parker to Anderson, Canton, Nov. 28 (misdated Nov. 18 by the ABC, as is clear from internal evidence), 1835, ABC, So. China, 1831–37, #198. The passage quoted is the only evidence on the contact between Parker and Howqua in that immediate period. It implies that Peter Parker did not see him in the fall of 1835, since Parker would in all likelihood have mentioned it to Anderson or recorded such a notable encounter in his journal. Neither of these appears to have been done in 1835. In a later journal Parker documents his subsequent friendship with Howqua; Yale Journal 8, passim.

52. See Arthur W. Hummel, *Eminent Chinese of the Ch'ing Period, 1644–1912* (Washington, 1943–44), II. For a very complimentary description of Howqua by a contemporary, see Hunter, *"Fan Kwae" at Canton,* pp. 48–49.

53. See the Map of the Canton Factories, 1840 (after W. Bramston), in William W. Cadbury and Mary Hoxie Jones, *At the Point of a Lancet: One Hundred Years of the Canton Hospital, 1835–1935* (Shanghai, 1935), facing p. 38, where the authors have marked the location of the hospital. For the engraved "Plan of the City of Canton & its Suburbs" by W. Bramston, see James Orange, ed., *The Chater Collection, Pictures Relating to China, Hong Kong, Macao, 1655–1860* (London, 1924), pp. 256–257. The usual variables are close at hand: the First Quarterly Report on Dr. Parker's new work mistakenly gives the street number as #7, and Fung-tae Hong is variously labelled elsewhere as Parsee (Collis, *Foreign Mud,* facing p. 42), or Chow-chow (Hunter, *"Fan Kwae" at Canton,* p. 22).

54. Parker, First Quarterly Report, pp. 461–473.

55. This passage and the following ones which deal with the medical events of November 1835 are quoted from ABC, So. China, 1831–37, #188, Nov. 4, 5, 9, 10, 21, 1835, pp. 5–9. Later on, in recounting the opening of the hospital, Dr. Parker repeatedly used a modified, and probably erroneous, version; e.g., in the chief piece of his publicity material for distribution in England and Scotland: "the first day no patients ventured to come; the second, a solitary female affected with glaucoma, came; the third day, half a dozen; and soon they came in crowd" (Parker, *Statements Respecting Hospitals,* p. 22). Lockhart, p. 122, reproduced this account virtually verbatim. Since these accounts by Parker and Lockhart were widely circulated, one finds their errors often repeated. Most of these details contradict Parker's own earliest account, written close to the events, where no mention is made of an empty opening day, and where four and not one came on the first day during which he did have patients. One might be tempted to accept the assertion that no patient ventured in on the first day and to assume, therefore, that Dr. Parker's opening day might possibly have been Tuesday, Nov. 3; but the other details of his revised standard version of later years appear to have been

the victims of a busy time with crowds of patients, a faulty memory, and the absence of his journal which had been sent off to the ABC. None of the usual accounts of the opening of the hospital gives support to Nov. 3 as an empty day; e.g., Williams' account declares: "It was opened for the admission of patients Nov. 4, 1835." (*Middle Kingdom*, I, 346.) Parker's late November letter to Rufus Anderson blandly stated — and this was only a few weeks after the event — that he had opened his eye clinic "on the 10th of November," which we know to have been quite wrong. (Parker to Anderson, Canton, Nov. 28 [misdated Nov. 18, 1835], ABC, So. China, 1831–37, # 198.) His British publicity, referred to above, compounded the errors by stating that the hospital "was opened by Rev. P. Parker, M.D., October, 1835." (Parker, *Statements Respecting Hospitals*, p. 22.) In the autobiographical chronology which he compiled during his voyage home on the *Niantic* in 1840 he recorded the opening date as Nov. 5. (Yale Journal 8, p. 93.)

56. Taylor, *Voyage around the World*, II, 149–150.

57. Harvard Journal 7, Dec. 6, 1835, ABC, So. China, 1831–37, # 188, p. 13a.

58. Harvard Journal 8, Dec. 29, 1835, ibid., # 189.

59. Harvard Journal 7, Dec. 6, 1835, ibid., # 188, p. 13.

60. Harvard Journal 8, Jan. 4, 1836, ibid., # 189. On the press of patients see also Taylor, *Voyage around the World*, II, p. 148.

61. Harvard Journal 7, Nov. 22, 1835, ABC, So. China, 1831–37, # 188, pp. 9a–10.

62. *Ch. Repos.* 4:391 (Dec. 1835).

63. Harvard Journal 7, Dec. 6, 1835, ABC, So. China, 1831–37, # 188, p. 13. "It is surprising with what fortitude they submit to the operation." Ibid., Dec. 17, 1835, p. 16a.

64. This is Dr. Parker's first mention of operating for cataract at Canton. He was often called upon for this work. For further details on his burgeoning medical practice, its nature, and decisions to diversify his surgery (esp. tonsils, tumors, and bladder stones) see below, Chap. 10.

65. Harvard Journal 8, Feb. 11, 1836, ABC, So. China, 1831–37, # 189. Much other evidence testifies to the remarkable fortitude of Chinese during operations. See, e.g., Williams, *Middle Kingdom*, II, 189.

66. Harvard Journal 8, April 5, 1836, ABC, So. China, 1831–37, # 189.

67. Harvard Journal 7, Dec. 6, 1835, ibid., # 188, pp. 12a–13.

68. Harvard Journal 8, April 5, 1836, ibid., # 189.

69. Enclosure D in Joint Mission Letter to Anderson, Canton, Sept. 8, 1836, ibid., # 17.

70. Lockhart to William Ellis, secretary of the LMS, Canton, Feb. 7, 1839, LMS Archives, South China, Box 3, Folder 3, Jacket Letter B; see also Cadbury and Jones, *At the Point of a Lancet*, p. 80.

71. Edward H. Hume, "Peter Parker and the Introduction of Anesthesia into China," *Journal of the History of Medicine and Allied Sciences* 1:671 (1946).

72. Hobson, Hospital Report, 1855; quoted by Lockhart, p. 188.

73. Parker, First Quarterly Report, p. 462. This first report covered the period of Nov. 4, 1835–Feb. 4, 1836. For a good generalized account of admissions and procedures see Parker, *Statements Respecting Hospitals*, pp. 22–23.

74. For this speculation, I am indebted to F. G. Kilgour, formerly Librarian of the Yale Medical Library; Kilgour to author Sept. 25, 1962.

75. Cullen's help was acknowledged in both the First & Fourth Reports: Parker, First Quarterly Report, p. 469; Fourth Quarterly Report, *Ch. Repos.* 5:331 (November 1836). This is probably the James Francis Downie Cullen identified in Crawford, *Roll of Indian Medical Service*, p. 445, as Assistant Surgeon for a few months in 1835.

76. Adee and Palmer were thanked in the First Quarterly Report, p. 469; Adee is briefly identified in *National Cyclopaedia of American Biography* (New York, 1892–1969), XII, 459.

77. Bonsall is mentioned late in 1836; see Fourth Quarterly Report, p. 329.

78. First Quarterly Report, p. 469, note; see also Fourth Quarterly Report, p. 331: "I should do injustice to my own feelings not to acknowledge the untiring interest which Dr. Cox has taken in the operations of the hospital during the past year, lending his assistance upon each day for operations, and with no other reward than that of *doing good.*" There are repeated references to his generous assistance in the preceding three reports: First Quarterly Report, p. 470; Second Quarterly Report, *Ch. Repos.* 5:42 (May 1836); Third Quarterly Report, *Ch. Repos.* 5:188 (August 1836); see also Harvard Journals 7, entry for Nov. 10, 1835, and 8, entries for Jan. 14 and 18, 1836.

79. First Quarterly Report, p. 469; Third Quarterly Report, p. 188; Fourth Quarterly Report, pp. 325–326, 331; and elsewhere.

80. Harvard Journal 8, Jan. 15, 1836, ABC, So. China, 1831–37, #189.

81. Williams, *Middle Kingdom*, II, 346. For other forms of the surveillance, see Harvard Journal 8, Jan. 28 and 30, 1836, ABC, So. China, 1831–37, #189.

82. Harvard Journal 7, ibid., #188, Oct. 15, 1835, p. 2; Oct. 17, 1835, p. 4.

83. Williams, *Middle Kingdom*, II, 346–347.

84. Lockhart, pp. 128, 166–167.

85. Parker to Anderson, Canton, Nov. 28 (misdated Nov. 18), 1835, ABC, So. China, 1831–37, #198.

86. Harvard Journal 7, ibid., #188, Dec. 19, 1835, pp. 16a–17. See also

Enclosure D in Joint Mission Letter to Anderson, Canton, Sept. 8, 1836, ibid., #17.

87. Parker to Anderson, Canton, Sept. 8, 1836, ibid., #17, p. 5.

88. Parker to Anderson, Canton, Dec. 23, 1835, ibid., #199.

89. Bridgman to Anderson, Canton, Jan. 29, 1836, ibid., #123. In April Bridgman warned again that "I have much more fear for his health than for my own. The hospital, which is gaining great eclat, will, I fear, undermine him ere he is aware of it, and compel him to quit Canton." (Bridgman to Anderson, en route to Macao, April 7, 1836, ibid., #126, pp. 3–4.)

90. Yale Journal 7, p. 84; and Parker to Anderson, Canton, June 18, 1836, ibid., not numbered as a separate item, but lies between #201 and #202.

91. Yale Journal 7, Aug. 14, 1836, p. 84.

92. ABC, *Twenty-fifth Anniversary Report* (Boston, 1834), pp. 55, 76, 85; and ABC, "Statistical View," *Missionary Herald* 36:17–38 (January 1840). Those men who began their medical work in the mission field after Dr. Parker, by however small a margin, are not included here. Some were essentially contemporaneous, such as Dan B. Bradley in Siam and Asahel Grant, who went to Asia Minor in 1835.

4 ◆ A Parcel of Shipwrecked Japanese Sailors

1. Parker, *Journal of an Expedition from Sincapore* [sic] *to Japan, with a Visit to Loo-choo; Descriptive of These Islands and Their Inhabitants; in an Attempt with the Aid of Natives Educated in England, to Create an Opening for Missionary Labours in Japan*, rev. by Rev. Andrew Reed (London, 1838), p. 2. This work will hereafter be cited as Parker-Reed, *Japan*. It should not be confused with Parker's longhand version, which will be discussed below.

There is still no solid evidence enabling us to define Reed's work as editor of Dr. Parker's published account of the voyage, beyond the obvious fact that his printed version is quite different from Parker's Yale Journal 8A. Parker may have sent the original journal to him in England, hoping to get it back safely. It is more likely that Parker or someone else made a copy for Reed, as indeed Parker said he might do. (Parker to Anderson, Canton, Sept. 30, 1837, ABC, So. China, 1838–44, #112.) We are unable to determine whether such a hypothetical copy altered the original, whether Reed was empowered to edit freely for English readers, or whether he simply went ahead on his own. We do know that Andrew Reed (1787–1862) was one of the foremost Congregational ministers of his day in London. (See the memoir in the *Evangelical Magazine and Missionary Chronicle*, [1862], p. 239.) He visited the American churches in 1834 and was present at Parker's ordination.

2. Charles W. King and G. Tradescant Lay, *The Claims of Japan and Malaysia upon Christendom Exhibited in Notes of Voyages Made in 1837* (New York, 1839), I, 77–78.

3. Ibid., p. xviii; S. Wells Williams, "Narrative of a Voyage of the Ship Morrison, Captain D. Ingersoll, to Lewchew and Japan, in the Months of July and August, 1837," *Ch. Repos.* 6:210 (1837).

4. Yale Journal 8A, pp. 113–115. The pages of Parker's longhand account (Yale Journal 8A) of the trip to Japan are very jumbled. The chronological narrative can be followed by observing the following sequence: Jan.[?]–, 1837, and Jan. 29, 1837, pp. 155–159; June 18 (birthday) – 25, 1837, pp. 165–170; June 25 continuing, pp. 111–120; June 30–July 5, pp. 20–75; journal skips from Liu-ch'iu to Edo Bay; July 28–31, pp. 76–108; Aug. 7–10, pp. 12–19; Aug. 10 continuing, pp. 109–110; crossed out, pp. 133–135; Aug. 11–12, pp. 135–154; Aug. 14–15, pp. 129–133; Dec. 10, pp. 120–128; Dec. 10 continuing, Dec. 31, and Jan. 7, 1838 (presumably), pp. 171–188; not dated, pp. 160–164; two important items not yet placed or dated.

5. Yale Journal 8A, pp. 4–5.

6. Ibid., pp. 31–32. Parker was not alone in these reactions. In the awful missionary clichés of his day, Williams found the islanders "debased by idolatry, and besotted by sin." Williams, "Voyage to Lewchew," p. 226.

7. Yale Journal 8A, p. 36.

8. Ibid., pp. 49–50.

9. Ibid., pp. 73–74. For Parker's medical remarks: ibid., pp. 68–69. Parker's entries in his journal include many observations on the inhabitants, their stature, dress, houses, canoes, language, and agriculture; ibid., pp. 52–57.

10. Ibid., p. 87.

11. Ibid., pp. 99–103.

12. The following account of the Kagoshima Bay events is taken from Yale Journal 8A, pp. 17–19 (Aug. 10, 1837); pp. 109–110, where the text is partly crossed out (Aug. 10, cont.); pp. 133–135, crossed out (Aug. 10, cont., Aug. 11); pp. 135–140 (Aug. 11); pp. 141–154, portions crossed out (Aug. 12). This original record by Parker is particularly chaotic with misspellings, incomplete sentences, and jumbled pagination — all quite understandable under the circumstances. Reed took many editorial liberties in the published version (Parker-Reed, *Japan*, pp. 55–69, for the Kagoshima section), presenting essentially the same material but in a different order, with substantial omissions (some of them interesting), and with some change of point of view.

13. Yale Journal 8A, pp. 128, 171, 173–174.

14. Parker's conclusions in favor of noninterference and turning the other cheek were curiously transformed in the published account, presum-

ably through free-wheeling editorial action, into a muscular Christianity which argued that "justice . . . may imperiously demand the interference of civilized nations" (Parker-Reed, *Japan*, p. 72). The edited version gives inadequate insight into the violent turmoil inside Dr. Parker resulting from the events in Japanese waters.

15. Yale Journal 8A, pp. 150–152.

16. See the important larger passage of which this is a part; ibid., pp. 123–128, recorded Dec. 10, 1837.

17. Williams, *Life and Letters*, p. 99.

5 ◆ The Institutionalization of Medical Missions

1. The Medical Missionary Society in China; Address, with Minutes of Proceedings (pamphlet, Canton, 1838), pp. 22–24. This work contains the Society's "Regulations and Resolutions," the minutes of the first two meetings (Feb. 21 and April 24, 1838), a list of officers and members, an address drawn up by Colledge, Parker, and Bridgman expounding the history and motivation of their efforts to establish the Society, a reprint of an 1836 "Paper of Suggestions," an audit statement, and a list of donors and their subscriptions.

2. Parker to ABC, March 7, 1837, no place of origin given, ABC, So. China, 1838–44, #10, Document D.

3. *Missionary Herald* 35:113 (March 1839).

4. Lockhart, p. 143.

5. Parker, *Statements Respecting Hospitals*, p. 6.

6 "First Report of the Medical Missionary Society's Hospital at Macao, for the quarterly term beginning 5th July, and ending 1st Oct., 1838," *Ch. Repos.* 7:411 (December 1838). A Chinnery sketch of the building may be seen in the Yale Medical Library.

7. Ibid., pp. 411–412.

8. Wong and Wu, p. 343, passim.; ABC, Vinton Book, I, 29.

9. Lockhart to William Ellis, Secretary of the LMS, Canton, Feb. 7, 1839, LMS Archives, South China, Box 3, Folder 3, Jacket Letter B. On Lockhart's career, see Wong and Wu, pp. 321, 322, 325, 350–352, 368–369, 382–383, 388; Lockhart, pp. 125–127, passim; Lockhart's Hospital Reports in *Ch. Repos.*

10. Lockhart to Ellis, Macao, May 1, 1839, LMS Archives, South China, Box 3, Folder 3, Jacket Letter B.

11. "First and Second Reports of the MMS in China . . . ," Second Report, July 1, 1841, pp. 6, 15.

12. Ibid., p. 16, Lockhart, p. 126.

13. Wong and Wu, pp. 321–322; *Missionary Herald* 36:187 (May 1840).

14. In the absence of a good biography of Benjamin Hobson, one can

garner information from several sources: extensive unpublished correspondence in the archives of the London Missionary Society; *Ch. Repos.*
11, 12, 13, 19 . . . for many of his hospital reports; Wong and Wu, pp. 322,
350, 359–369, passim.; the *Chronicle* of the London Missionary Society,
1873, pp. 83–84; Lockhart, passim. Extracts of a Hobson journal are
enclosed in a letter (Hobson to Tidman, Canton, July 19, 1848, LMS
Archives, South China, Box 5, Folder 1, Jacket Letter A), but the location
of the journal itself is unknown.

15. For identifications of these six men see Wong and Wu, passim.

16. T. R. Colledge, *The Medical Missionary Society in China* (pamphlet,
Philadelphia, 1838), p. 6.

17. Editor's prefatory remarks to Colledge, "Suggestions with Regard to
Employing Medical Practitioners as Missionaries to China," *Ch. Repos.*
4:387 (December 1835).

18. Among the early physicians in the Sandwich Islands, Baldwin was
the most sensitive to the need for separation; his mission generally
contended against a variety of employments for one individual. Baldwin to
Anderson, Lahaina, Nov. 15, 1836, ABC, Sandwich Is. Mission, 1831–37,
#10.

19. Lockhart, pp. 117–118.

20. Sir Henry Halford, from an address before the Royal College of
Physicians, early 1838, quoted in W. H. Medhurst, *China: Its State and
Prospects, With Especial Reference to the Spread of the Gospel* (London,
1840), pp. 541–542; see Parker, "First Report of the Medical Missionary
Society's Hospital at Macao, for the quarterly term beginning 5th July, and
ending 1st October, 1838," *Ch. Repos.* 7:419 (December 1838).

21. Bridgman to Anderson, Canton, March 26, 1835, ABC, So. China,
1831–37, #112, p. 4.

22. One of the most confident and articulate statements in support of
their position came in a series of lectures in Edinburgh in the 1840's,
published as *Lectures on Medical Missions* . . . (Edinburgh, 1849[?]).

23. Lockhart, pp. 133–134.

24. Ibid., pp. 116–117, 281.

25. For the text of Lay's speech see "First and Second Reports of the
MMS in China . . . ," First Report, pp. 7–10.

26. *Statements Respecting Hospitals*, p. 5.

6 ◆ Opium and the Approach of War

1. For a helpful discussion of estimates of the number of smokers, see
Chang Hsin-pao, *Commissioner Lin and the Opium War* (Cambridge, 1964),
pp. 34–36. For a radically lower estimate, see John K. Fairbank, *Trade and
Diplomacy on the China Coast: The Opening of the Treaty Ports, 1842–1854*

(Cambridge, 1953), I, 64 and 64n17. For chronology, insights, and material on the period of the First Opium War, I have relied especially on Chang Hsin-pao's fine work, *Commissioner Lin*; and the absorbing treatment of Commissioner Lin Tse-hsü in Waley, *Opium War*. Waley's account relies heavily on "Lin Tse-hsü jih-chi" (The diary of Lin Tse-hsü [1839–1841]), in *Ya-p'ien chan-cheng* ([Collected materials on] The Opium War), ed. Ch'i Ssu-ho et al. (Shanghai, 1954), II, 1–85. The editors of the diary published only those sections dealing with Lin's involvement in the Opium War. These excerpts cover 1839 rather extensively, treating the next two years more sporadically, with unexplained gaps.

2. See Robert Bennet Forbes, *Personal Reminiscences*, 3rd ed., rev. (Boston, 1892), pp. 145–154, for details on life in Canton during the spring crisis of 1839.

3. General Letter from the Mission, July 14, 1839, *Missionary Herald* 36:81 (March 1840).

4. Williams to ABC, Macao, May 17, 1839, ibid., 35:464 (December 1839).

5. *The First and Second Reports of the Medical Missionary Society in China: with Minutes of Proceedings, Hospital Reports, etc.* (pamphlet, Macao, 1841), p. 14.

6. General Letter from the Mission, Canton, July 14, 1839, *Missionary Herald* 36:81–82 (March 1840).

7. Taylor, *Voyage around the World*, II, 147.

8. H. B. Morse, *The International Relations of the Chinese Empire*, 3 vols., vol. I: *The Period of Conflict, 1834–1860* (Shanghai, 1910), p. 245n144.

9. Chang Hsin- pao, *Commissioner Lin*, pp. 193–194.

10. Yale Journal 8, June 10, 1839; in this entry, his first for 1839, he writes in a kind of shorthand, as though he wanted a record to jog his own memory but wished to veil it from other eyes. It is not likely that he merely wrote in great haste, because in that period, with his hospital closed, he had time on his hands.

11. Yale Journal 8, June 11, 1839. See also Parker, Semi-Annual Report, to Anderson, July 4, 1839, ABC, So. China, 1838–44, vol. Ia.

12. Yale Journal 8, July 29, 1839. Parker wrote up these items near the end of the month, but they apparently took place about mid-July. His letter to Anderson under the date of July 24, 1839 (ABC, So. China, 1838–44, vol. Ia, #121), places the initial requests "a little more than a week since," ambiguously referring either to lapsed time since Parker's last letter to Anderson on July 4 or to the amount of time earlier than his current writing, July 24. The ambiguity raises no real difficulty, because either reading works out to mid-July.

13. Yale Journal 8, July 29, 1839.

14. Parker to Anderson, Canton, July 24, 1839, ABC, So. China, 1838–44, vol. Ia, #121.

15. For Parker's notes on his relationship with Commissioner Lin see his report on case "No. 6565. Hernia," pp. 634–637 of Parker, "Hospital reports of the Medical Missionary Society in China for the year 1839," *Ch. Repos.* 8:624–639 (April 1840).

16. Yale Journal 8, July 29, 1839; see also Parker to Anderson, Canton, July 24, 1839, ABC, So. China, 1838–44, vol. Ia, #121.

17. Parker, "Hospital Reports of the MMS . . . for the year 1839," *Ch. Repos.* 8:634–637 (April 1840).

18. Ibid., p. 635.

19. Yale Journal 8, Aug. 23, 1839.

20. Parker to Anderson, Canton, Sept. 5, 1839, ABC, So. China, 1838–44, vol. Ia, #122.

21. Immanuel C. Y. Hsü, *China's Entrance into the Family of Nations: The Diplomatic Phase, 1858–1880* (Cambridge, Mass., 1960), pp. 123–125.

22. The translations by both men may be found in "Hua ta-erh ko-kuo lü-li" (Vattel's *Law of Nations*), trans. Po-chia (Peter Parker) and Yüan Te-hui, in Wei Yüan, *Hai-kuo t'u-chih* (An illustrated gazetteer of the maritime countries; 100 *chüan,* 1852), 83:18–21b. The incomplete, published version of Lin's diary contains no allusion to his requests of Dr. Parker for medical assistance and for help in translating Vattel. Similarly the recent biography of Lin Tse-hsü by a descendant reveals nothing of the Lin-Parker connection: Lin Ch'ung-yung, *Lin Tse-hsü chüan* (Biography of Lin Tse-hsü; Taipei, Chung-hua ta-tien pien yin hui, 1967).

23. On the intricacies of the drafts and modifications see Chang Hsin-pao, *Commissioner Lin,* pp. 134–136, esp. the information in the relevant footnotes.

24. Parker to Anderson, Canton, Aug. 29, 1839; ABC, So. China, 1838–44, vol. Ia, #123.

25. Chang Hsin-pao, *Commissioner Lin,* p. 138. Waley, *Opium War,* pp. 82, 93, implies that the *Royal Saxon,* whose captain also signed the guarantee, was the ship which took Lin's letter to England.

26. Parker to ABC, April 12, 1840, *Missionary Herald* 36:431 (November 1840).

27. Yale Journal 8, June 15, 1840.

28. Waley, *Opium War,* p. 103.

29. Chang Hsin-pao, *Commissioner Lin,* pp. 211–212.

30. Fortunately for the biographer of Peter Parker, Forbes kept a full and animated diary of the 1840 voyage home: R. B. Forbes, Ms. "Journal of return from China on the *Niantic*: sailed from Macao July 5, arrived New York Dec. 10, 1840"; in collection of R. Forbes Perkins. This offers the best glimpses of any of the available documentation into the human qualities of Dr. Parker, his virtues, and shortcomings.

31. Ibid., July 9, 1840.

32. Ibid., July 12, 1840.

33. Ibid., Oct. 7, 1840.

34. Ibid., Oct. 18, 1840.

35. Yale Journal 8, Dec. 3, 1840. Parker's account of the voyage is found on pp. 71–95 and 98–195 of this Yale Journal; pp. 96–97 are out of place and obviously apply to Dr. Parker's 1842 voyage on the *Mary Ellen* when he was returning to China.

7 ◆ Washington, Marriage, and London

1. Yale Journal 8, Dec. 10, 1840; Yale Journal 8, Dec. 13, 15, 16, 1840.

2. Ibid., Dec. 29, 1840, gives the name in execrable handwriting; it could be Chin Sung or (less likely) Chiu Sung (or Sing). In a letter to President Day it seems to be "Chin Sang." (Parker to Day, Washington, Jan. 21, 1841, Yale, Beinecke Library, Day Papers, vol. 15). The entry for Feb. 4, 1841, refers to Parker's teacher sitting for a portraitist, but the whereabouts of the portrait is not known.

3. Yale Journal 8B, Dec. 25, 1840.

4. Ibid., Dec. 29, 1840.

5. Ibid., Jan. 24, 1841.

6. Ibid., Jan. 31, 1841. For a brief reference in a letter, see Anson Phelps Stokes, *Memorials of Eminent Yale Men* (New Haven, 1914), I, 95.

7. Yale Journal 8B, entry for Jan. 23, 1841, recapping the highlights of the two previous days.

8. Parker to Daniel Webster, Jan. 30, 1841, Washington, Peter Parker Collection, Yale Medical Library.

9. Parker, Yale speech, 1872, at semicentennial of the Yale Divinity School; Stevens, p. 327.

10. Yale Journal 8B, Jan. 23, 1841.

11. Genealogical research shows that Harriet and Daniel came from entirely different lines of Websters: Harriet from the John of Ipswich (Mass.) line, Daniel from the Thomas of Ormsby (England) line. Difficulties arise in tracing, because both lines settled in the same communities in New England and probably thought themselves related. Mable Fern Faling, *Genealogy of the Webster Family to Which Daniel Webster Belonged* (Boston, 1927).

12. Our evidence consists of his journal entry recording that he sought through fasting and prayer to decide some important question involving his "happiness and usefulness for life." (Yale Journal 8B, Feb. 20, 1841.)

13. For Parker's account of the emotions and events of these days, see ibid., Feb. 23–25, 1841.

14. Ibid., March 15, 1841. Adams records the interview in his own journal; see Charles Francis Adams, ed., *Memoirs of John Quincy Adams* (Philadelphia, 1876), X, 444–445.

15. Yale Journal 8B, March 6, 1841. This operation is related to the Yale "legend" about Dr. Parker's nonpractice of surgery in the United States. See Chap. 1.

16. Yale Journal 8B, March 29, 1841.

17. Written after Parker's death in the margin of ibid., Feb. 28, 1841.

18. See the minutes of the Medical Association of Boston as published in Parker, *Statements Respecting Hospitals,* pp. 29–31.

19. Yale Journal 8B, May 16, 1941, p. 60.

20. Ibid., p. 65.

21. Lockhart, Milne, and Hobson to LMS, Macao, Aug. 18–31, 1840, LMS Archives, South China, Box 4, Folder 1, Jacket Letter B.

22. LMS Archives, Board Minutes, 1840–41, vol. 27, May 11, 13, 17, 1841.

23. Parker to Anderson, London, July 2, 1841, ABC, So. China, 1838–44, vol. Ia, #135. The Board Minutes of the LMS contain no reference to Parker's "visit before the Directors," and the minutes of the Eastern Committee no longer exist, having been destroyed during the blitz in World War II.

24. Yale Journal 8B, p. 71, May 29, 1841; the pamphlet—a very useful source—evolved further, and in its final form became *Statements Respecting Hospitals in China Preceded by a Letter to John Abercrombie, M.D., V.P.R.S.E.* (Glasgow, 1842).

25. Yale Journal 8B, p. 59, May 15, 1841; May 18, 1841, pp. 62–63; June 8, 1841, p. 82.

26. Parker to Anderson, London, July 2, 1841, ABC, So China, 1838–44, vol. Ia, #135; this letter contains an informative resumé of Parker's activities on mission business in London.

27. Yale Journal 8B, June 5, 1841, p. 79.

28. Ibid., June 14, 1841, p. 84; June 16, 1841, p. 85.

29. The text of the address has not been preserved, but quotations from it appear in Medhurst, *China,* pp. 541–542, and Parker, "First & Second Reports of the MMS in China . . . ," First Report, Nov. 29, 1838, pp. 5–6. According to Parker the address was reported in the *London Medical Gazette,* Feb. 1, 1838. See Yale Journal 8B, May 19, 1841, p. 64, where Parker records Sir Henry's reference, during one of their encounters in 1841, to his 1838 address.

30. Yale Journal 8B, May 19, 1841, p. 64.

31. See *DNB* for biographies of these prominent physicians.

32. Yale Journal 8B, May 28–29, 1841, p. 70.

33. The reference here is to a namesake nephew and successor of the celebrated Astley Paston Cooper (1786–1841) of Guy's Hospital.

34. Yale Journal 8B, July 13, 1841, p. 99.

35. Ibid., June 7, 1841, p. 82.

36. Ibid., June 1, 1841, p. 76; for a discussion of the paintings, see below, Chap. X.

37. Yale Journal 8B, June 25, 1841, p. 89.

38. Ibid., June 25, 1841, p. 88. The surgeon's name is mercifully withheld from us by Parker's inscrutable handwriting.

39. Ibid., June 26, 1841, pp. 90–91.

40. Ibid., June 27, 1841, p. 91.

41. Ibid., June 28, 29, 1841, pp. 91–93; Parker to Mrs. Peter Parker, Paris, June 29, 1841; Stevens, pp. 207–209.

42. Parker, *Statements Respecting Hospitals,* pp. 9–12.

43. Ibid., pp. 13–14; refers to the *Liverpool Standard* of Aug. 3, 1841. H. F. Taylor, *A Century of Service (1841–1941): A Sketch of the Contribution Made by the Edinburgh Medical Missionary Society to the Extension of the Kingdom of God at Home and Abroad* (pamphlet, Edinburgh, 1941). It was this society which was responsible for the excellent *Lectures on Medical Missions.*

44. There is no account in his journal or in any known, surviving record of either his departure or voyage. It is not clear from which city he sailed, although a Liverpool departure about August 4 would have been especially convenient.

45. *Missionary Herald* 37:442 (November 1841).

46. For Parker's account of the interview with President Tyler, see Yale Journal 8B, Sept. 16, 1841, pp. 101–102.

47. Ibid., Sept. 16, 1841, pp. 102–105.

48. Thomas Sewall to Isaac Hays, Washington, Dec. 30, 1841; Library, College of Physicians of Philadelphia.

49. At which one we cannot be sure. There was a third possibility—the Medical Institute of Philadelphia, but this appears to have been a summer institute, whereas Parker attended in the winter. See W. B. McDaniel, 2nd, to the author, Philadelphia, Aug. 11, 1961, for a most helpful letter from an expert curator. Both Stevens, p. 225, and Cadbury and Jones, *At the Point of a Lancet,* p. 75, by assigning Parker a diploma from the "College of Medicine in Philadelphia" (there was no such institution), have confused Parker's unidentified affiliation with the identifiable College of Physicians of Philadelphia, to which he was elected an associate member. For his certificate of election, see Peter Parker Collection, Yale Medical Library. The source of confusion lay in the mistranslation of the certificate's phrase: "Collegii Medicorum Philadelphiensis."

50. *The First and Second Reports of the MMS in China: with Minutes of Proceedings, Hospital Reports, etc.* (pamphlet, Macao, 1841), p. 16.

51. The voyage is covered in Yale Journal 8, June 13–Nov. 5, 1842, pp. 196–221, although in the usual fashion, with very few interesting entries on such matters as Mrs. Parker and the ship. The near-shipwreck of September 20 receives several pages; see the entry for Sept. 24.

52. ABC, *Annual Report: 1845,* p. 158.

53. See Frederick Wakeman, Jr., *Strangers at the Gate* (Berkeley, 1966), pp. 52–58, for a perceptive discussion of Cantonese xenophobia in the 1841–42 period.

54. Lockhart, pp. 130–131. See also Circular Letter, Hobson to Tidman, Hong Kong, Jan. 26, 1843, LMS Archives, South China, Box 4, Folder 3, Jacket Letter A, item 53.

55. Diary, 1842, Nov. 5, 1841, FDR Library, Hyde Park. Edward Delano was a great-uncle of President Franklin Delano Roosevelt. For Parker's description of the arrival, see Yale Journal 8, Nov. 5–6, 1842, pp. 221–222.

56. Delano, Diary, 1842, Oct. 10, Nov. 19, 20; Diary, 1843–44, Jan. 22, 1843.

57. Delano, Diary, 1842, Dec. 10, 28, 1842.

58. Delano, Diary, 1843–44, April 1, 1843.

59. When Harriet died, her daughter-in-law burned her letters and diaries as being "too personal for other eyes to see." (Peter Parker III to the author, Barrington, Ill., Nov. 29, 1963.)

60. Delano, Diary, 1843–44, Feb. 21, 1843. See also Yale Journal 8B, March 11, and 18, 1843, where Parker refers to her improved — and then restored — health.

61. Hobson to Tidman, Hong Kong, Nov. 26, 1844, LMS Archives, South China, Box 4, Folder 4, Jacket Letter B.

8 ◆ The Caleb Cushing Interlude

1. Yale Journal 8, Sept. 1, 1844, on board U.S. *St. Louis,* pp. 233–234.

2. John Tyler (written by Webster) to the House of Representatives, Dec. 30, 1842, as found in J. W. McIntyre, ed., *The Writings and Speeches of Daniel Webster* (Boston, 1903), XII, 140–141.

3. Claude M. Fuess, *Life of Caleb Cushing* (New York, 1923), passim.; for an excellent brief account of the Cushing mission to China see D. H. Miller, ed., *Treaties and Other International Acts of the United States of America* (Washington, 1931–1948), IV (1934), 558–662. Relevant items in the Cushing papers at the Library of Congress may be found in Boxes 42–47 and 164.

4. Anderson to S. T. Armstrong, Boston, June 8, 1843; ABC, Letters: Domestic, XVIII, 105–106; cited by C. J. Phillips, *Protestant America,* p. 192.

5. Parker to Anderson, Canton, June 22, 1846, ABC, So. China, 1846–60, vol. II, #241.

6. Yale Journal 8B, June 18 and 25, Dec. 31, 1843; Jan. 4, 1844.

7. Ibid., March 7, 1843.

8. Ibid., March 12, 1843.

9. Ibid., March 18, 1843.

10. Yale Journal 8, Sept. 1, 1844, on board U.S. *St. Louis,* p. 232; see also Stevens, p. 327, for Parker's similar assertion in his address in 1872 at the semicentennial of the Yale Divinity School.

11. Yale Journal 8, Sept. 1, 1844, on board U.S. *St. Louis,* pp. 232–233; see also Parker to David Green, Canton, Aug. 1, 1844, ABC, Amoy, Siam, Borneo, 1820–46, #71, pp. 3–4.

12. Instructions of Secretary of State Webster to Caleb Cushing, May 8, 1843; for long excerpt, see Miller, *Treaties,* IV, 638–641; full text in 28th Cong., 2nd sess., Sen. Doc., No. 138 (1845), Ser. 457, Department of State, 1 Instructions China, 5–13.

13. Parker to Cushing, May 7, 1844; Library of Congress, Cushing Papers, Box 44.

14. Parker to Cushing, dated only May, 1844; LC, Cushing Papers, Box 44, May 27–31 (1844) file.

15. Delano, Diary, 1843–44, May 2, 1844.

16. Parker to Cushing, June 10, 1844, Macao; LC, Cushing Papers, Box 44.

17. Cushing to A. P. Upshur, Macao, June 12, 1844; LC, Cushing Papers, Box 44.

18. Cushing, despatch #72, July 8, 1844, D.S., 2 Despatches, China; Miller, *Treaties,* IV, 646.

19. Hummel, *Eminent Chinese,* p. 132; Te-kong Tong, *United States Diplomacy in China, 1844–60* (Seattle, 1964), p. 8.

20. Hummel, *Eminent Chinese,* p. 606; Tong, *United States Diplomacy,* p. 11n.

21. Yale Journal 8, Sept. 1, 1844, on board U.S. *St. Louis,* pp. 234–235.

22. Miller, *Treaties,* IV, 644.

23. Parker, "Minutes of a meeting of the American and Chinese Commissioners at the House of Legation at Macao. June 24th, 1844," LC, Cushing Papers, Box 44, in June 17–21 (1844) file. These minutes are a part of: Parker's "Minutes of Discussions before the Treaty of Wang Hiya," comprising 18 longhand pages. They cover the meetings of June 18–27 in some detail and constitute a good first-hand source, which I have closely followed. They break off without explanation, after supplying a lively account of the discussions of June 27. For the period of June 28–July 2, there is no comparable source.

24. Parker, "Minutes of a meeting . . . June 24th, 1844," LC, Cushing Papers, Box 44, in June 17–21 (1844) file.

25. Cushing, despatch #72, July 8, 1844, Macao, D.S., 2 Despatches, China; quoted by Miller, *Treaties,* IV, 647.

26. Ch'i-ying to Cushing, July 2, 1844; LC, Cushing Papers, Box 45.

27. Fairbank, *Trade and Diplomacy,* I, 196.

28. Fuess, *Caleb Cushing,* I, 425.

29. See text of the letter in Miller, *Treaties,* IV, 660–661.

30. Ch'i-ying to Cushing, July 9, 1844, LC, Cushing Papers, Box 45.

31. Parker, Yale Speech, 1872, Yale Divinity School Semicentennial; Stevens, p. 328. For Parker's earlier account, close to the event, see Yale Journal 8, Sept. 1, 1844, on board U.S. *St. Louis,* p. 235, where he put together (pp. 231–237) retrospective remarks on his work for Caleb Cushing. These pages comprise the best account by Parker of his previous six months' work, a period during which he did not make detailed diary notations.

32. For material on these, see LC, Cushing Papers, Box 44, in June 23–26 and 27–30 files.

33. Miller, *Treaties,* IV, 565. This is the article on which Parker later based his claims in the Roberts case; see below, Chap. XI.

34. Parker to Cushing, Aug. 5, 1844, LC, Cushing Papers, Box 46.

35. Copy of this agreement was enclosed with Cushing, despatch #84, Aug. 15, 1844, D.S., 2 Despatches, China; quoted in Miller, *Treaties,* IV, 656–657.

36. Humphrey Marshall to State Dept., No. 16, Shanghai, May 26, 1853, House Docs., No. 123 (1854), 33rd Cong. 1st sess., p. 140; quoted by Tong, *United States Diplomacy,* pp. 32–33. Tong's conclusion is that "Parker's Chinese was very poor and hardly suitable for official use," ibid., 32.

37. Earl Swisher, *China's Management of the American Barbarians: A Study of Sino-American Relations, 1841–1861, with Documents* (New Haven, 1953), p. 49.

38. See, e.g., Hobson to Tidman[?], Canton, June 22, 1848, LMS Archives, South China, Box 5, Folder 1, Jacket Letter A.

39. Cushing to Parker, Macao, July 25, 1844; LC, Cushing Papers, Box 45.

40. Parker to Cushing, Canton, Sept. 19, 1844, LC, Cushing Papers, Box 47.

41. Yale Journal 8, Sept. 1, 1844, on board U.S. *St. Louis,* pp. 236–237.

42. Parker et al. to Cushing, Canton, Aug. 19, 1844, LC, Cushing Papers, Box 46; see also Parker's rejoinder to what seems to have been a note of appreciation to him: Parker to Cushing, Aug. 22[?], 1844; LC, Cushing Papers, Box 46.

43. Cushing, despatch #101, D.S., 2 Despatches, Jan. 25, 1845; quoted in Miller, *Treaties,* IV, 645. See also Cushing's lavish praise in his letter to Rev. Septimus Tustin, chaplain of the U.S. Senate, Feb. 17, 1845, Washington: Bridgman, *Life and Labors,* pp. 132–134, and Cushing to Bridgman, Washington, Feb. 10, 1845, in Bridgman, ibid., p. 131.

44. Parker to David Green, Canton, Aug. 1, 1844, ABC, Amoy, Siam, Borneo, 1820–46, #71, pp. 3–6.

45. Fairbank, *Trade and Diplomacy,* p. 208.

46. Yale Journal 8, Canton, Oct. 27, 1844.

9 ◆ Schism in the MMS and Severance from the ABC

1. Parker to Anderson, Canton, Feb. 10, 1845, ABC, Amoy, Siam, Borneo, 1820–46, #73, pp. 18–19.

2. *China Mail,* no. 9 (April 17, 1845), p. 33.

3. Ibid., no. 7 (April 3, 1845), p. 27.

4. Ibid., no. 3 (March 6, 1845), p. 9.

5. Ibid., no. 9 (April 17, 1845), p. 33.

6. Ibid.

7. The regulations are printed in *Ch. Repos.* 7:32–36 (May 1838); adopted on Feb. 21, 1838, they were supplemented on March 27, 1843.

8. *China Mail,* no. 7 (April 3, 1845), p. 27.

9. Ibid., no. 10 (April 24, 1845), p. 37.

10. *Report of the MMS in China for the Year 1845* (pamphlet, Victoria, 1846), p. 4.

11. Hobson to Tidman and Freeman, foreign secretaries, Hong Kong, May 29, 1845, LMS Archives, South China, Box 4, Folder 4, Jacket Letter D. For Lockhart's published version of the schism, a study in blandness and discretion, see Lockhart, pp. 144–145.

12. Hobson to Tidman, Hong Kong, Nov. 26, 1844, LMS Archives, South China, Box 4, Folder 4, Jacket Letter B.

13. *China Mail,* no. 12 (May 8, 1845), p. 46.

14. See Lists of Officers, MMS, appended to *Report of the MMS in China, for 1843–44* (pamphlet, Macao, 1844), p. 31. There is some ambiguity about the "List of Officers" applying to 1843–44 or 1844–45; I am assuming the report's list applies to the coming year and not the past year. See also, *Report of the MMS in China for the Year 1845,* p. 37.

15. Lockhart, pp. 144–145.

16. Hobson to Tidman, Canton, Dec. 24, 1848, LMS Archives, South China, Box 5, Folder 1, Jacket Letter A.

17. Cleland to Tidman, Canton, Sept. 27, 1849, LMS Archives, South China, Box 5, Folder 1, Jacket Letter B; Hobson to Tidman, Canton, July 19, 1846, LMS Archives, South China, Box 5, Folder 1, Jacket Letter A; Hobson to Tidman, Canton, Jan. 27, 1849, LMS Archives, South China, Box 5, Folder 1, Jacket Letter B.

18. See *Report of the MMS in China for the Year 1847* (pamphlet, Victoria, 1848).

19. Legge to Tidman, Hong Kong, 22 Nov., 1852, LMS Archives, South China, Box 5, Folder 3, Jacket Letter B. Wong and Wu, p. 338, suggest that the Hong Kong Medical Missionary Society lingered longer and quietly passed away with the death of Dr. Colledge in 1879.

20. *Report of the MMS in China; Including the Thirteenth Report of the Ophthalmic Hospital in Canton* (pamphlet, Canton, 1845).

21. Report of the Thirteenth Annual Meeting of the MMS in China; in *Minutes of Two Annual Meetings of the MMS in China, Including the Sixteenth Report of Its Ophthalmic Hospital at Canton for the Years 1850 and 1851* (pamphlet, Canton, 1852).

22. *China Mail,* no. 16 (June 5, 1845), p. 60; see also *Transactions of the China Medico-Chirurgical Society for the Year 1845–46* (Hong Kong, 1846).

23. Printed *Minutes of the Chinese Missionaries . . . 1843,* LMS Archives, South China, Box 4, Folder 3, Jacket Letter D.

24. William Appleton et al. to Parker, Boston, Nov. 17, 1846, *Minutes of the Annual Meeting of the Medical Missionary Society in China,* for the years 1848 and 1849 (pamphlet, Canton, 1850), p. 4.

25. Parker to Anderson, Canton, May 30, 1843, ABC, So. China, 1838–44, vol. Ia, #150.

26. See, e.g., Parker to Anderson, Canton, Nov. 28, 1835, and March 27, 1836, in ABC, So. China, 1831–37, #198 and #201.

27. A distillation of these oft-repeated arguments may be found in his 1872 address at the semicentennial of the Yale Divinity School; quoted in Stevens, pp. 329–330.

28. See chart in Williams, *Middle Kingdom,* II, 375–376. Dyer Ball, here counted as one of the eight, had medical training, but may not have had much of a medical practice in this first decade during his residence in Singapore, Macao, and Hong Kong.

29. Parker to Anderson, Canton, Nov. 28 (misdated Nov. 18), 1835, ABC, So. China, 1831–37, #198; Anderson to Canton mission, Boston, June 17, 1836, ABC, Letters: Foreign, I, 51–52.

30. Rufus Anderson, *A Sermon on the Present Crisis in the Missionary Operations of the ABCFM* (pamphlet, Boston, 1840), p. 5.

31. The quotation, exquisitely Anderson-oriented, is from the *Constitution, Laws, and Regulations of the ABCFM,* pp. 21–22.

32. Anderson, *Foreign Missions: Their Relations and Claims,* 3rd ed. (New York, 1876), p. 29.

33. Ibid., p. 294; see also p. 49.

34. From Anderson's report at the 32nd Annual Meeting of the ABC, Philadelphia, 1841: "Citizenship of Missionaries and their Children," *Missionary Herald* 37:445 (November 1841).

35. Anderson to China Mission, Boston, Oct. 23, 1844, ABC, Letters: Foreign, XIV, 363.

36. Anderson to China Mission, Boston, Jan. 23, 1845, ibid., XV, 131.

37. Bridgman to Anderson, Canton, May 31, 1834, ABC, So. China, 1831–37, #98.

38. Records of the Prudential Committee, VI (1841–45), 414.

39. Parker to David Green, Canton, Aug. 1, 1844, ABC, Amoy, Siam, Borneo, 1820–46, #71, pp. 8–9. For the committee ruling of Dec. 10, 1844, see: ABC, Records of the Prudential Committee, VI (1841–45), 387; and for Williams' dissatisfaction concerning the sums actually paid over by Parker: Williams to Anderson, Canton, Oct. 25, 1849, ABC, So. China: 1846–60, vol. II, #300, pp. 2–3. In 1850 Dr. Parker paid to Williams as treasurer a final installment on his 1844 government stipend: Parker to Anderson, Canton, April 20, 1850, ABC, So. China, 1846–60, vol. II, #246. Parker further confused the scene in the late 1840's by offering a gift of $1000 to ABC for the purchase of land in Shanghai toward the establishment there of an American Board mission. This gift was the source of concern and letter writing, because Williams opposed creating a mission there and did not want to acknowledge the gift lest it commit the Board to it. Letters sailed to and fro while Dr. Parker remained unthanked. Also related to the correspondence is: Anderson to Parker, Boston, Jan. 28, 1850, ABC, Letters: Foreign, XXIV, pp. 35–38.

40. Records of the Prudential Committee, VI (1841–45), 419–21.

41. Anderson to Brethren at Hong Kong and Canton, Boston, March 14, 1845, ABC, Letters: Foreign, XV, 223–30.

42. Parker to the Prudential Committee, Canton, Jan. 1, 1846, ABC, Amoy, Borneo, Siam, 1820–46, #79.

43. Bridgman to Anderson, Canton, Dec. 25, 1845, ABC, Amoy, Siam, Borneo, 1820–46, #63.

44. Anderson to Rev. Messrs. Bridgman and Ball, Boston, July 17, 1845, ABC, Letters: Foreign, XVI, 68–69. The ensuing struggle over the discontinuance of the *Repository* was long and unpleasant, lies essentially outside an account of Dr. Parker's career, and is not covered here.

45. Anderson to Parker, Boston, July 17, 1845, ABC, Letters: Foreign, XVI, 72.

46. Parker to Anderson, Canton, July 22, 1846, ABC, Amoy, Borneo, Siam, 1820–46, #81.

47. Webster, *Duchess of Malfi*, III, iii, lines 60–61.

48. Parker to the Prudential Committee, Canton, Jan. 1, 1846, ABC, Amoy, Borneo, Siam, 1820–46, #79.

49. Ibid., pp. 4–5.

50. Records of the Prudential Committee, VII (1845–49), 86.

51. Bridgman to Anderson, Canton, Dec. 25, 1845, ABC, Amoy, Borneo, Siam, 1820–46, #63.

52. Parker to Anderson, Canton, Jan. 31, 1846; ibid., #82.

53. Anderson to Brethren of the Canton Mission, Boston, Dec. 17, 1845, ABC, Letters: Foreign, XVI, 500–501; Anderson to Parker, Boston, Dec. 19, 1845; ibid., p. 511.

54. For emphasis on it in this particular period, see: Bridgman to

Anderson, Canton, Jan. 1, 1846, ABC, Amoy, Borneo, Siam, 1820–46, #45, p. 3; private letter, Parker to Anderson, Canton, June 22, 1846, ABC, So. China, 1846–60, vol. II, #241. Anderson returned to his suggestion in his letter of Oct. 3, 1846, to Parker, ABC, Letters: Domestic, XXV, 98–100.

55. Williams to Anderson, Canton, Jan. 29, 1849, ABC, So. China, 1846–60, II, 6.

56. A.C.T., *New York Observer*, June 3, 1880.

57. See Anderson to Parker, Boston, June 15, 1846, ABC, Letters: Foreign, XVII, 432–433; and Anderson to Brethren of the Canton Mission, Boston, July 15, 1846; ibid., pp. 419–430.

58. Anderson to Parker, Boston, June 15, 1846; ibid., p. 433.

59. Anderson to Parker, Boston, Oct. 3, 1846, ABC, Letters: Domestic, XXV, pp. 98–100.

60. Records of the Prudential Committee, VII (1845–49), 212.

61. Anderson to Parker, Boston, Sept. 29, 1847, ABC, Letters: Foreign, XX, 66–70.

62. ABC, *38th Annual Report* (Boston, 1847), pp. 163–164.

63. Anderson to Parker, Boston, Sept. 29, 1847, ABC, Letters: Foreign, XX, 66–70.

64. Parker to Anderson, Canton, May 22, 1847, ABC, So. China, 1846–60, II, #243.

65. Parker to Anderson, Canton, June 22, 1848; ibid., #245.

66. William E. Soothill, *Timothy Richard of China: Seer, Statesman, Missionary* (London, 1924), p. 156, as applied to Richard.

67. Tidman to Hobson, London, Nov. 24, 1851, LMS Archives, Eastern Outgoing Letters, China-Ultra Ganges, Box 4, p. 609.

10 ◆ Pioneer Physician, Teacher, and Surgeon

1. Arturo Castiglioni, *A History of Medicine*, trans. E. B. Krumbhaar (New York, 1941), pp. 680, 724, 744.

2. See Fielding H. Garrison, "The History of Bloodletting," *New York Medical Journal* 97:498–501 (March 1913), and G. Garwood, "The Leech: Past, Present, and Future," *University of Western Ontario Medical Journal* 22:168–170 (November 1952).

3. Marshall Hall, *Researches Principally Relative to the Morbid and Curative Effects of Loss of Blood* (London, 1830), p. 251.

4. Parker, Eleventh Hospital Report, *Ch. Repos.* 13:245 (May 1844).

5. Leon S. Bryan, Jr., "Bloodletting in American Medicine, 1830–1892," *Bulletin of the History of Medicine* 38:517, 518, 520 (1964).

6. Harvard Journal 6, ABC, So. China, 1831–37, #187, p. 12a.

7. First Quarterly Report, *Ch. Repos.* 4:471 (February 1836).

8. Harvard Journal 8, Dec. 31, 1835, ABC, So. China, 1831–37, #189.

9. Fifth Hospital Report, *Ch. Repos.* 5:462 (February, 1837).

10. Castiglioni, *History of Medicine*, p. 632. I am indebted to Dr. Richard M. Robb for clarification of the couching technique and of recent advances in eye treatment.

11. Roy O. Scholz, *Sight: A Handbook for Laymen* (Garden City, N.Y., 1960), p. 135.

12. Harvey, "Peter Parker," p. 236. Dr. Parker supplies some details of a less successful case in Harvard Journal 7, Nov. 29, 1835, ABC, So. China, 1831–37, #188, pp. 10–10a.

13. George H. Werner, Bachisio Latte, and Andrea Contini, "Trachoma," *Scientific American* 210:79 (January 1964).

14. Parker, Eleventh Hospital Report, *Ch. Repos.* 13:240 (May 1844).

15. Parker, Eighth Hospital Report, *Ch. Repos.* 7:95 (June 1838).

16. Harvard Journal 8, Jan. 7, 1836, ABC, So. China, 1831–37, #189.

17. Parker, Fourth Hospital Report, *Ch. Repos.* 5:329–331 (November 1836). This was Parker's case #2152; the patient, a man aged twenty-three, had fallen from a house six years earlier and broken the humerus of his left arm. Union having taken place, the arm was rebroken six months before Parker saw it. The latter found the skin tight and fluid present in an aneurysmal condition which required amputation at the shoulder. This patient may be observed among Parker's medical portraits (for a description of these, see below) at both the Yale Medical Library (Gulick code reference: II, 22–22A) and the Gordon Museum, Guy's Hospital, London (Gulick code reference: Dr. Missen #6).

As to Dr. Parker's statement that this was the first voluntary amputation of a limb in China, Dr. Joseph Needham has kindly supplied me with clarifying comments. Although it appears that amputation surgery was not regularly practiced in traditional Chinese medicine, there must have been times in war when Chinese military physicians completed the removal of injured extremities. In such cases their emphasis is likely to have centered on preventing bleeding, effecting antisepsis, and inducing healing, all critical elements in the amputation process. Secondly, the long history of punishment by amputation, very common in the Han period, for example, suggests that physicians must have evolved techniques for securing safe and quick healing after such amputation. Subject to these provisos and with the understanding that research is incomplete, Dr. Needham believes that Parker's statement about his operation is correct.

18. Parker, Twelfth Hospital Report, *Ch. Repos.* 13:302–303 (June 1844).

19. Delano, Diary, 1846, entries for Aug. 31–Sept. 2.

20. General Letter from . . . Canton, March 7, 1838, *Missionary Herald* 34:339 (September 1838).

21. Yale Journal 8B, December 31, 1843; Parker's handwriting raises a question as to whether the weight he was recording was two or three pounds.

22. Semiannual Report, Parker to Prudential Committee, Canton, Jan. 1, 1845, ABC, Amoy, Siam, Borneo, 1820–46, #41, pp. 15–16.

23. Parker, *Minutes of Two Annual Meetings of the MMS in China; including the Sixteenth Report of its Ophthalmic Hospital at Canton for the Years 1850 and 1851* (pamphlet, Canton, 1852), p. 32.

24. Bridgman to Anderson, Canton, Jan. 1, 1846, ABC, Amoy, Siam, Borneo, 1820–46, #45, p. 3.

25. Lockhart, p. 140; refers to Hobson's 1845 report.

26. Harvard Journal 8, Jan. 4 and 14, 1836, ABC, So. China, 1831–37, #189.

27. Ibid., Jan. 18, 1836.

28. Ibid., Jan. 22, 1836. There appear to be two portraits of Akae, this famous young patient of Dr. Parker: one is found in the Gordon Museum, Guy's Hospital, London; the other, in the Lamqua collection of the Yale Medical Library. The Yale portrait is marked "0–1911 #1 92" on the back. (See below for description and discussion of the Yale collection of which it is a part.) Although it is not entirely certain that these are Akae's portraits, the evidence for such a supposition is quite good. It is clear that a portrait was done of Akae in the period when she was Dr. Parker's patient. Parker's longhand version of his First Quarterly Report contains material on Akae's mother, who is listed as Dr. Parker's case #445, described as a respectable boat-woman and mother of four, and shown to be afflicted with tumors similar to Akae's. Then, after Parker's coverage of #446 (Akae), his longhand directions for printing refer to the "painting" of Akae before the first operation. Since the printer did not include the illustration, we do not have it as evidence of a clear connection between the case history description of Akae and the portrait in question. The portrait does tally with the doctor's description. For later information on Akae's case with a description of the recurrence of fast-growing tumors and a subsequent operation, see Parker, longhand version of First Quarterly Report, following case #446. (This section contains its own puzzles. It appears from internal evidence to have been added after the passage of some years — a practice of the doctor's as he reviewed his own writings — but externally it fits into the February 1836 material.) I have retained Parker's rendering of Akae's name.

29. Harvard Journal 8, Jan. 24, 1836, ABC, So. China, 1831–37, #189.

30. Ibid., Feb. 1, 1836.

31. The 86 portraits at Yale have numbers on the front of each painting, a sequence appearing to have been established by Prof. Moses White of the Yale Medical School. The 86 were photographed by this author in a different sequence — the unsystematic order in which they happened to be filed. Someone using the Gulick filmstrip of the Yale portraits, which is available at the Yale Medical School Library and the Gordon Museum,

can readily orient himself by consulting a "Key to Numbering on front and back of Lamqua Paintings of Yale Medical Library as photographed by Prof. E. V. Gulick, Wellesley College," copies of which are available in both those collections. The "Key" observes the Gulick photographic order.

Among the 110 known Lamqua paintings of Dr. Parker's patients, there are over 20 duplicate portraits. All except one of the Guy's 23 fall into this category, as do a handful within the Yale collection and the single painting at Countway. Two Yale paintings are marked #36 on the front and are identical, recording Dr. Parker's case #2986.

Among the Yale 86 there is apparently one before-and-after pair of paintings (PP #2152. Before: Gulick code reference II:22–22A; at Guy's also. After: Gulick code reference II:23–23A; also at Guy's) and possibly more. The overall collection of Lamqua medical portraits deals with about 80 different patients, all of whom with only one exception can be studied in the Yale 86.

32. C. Toogood Downing, *The Stranger in China; or, the Fan-Qui's Visit to the Celestial Empire, in 1836–7* (Philadelphia, 1838), I, 210–222.

33. Parker, Seventh Hospital Report, *Ch. Repos.* 6:438–439 (January 1838), quoted by C. J. Bartlett, "Peter Parker, the Founder of Modern Medical Missions: A Unique Collection of Paintings," *Journal of the American Medical Association* 67:407–411 (August 1916). The illustrations used by Dr. Bartlett are from the Yale group of 86; for this particular one there is an identical painting at Guy's, probably a copy, but cleaned and in much better condition when last seen by the author (1964) than the "original" at Yale.

34. Acting with courtesy and generosity, four members of the faculty of Guy's Hospital Medical School — Dr. G. A. K. Missen, Prof. I. Doniach, Prof. Keith Simpson (then Curator of the Gordon Museum), and the late Prof. G. Payling Wright, supplied this author with diagnoses of the 23 portrait cases at Guy's. Since Dr. Missen recorded their diagnostic comments and appraisals, the latter are here referred to under his name.

The initiative in making these diagnoses arose from the response of Professor Wright to a letter from the author. The original diagnoses, covering 21 paintings, were conveyed by letter, G. Payling Wright to the author, London, Aug. 8, 1962. Subsequently the Gordon Museum discovered two more paintings, concerning which Dr. Missen added his diagnoses; Missen to the author, 14 April, 1967.

35. Parker, Fourth Hospital Report, *Ch. Repos.* 5:325–327 (November 1836); Yale: Gulick code reference 23A–24; Missen #11.

36. Parker, Eighth Hospital Report, *Ch. Repos.* 7:102–103 (June 1838); Missen #20; Yale: Gulick code reference 27A–28.

37. Parker case #3000; Yale: Gulick code reference II:7–7A; Missen #16; Bartlett #4.

38. Parker case #3488; Yale: Gulick code reference II:32–32A; Missen #3; Bartlett #5.

39. Parker case #2152; Yale: Gulick code reference 22–22A; Missen #6; Bartlett #2.

40. Parker case #4605; Yale: Gulick code reference III:14–14A; Missen #8.

41. Parker, Thirteenth Hospital Report: as pamphlet, pp. 4–6; or in *Ch. Repos.* 14:450–452 (October 1845). Also recorded in Semiannual Report, Parker to Prudential Committee, Canton, Jan. 1, 1845, ABC, Amoy, Siam, Borneo, 1820–46, #41, pp. 5–9.

42. Semiannual Report, Parker to Prudential Committee, Canton, Jan. 1, 1845, ABC, Amoy, Siam, Borneo, 1820–46, #41, pp. 9–13.

43. Ibid., pp. 14–15.

44. Yale Journal 8, June 22, 1845, p. 241.

45. His figures are helpful but incomplete; e.g., his report on the period of July 1845 to December 1847 records 31 cases of urinary calculus but does not indicate how many involved lithotomy. The next report, covering 1848 and 1849, shows 8 lithotomies out of 54 calculus cases.

46. Parker, Fifteenth Hospital Report: as pamphlet, p. 10; or in *Ch. Repos.* 19:262–263 (May 1850).

47. Parker, *Sixteenth Hospital Report (1850–51)*, pp. 9–11.

48. Parker, Fifteenth Hospital Report (1848–49), *Ch. Repos.* 19:260 (May 1850).

49. Parker, Ninth Hospital Report: as pamphlet, p. 14; or in *Ch. Repos.* 7:575 (March 1839).

50. Parker, Twelfth Hospital Report, *Ch. Repos.* 13:311–312 (June 1844); he appears to refer to the same case in Yale Journal 8B, Dec. 31, 1843. For a sampling of other reported losses, see case #29,015 in Parker, Fifteenth Hospital Report (1848 and 1849) and case #38,000 in Sixteenth Hospital Report (1850–51).

51. Note the typical contents of standard surgical texts of the general period of Parker's training; e.g., John Syng Dorsey, *Elements of Surgery* (Philadelphia, 1818) covers such conditions as gangrene, burns, wounds, fractures, dislocations, hernia, urinary tract, bloodletting, and harelip. The inner malfunctioning of organs was generally left alone. The same was true of the 25 discourses in John Bell, *The Principles of Surgery* (New York, 1812).

52. E.g., his case #3438 — aneurism (portrait: Peter Parker Collection, Yale Medical Library), Gulick code reference 25A–26.

53. Parker, Fourteenth Hospital Report: as pamphlet, pp. 12–13; or in *Ch. Repos.* 17:143 (March 1848). Parker's donor in the States was a Mr. Spooner. John M. Forbes was involved in sending one of the early supplies of ether to Howqua. See John M. Forbes to Paul Forbes, July 25, 1847,

Boston; in volume of typed letters, Forbes Collection, Baker Memorial Library, Harvard.

54. Parker, Fourteenth Hospital Report: as pamphlet, pp. 13–14; or in *Ch. Repos.* 17:143–144 (March 1848).

11 ◆ Chargé

1. Fairbank, *Trade and Diplomacy*, I, 365–366.

2. Despite the fact that he so identified himself in his detailed Amherst biographical description; Archives, Amherst College.

3. Fairbank, *Trade and Diplomacy*, II, ch. 22, n. 15.

4. Ibid., p. 415.

5. Marshall to Marcy, Shanghai, July 6, 1853; House Exec. Doc. No. 123 (1855), 33rd Cong., 1st sess., p. 198; cited by Phillips, *Protestant America*, p. 200.

6. Tong, *United States Diplomacy*, pp. 91–92.

7. Sir John Bowring, *Autobiographical Recollections of Sir John Bowring* (London, 1877), pp. 222–224, recording an interview with Yeh.

8. So Kwan-wai and Eugene P. Boardman, "Hung Jen-kan, Taiping Prime Minister, 1859–1864," *Harvard Journal of Asiatic Studies* 20:279 (1957).

9. For coverage of the trip, see Swisher, *China's Management*, pp. 269–83, and Tong, *United States Diplomacy*, pp. 161–172. No scholar yet has adequately utilized British archives on this and related diplomatic problems.

10. This 1845 letter of Forbes may be found in Eldon Griffin, *Clippers and Consuls: American Consular and Commercial Relations with Eastern Asia, 1845–1860* (Ann Arbor, 1938), p. 57. Griffin's work is very detailed and helpful on consular personnel, duties, and performances in the period when Dr. Parker had so many connections with that group. Griffin's account is defensive about them and given to lambasting those who had the temerity to challenge the often dubious and independent ways of the consuls.

11. For the following information I am indebted to Robert L. Irick for generously allowing me to use material from chap. 1 of his unpublished ms., "The Chinese Emigrant in Sino-American Diplomacy," an early form of his dissertation at Harvard University.

12. Griffin, *Clippers and Consuls*, pp. 189–90.

13. Counting consuls and acting consuls, one gets the following numbers: 8 for Amoy (1849–59); 6 for Canton (1843–60); 7 for Foochow (1853–60); 8 for Hong Kong (1844–60); 4 for Macao (1849–60); 6 for Ningpo (1854–60); and 11 for Shanghai (1846–60). Griffin, *Clippers and Consuls*, pp. 358–364.

14. Griffin manages to suggest Parker was wrong without saying more than that Bradley had a good record. The fact that Parker later accepted the nomination of the consul's own son suggests that the doctor had not acted out of rancor toward Bradley in vetoing his earlier choice of a substitute.

15. Griffin, *Clippers and Consuls*, pp. 131–133. Relying almost exclusively on the dispatches from the consular officers themselves, Griffin conveys the impression of consular unanimity in opposition to Dr. Parker, but his case against the latter is based upon the antagonism of only 4 out of some 50 American consuls. (See ibid., pp. 129–133.) And 2 of the 4 — Robert S. Sturgis (vice-consul, Canton, in 1855) and James Keenan at Hong Kong — seem unimpressive as consular officers, even in Griffin's complimentary handling of the service. Whatever may have been Dr. Parker's undisclosed relations with the remaining 46 consuls, it is true that he had substantial run-ins with the above-mentioned foursome. If these were not daily rows, they nevertheless occurred with reassuring regularity and have left us some lively reports in the National Archives in Washington.

16. Griffin, *Clippers and Consuls*, p. 94.

17. *China Mail*, no. 430 (May 12, 1853), p. 75. The ensuing account of the wreck of the *Larriston* is based on material in the *North China Herald*, no. 149 (June 4, 1853), where a news account is accompanied by a long letter from Capt. Baylis to a friend. Further data and comment are found in the *China Mail* of 1853: no. 432 (May 26); no. 433 (June 2); no. 434 (June 9); no. 445 (Aug. 25); and no. 446 (Sept. 1). Dr. Parker's account is published in Stevens, pp. 285–287.

18. *North China Herald*, no. 149 (June 4, 1853).

19. Griffin, *Clippers and Consuls*, Appendix 11, pp. 424–431 goes with extraordinary care into the duty question at Shanghai. His footnote "a," covering much of pp. 424–426, has an excellent summary; the text itself is a chronology of the question and incidentally of the struggle between Parker and Consul Murphy. Griffin presents Parker as pro-U.S. merchants and a bit of a "bad guy"; he presents Murphy as hewing honorably to the line of the McLane award and makes it fairly clear that Murphy had the sounder understanding of the question. For an authoritative summary of the back duty settlement, see Fairbank, "The Creation of the Foreign Inspectorate of Customs at Shanghai," *Chinese Social and Political Science Review*, Peking, 20:70–89 (April 1936); also covered in Fairbank, *Trade and Diplomacy*, I, 453–461.

20. Fairbank, ibid., p. 394.

21. Swisher, *China's Management*, passim.

22. Lockhart, p. 175. On the diminished activity at the Canton Hospital, see also Hobson to Tidman, Canton, May 8, 1855, LMS Archives, South China, Box 5, Folder 4, Jacket Letter B.

23. Hobson to Tidman, Aug. 20, 1851, LMS Archives, South China, Box 5, Folder 2, Jacket Letter A.

24. *Minutes of three Annual Meetings of the MMS in China, for the years 1854, 1855, and 1856* with Dr. Kerr's Report of 1855–56 (pamphlet, Macao, 1857), p. 4.

25. See the long retrospective entry in Yale Journal 8, pp. 246–249, Macao, April 22, 1855.

26. Wong and Wu, p. 826.

12 ◆ Commissioner

1. Supplement to *China Mail*, no. 539 (June 14, 1855), p. 97.

2. Edward Everett to Hon. J. M. Clayton, Cambridge, April 20, 1849, in Everett letterbook, Massachusetts Historical Society.

3. Hobson to Tidman, Canton, Jan. 7, 1856, LMS Archives, South China, Box 5, Folder 4, Jacket Letter C. For another disparaging mission letter on Parker in the same period, see W. A. Macy to Anderson, Macao, Aug. 8, 1857, in ABC, So. China, 1846–60, vol. II, #230; quoted by Phillips, *Protestant America*, p. 203. Macy served the ABC in China during parts of the 1840's and 1850's.

4. *China Mail*, no. 569 (Jan. 10, 1856), p. 6.

5. Reported in Delano, Diary, 1846, Sept. 5.

6. Both the letter of invitation and Parker's refusal may be found in *North China Herald*, no. 287 (Jan. 26, 1856), pp. 102–103. Although the Forbeses were not among the signers, they do seem to have relaxed their earlier opposition to Parker — the volume of typed letters of John M. Forbes to Paul S. Forbes at Baker Memorial Library does not reveal any effort by them in 1855 to block Parker's appointment as commissioner. For a recent scholarly appraisal of the appointment, see Tong, *United States Diplomacy*, pp. 173–174.

7. Marcy to Parker, Washington, D.C., Sept. 27, 1855; cited in Tong, *United States Diplomacy*, p. 174.

8. Parker, "Minutes of an interview with the Earl of Clarendon," Oct. 26, 1855, London, Sen. Exec. Docs., No. 22 (1859), 35th Cong., 2nd sess., Ser. 982, pp. 619, 620; and Parker to Marcy, Nov. 8, 1855, Paris, ibid., p. 621.

9. Published on the front page of *China Mail*, no. 570 (Jan. 17, 1856).

10. Consult an excellent page of clarifying generalization in Tong, *United States Diplomacy*, p. 283.

11. Griffin, *Clippers and Consuls*, p. 429.

12. See, e.g., J. M. Forbes to William B. Reed, Boston, May 22, 1857, "Letters of J. M. Forbes, 1843–1867," MS Div., Baker Memorial Library.

13. Fairbank, *Trade and Diplomacy*, I, 460–461.

14. Swisher, *China's Management*, p. 314.

15. Tong, *United States Diplomacy*, p. 184.

16. See "A Letter to the Editor," *China Mail*, no. 608 (Oct. 9, 1856), p. 162.

17. Marcy to Parker, Feb. 2, 1857, Washington; National Archives, Records of the Department of State, Diplomatic Instructions, China, 1:148–149. Many items are in Consular Dispatches, Hong Kong, vols. 3 and 4. More may be found in Sen. Exec. Docs., No. 22 (1859), 35th Cong., 2nd sess., Ser. 983, pp. 1319–20, 1383–84. Ibid., pp. 1384–85, has a partial record of the correspondence concerning Keenan.

18. *China Mail*, no. 614 (Nov. 20, 1856), pp. 186–187. The commissioner's account may be found in Parker to Marcy, no. 31, Nov. 22, 1856, Whampoa, in Senate Exec. Docs., No. 22 (1859), 35th Cong., 2nd sess., p. 1020.

19. Comparable action in the previous year had earned him a letter to the editor in which he was described by its author, "Reason," as a supporter of pirates. *China Mail*, no. 522 (Feb. 15, 1855), p. 26.

20. Tong, *United States Diplomacy*, pp. 186–187.

21. Ibid., pp. 194–195.

22. Ibid., p. 198.

23. Harold D. Langley, "Gideon Nye and the Formosa Annexation Scheme," *Pacific Historical Review* 34:397–420 (November 1965).

24. Parker to Bowring, Macao, March 21, 1857; "Letters and Despatches of Peter Parker, 12 May, 1856–May, 1857" in Manuscript Collection, Papers of Commodore James Armstrong, Misc. Papers, Peabody Museum, Salem, Mass. Most of the items in this collection seem to be rather pleading letters by Parker to Armstrong; there is also one letter to Bowring, and one by Caleb Jones, U.S. Consul, Foochow. Many were written from Macao; some from Shanghai and Hong Kong. Among the subjects dealt with were: the desecration by Chinese of foreign graves on Dane's Island; piracy in Chinese waters by Chinese vessels; an attempt to introduce poison into the bread at Hong Kong; pending negotiations for revision of the treaty; minor incidents involving American property, especially at Canton; and disrespect paid to the American flag. The general tone is somewhat hysterical over the flag, American national honor, private property, and hostile incidents. He wanted from Armstrong the use of one or more ships for his (Parker's) own inspection tours and general prestige; Armstrong seems to have been reluctant. I am indebted to Francis B. Lothrop and, back of him, to Prof. Harold D. Langley, for directing me to these materials.

25. Tong, *United States Diplomacy*, p. 207.

26. Ibid., p. 202.

27. Ibid., p. 209.

28. *China Mail*, no. 632 (March 26, 1857), p. 51.

29. Lockhart, p. 178.

30. The argument is plausibly presented in Tong, *United States Diplomacy*, pp. 189–192.

31. Hunter, *"Fan Kwae" at Canton*, p. 26.

32. See Marcy instruction of Feb. 27, 1857, printed in Sen. Exec. Docs., No. 30 (1859–60), 36th Cong., 1st sess., Ser. 1032, pp. 5–6.

33. Morse, *The International Relations of the Chinese Empire*, I, *Conflict*, 485; Fairbank, *Trade and Diplomacy*, II, ch. 22, n. 9. Parker sometimes incorrectly referred to himself as minister plenipotentiary; see, e.g., Parker to Yeh, Jan. 31, 1857, Macao, Sen. Exec. Docs., No. 22 (1859), 35th Cong., 2nd sess., p. 1184.

13 ◆ Retirement and Epitaph

1. There are occasional references to his health, to improvement of it, to joy over its having been good, and so on, in the unpublished letters of S. Wells Williams to Parker in the MS Div., Sterling Library, Yale University, e.g., those from Peking and Shanghai, Sept. 5, 1863, and June 12, 1872.

2. Hobson to Tidman, Aug. 20, 1851, LMS Archives, South China, Box 5, Folder 2, Jacket Letter A.

3. See Parker to R. B. Forbes, Canton, 21 July, 1851, Forbes Papers, Museum of the China Trade, pt. II, reel 12, no. 4, folder 9.

4. For information on Parker and J. M. Forbes, I am indebted to Crosby Forbes. See Crosby Forbes to author, Dec. 7, 1966.

5. Will no. 41203, Register of Probate Court, Cambridge, Massachusetts.

6. Yale Journal 10, June 18, 1859; cited in Stevens, p. 316.

7. Variously designated in Boyd's *Directory of the District of Columbia* as Jackson Place cor. Penn. Ave., 16½ west cor. Penn. Ave., 700 Jackson Place, N.W., 2 Jackson Square N.W., 2 Jackson Place, 2 Lafayette Square, 2 16½ N.W.; all refer to the same dignified, three-storied structure.

8. *The Nation's Capitol, Washington City, D.C., Bird's Eye View,* a map published by A. Sachse & Co., Baltimore, ca. 1883.

9. Peter Parker III to author, July 17, 1960, Barrington, Ill.

10. Williams to Parker, New Haven, June 8, 1880, Sterling Library, Yale.

11. Wilhelmus B. Bryan, *A History of the National Capitol* (New York, 1914–1916), II, 328; *Smithsonian Contributions to Knowledge*, XVI (Washington, 1870), x–xi.

12. Williams to Parker, Macao, Nov. 28, 1861, Feb. 26, 1862, and Peking, Sept. 1, 1864, Sterling Library, Yale.

13. Williams to Parker, Macao, Feb. 26, 1862; ibid.

14. Williams to Parker, Peking, Sept. 1, 1864; ibid.

15. Williams to Parker, Peking, Jan. 6, 1875; ibid.

16. *Constitution, Laws and Regulations of the ABCFM*, p. 6.

17. Stevens, pp. 346–347.

18. Cadbury and Jones, *At the Point of a Lancet,* p. 100.

19. Morse, *International Relations of the Chinese Empire,* vol. I: *Conflict,* p. 416n71.

20. Yale Journal 8B, March 8, 1843.

21. Press release, "The Peter Parker Centennial of Medical Missions in the Far East," October 1934, prepared by the Medical Committee of the Foreign Missions Conference of N.A., 419 Fourth Ave., NYC; in American Baptist Foreign Mission Societies' Collection, Valley Forge, Pa.; B-1046.

22. *Re-thinking Missions: A Layman's Inquiry after 100 Years,* ed. William Ernest Hocking (New York, 1932), p. 201.

23. Whitmore, "Western Medicine in China," p. 299.

24. Dr. William Lennox, "Medical Missions," in Orville A. Pelty, ed., *Layman's Foreign Missions, Inquiry, Fact-finders Reports: China.* V, suppl. ser., pt. II (New York, 1933), pp. 454, 456, 472, and passim.

25. Ibid., pp. 429–430.

26. Soothill, *Timothy Richard of China,* p. 37.

27. Fairbank, *Trade and Diplomacy,* I, 53.

◆ Works by Peter Parker

Amherst Memoir-Journal. Contains a "Memoir," written during his freshman year at Amherst College, covering his life up to departure for Wrentham (in March 1826) in 26 pp.; and a "Journal," beginning with March 20, 1826, at Wrentham and carrying on to September 30, 1827, at Amherst, with long gaps between entries. Yale Medical Library.

First Quarterly Report: "Ophthalmic Hospital at Canton; first quarterly report, from 4th November, 1835 to the 4th February, 1836," *Ch. repos.* 4:461–473 (February 1836). The longhand version of this report is in the Peter Parker Collection, Yale Medical Library.

First Report of the Hospital at Macao (July 5–Oct. 1, 1838); see *Ch. Repos.* 7:411–419 (December 1838). Also issued as pamphlet, Canton, 1838.

Harvard Journals. The American Board Archives at Harvard University contain in the volume marked "South China, 1831–37" (ABC 16.3.8, vol. I) a cluster of Parker journals for 1834–1836. Voluminous and rather jumbled, they can be treated as eight "Harvard Journals," the first consisting of the entries which deal with the voyage out to China and the others comprising separately mailed excerpts from (or parallel passages to) the "Yale Journal," which he retained for his own use.

> Harvard Journal 1: generally a duplication of Yale Journal 6 covering the 1834 trip to China. Mailed as a series of extracts to Boston and now found as items #175 (there are two items under this number) and #180 in ABC, South China, 1831–37.

> Harvard Journal 2: item #181 covering Canton and the voyage on the *Fort William* (Oct. 28–Dec. 22, 1834).

> Harvard Journal 3: item #182 covering the straits of Singapore and Singapore itself (Dec. 24, 1834–March 27, 1835).

> Harvard Journal 4: item #184 covering Singapore–Malacca–Singapore (April 12–July 5, 1835).

Harvard Journal 5: item #185 for Singapore (July 12–Aug. 5, 1835).
Harvard Journal 6: item #187 covering Singapore and the *Fort William* trip back to China (Aug. 11–Sept. 9, 1835).
Harvard Journal 7: item #188 covering Canton and the opening of the hospital (Oct. 11–Dec. 19, 1835).
Harvard Journal 8: item #189 covering Canton (Dec. 26, 1835–April 5, 1836).

Hospital Casebooks. Peter Parker Collection, Yale Medical Library.

Journal of an Expedition from Sincapore to Japan, with a Visit to Loo-choo; Descriptive of These Islands and Their Inhabitants; in an Attempt with the Aid of Natives Educated in England, to Create an Opening for Missionary Labours in Japan, revised by Rev. Andrew Reed. London, 1838.

"Journal of Mr. Parker on a Voyage to Japan," *Missionary Herald* 34:203–207 (1838).

Letters. Few have been published. Although there are some important ones in the Peter Parker Collection, Yale Medical Library, and a scattering here and there, the main body resides in the American Board collection at Houghton Library, Harvard. See American Board in Bibliography.

Medical Missionary Society, Reports. Portions by Dr. Parker.

"Notes of Surgical Practice amongst the Chinese," *Monthly Journal of Medical Science* 66:393–398 (1846).

Parker Correspondence. 35th Congress, 2nd Session, Senate Exec. Docs., No. 22 (1859), 2 vols., Ser. 982–983, pp. 495–1424.

Report to the Medical Missionary Society in "Report to the Medical Missionary Society containing an abstract of its history and prospects; and the Report of the Hospital at Macao, for 1841–42; together with Dr. Parker's statement of his proceedings in England and the United States." Macao, Press of S. Wells Williams, 1843, pp. 40–54.

Reports (quarterly and otherwise) of the Ophthalmic Hospital at Canton. These form the central pieces of Dr. Parker's medical writings. His account of the voyage to Japan contained medical observations of the Liu-ch'iu islanders, and his publicity pamphlet of 1842 included "Notes of Surgical Practice amongst the Chinese," but neither of these was as solidly professional as the collection of his hospital reports. Even the latter were aimed at an audience which included lay members as well as professionals, a fact which may have forced him to minimize jargon and maximize human interest. His hospital reports typically included an introductory paragraph, statistics on the medical conditions treated at the hospital, and brief descriptions of the several cases which Parker deemed of special interest.

In the later reports he often included appendices dealing with such matters as medical pupils, use of chloroform, or the quality of the evangelistic activities within the hospital. Usually the reports appeared in the *Chinese Repository* and also as pamphlets (with their own pagination). Although Dr. Parker left money in his will to have the hospital reports published in book form, there is no evidence that such publication ever took place.

No. of Report	Period covered	Where found
I	Nov. 4, 1835–Feb. 4, 1836	*Ch.Repos.* 4:461–473.
II	Feb. 4, 1836–May 4, 1836	*Ch.Repos.* 5:32–42.
III	May 4, 1836–Aug. 4, 1836	*Ch.Repos.* 5:185–192.
IV	Aug. 4, 1836–Nov. 4, 1836	*Ch.Repos.* 5:323–332.
V	Nov. 4, 1836–Feb. 4, 1837	*Ch.Repos.* 5:456–462.
VI	Feb. 4, 1837–May 4, 1837	*Ch.Repos.* 6:34–40.
VII	May 4, 1837–Dec. 31, 1837	*Ch.Repos.* 6:433–445.
VIII	Jan. 1, 1838–June 30, 1838	*Ch.Repos.* 7:92–106.
IX	July 1, 1838–Dec. 31, 1838	*Ch.Repos.* 7:569–588.
X	Jan. 1, 1839–Dec. 31, 1839	*Ch.Repos.* 8:628–639.
XI	Jan. 1, 1840–June 17, 1840	*Ch.Repos.* 13:239–247.
XII	Nov. 21, 1842–Dec. 31, 1843	*Ch.Repos.* 13:301–319.
XIII	Jan. 1, 1844–July 1, 1845	*Ch.Repos.* 14:449–461.
XIV	July 1, 1845–Dec. 31, 1847	*Ch.Repos.* 17:133–150.
XV	Jan. 1, 1848–Dec. 31, 1849	*Ch.Repos.* 19:253–280.
XVI	Jan. 1, 1850–Dec. 31, 1851	pamphlet, Canton, 1852.
XVII?	No report available on 1852–1854 as far as Yale Collection indicates.	
(no number)	June 1, 1855–October, 1856	pamphlet, Canton, 1857(?), by Parker's successor, Dr. Kerr.

Speech, in *The Semi-Centennial Anniversary of the Divinity School of Yale College, May 15th and 16th, 1872.* New Haven, 1872.

Statements Respecting Hospitals in China, Preceded by a Letter to John Abercrombie, M.D., V.P.R.S.E. Glasgow, 1842.

Yale Journals: these comprise most of the original diaries which Parker kept; unpublished, Peter Parker Collection, Yale Medical Library.

Yale Journal 1: "Journal," with entries for 1827–1830.

Yale Journal 2: "Diary of Senior Year in Yale College," with entries for Oct. 16, 1830–Jan. 25, 1831.

Yale Journal 3: "Diary Sec^d Term Senr Year in Yale College," with entries for Jan. 28–June 18 (his birthday), 1831.

Yale Journal 4: "Diary Last Term of Senr Year" in Yale College, with entries for June 18–Oct. 30, 1831.

Yale Journal 5: "Theological Seminary of Yale College," covering his graduate work, with entries from Dec. 25, 1831, to April 13, 1834; pp. 109–113 contain tantalizing sections systematically crossed out.

Yale Journal 6: "Sailing from N. York for China," with entries for May 16–Oct. 28, 1834.

Yale Journal 7: "Journal, Private," covering the Singapore trip and sojourn, plus Canton and Macao, with entries for Dec. 23, 1834–Aug. 14, 1836.

Yale Journal 8: "Journal, 1836," pp. 1–70 cover 1836–1840, Canton; pp. 71–195, Parker's return in 1840 on the *Niantic*; pp. 196–223, Dr. and Mrs. Parker returning to China on the *Mary Ellen* (pp. 96–97, out-of-place, also apply to this voyage); pp. 224–250, miscellany from 1844, 1845, 1854, 1855, 1877.

Yale Journal 8A: "1837 Voyage to Japan." For a key to disentangling these jumbled pages, see notes to Chap. 4.

Yale Journal 8B: "Arrival in America Dec. 1840," with entries for the United States, Europe, and Philadelphia in 1840–1842, and for China in 1844, 1848, 1849.

Yale Journal 9: "Journal," an 1854 private diary which quickly peters out; some miscellaneous entries for 1876.

Yale Journal 10: "Last Journal," 1856 and a few scattered entries to 1880.

◆ Bibliography

(Abeel, David). *Memoir of the Rev. David Abeel, D.D.*, ed. G. R. Williamson, New York, 1849.

Abeel, David. *Residence in China and Neighboring Countries.* New York, 1836.

(Adams, John Quincy). *Memoirs of John Quincy Adams,* ed. Charles Francis Adams. 10 vols. Philadelphia, 1876; vol. 10 used.

American Board of Commissioners for Foreign Missions. Papers. Houghton Library, Harvard University. The following volumes contain important Parker and Canton Mission letters, and have been especially useful:

    ABC   16.3.3.   Amoy, Siam, Borneo, 1820–1846, vol. I

    ABC   6.   vol. XI (Candidates, M-P)

    ABC   16.3.1.   Canton Mission

    ABC   1.1.   Letters: Domestic, vols. XVI–XXI, XXV

    ABC   2.1.   Letters: Foreign (copy book series), vols. I, XIV–XVII, XX, XXIV

    ABC   16.8.7.   Mission to Nestorians, Letters of Asahel Grant

    ABC   30.   Private Papers of Rufus Anderson, vol. XI

    ABC   19.1.   Sandwich Island Mission, 1831–1837

    ABC   16.3.8.   South China, 1831–1837, vol. I

    ABC   16.3.8.   South China, 1838–1844, vol. Ia

    ABC   16.3.8.   South China, 1846–1860, vols. I, II

    ABC   (no call number assigned). Vinton Book, vol. I

    ABC   Records of the Prudential Committee, vol. II (1825–1831), vol. IV (1834–1837), vol. VI (1841–1845), vol. VII (1845–1849).

    ABC   Sub-Committee Reports (1848–1866).

―――― *Annual Reports,* 1811ff. Report year irregular. Title varies slightly. Reports generally include the minutes of the Board's annual meeting. First ten reports published in one volume, 1834.

———— *Missionary Herald.* Boston, monthly, 1821–1951.

———— *Twenty-fifth Anniversary Report.* Boston, 1834.

———— *Constitution, Laws and Regulations of the American Board of Commissioners for Foreign Missions.* Boston, Crocker and Brewster, 1839.

———— "Statistical View of the Officers, Missions and Missionaries of the Board," *Missionary Herald* 36:17–38 (January 1840).

———— *The Divine Instrumentality for the World's Conversion.* Boston, 1856, pamphlet.

———— *The Haystack Prayer Meeting, An Account of Its Origin & Spirit.* Boston, 1906, Haystack Centennial pamphlet.

Amherst College Biographical Record. Amherst, Mass.

Anderson, Rufus. *A Sermon on the Present Crisis in the Missionary Operations of the ABCFM.* Boston, 1840, pamphlet.

———— "Leading Object of the Mission to the Oriental Churches," in American Board of Commissioners for Foreign Missions. *Annual Report:* 1842.

———— *Memorial Volume of the First Fifty Years of the American Board of Commissioners for Foreign Missions.* Boston, 1861.

———— *History of the Sandwich Island Mission.* Boston, 1870.

———— *History of the Missions of the American Board of Commissioners for Foreign Missions to the Oriental Churches.* 2 vols. Boston, 1872.

———— *Foreign Missions: Their Relations and Claims*, 3rd ed. New York, 1876.

Annals of Medical History, ed. F. R. Packard. 24 vols. New York, P. B. Hoeber, 1917–1942.

Appleton's Cyclopaedia of American Biography, ed. J. G. Wilson and J. Fiske. 7 vols. New York, Appleton, 1894–1900.

Armstrong, Commodore James. Papers. Manuscript Collection, Peabody Museum, Salem, Mass.

Bailyn, Bernard. *Education in the Formation of American Society.* Chapel Hill, University of North Carolina Press, 1960.

———— *Ideological Origins of the American Revolution.* Cambridge, Mass., Harvard University Press, 1965.

Bainton, Roland H. *Yale and the Ministry: A History of Education for the Christian Ministry at Yale from the Founding in 1701.* New York, Harper, 1957.

Balme, Harold. *China and Modern Medicine: A Study in Medical Missionary Development.* London, United Council for Mission Education, 1921.

Barber, John W. *Historical Collections . . . Relating to the History and Antiquities of Every Town in Massachusetts . . .* Worcester, 1841.

Bartlett, C. J. "Peter Parker, the Founder of Modern Medical Missions: A

Unique Collection of Paintings," *Journal of the American Medical Association* 67:407–411 (1916).

Beau, G. *La Médecine chinoise*. Paris, Editions du Seuil, 1965.

Bell, John. *The Principles of Surgery*. Abridged by J. Augustine Smith. 2nd ed. New York, 1812.

Bettelheim, B. J. *Letter from B. J. Bettelheim, M.D., Missionary in Lew Chew, Addressed to Rev. Peter Parker, M.D.* Canton, 1852, pamphlet.

Black's Guide to London and Its Environs, ed. Adam and Charles Black. Edinburgh, 1863.

Blake, E. M. "Yale's First Ophthalmologist — the Reverend Peter Parker, M.D.," *Yale Journal of Biology and Medicine* 3:386–396 (1931).

Bowring, Sir John. *Autobiographical Recollections of Sir John Bowring*. London, 1877.

Boxer, C. R. *Fidalgos in the Far East 1550–1770: Fact and Fancy in the History of Macao*. The Hague, Martinus Nijhoff, 1948.

Boyd's Directory of the District of Columbia 1858, 1860, 1862 . . . Washington, D.C., 1858, 1860, 1862 . . .

(Bridgman, Elijah Coleman) *The Life and Labors of Elijah Coleman Bridgman*, ed. Eliza J. Gillett Bridgman. New York, 1864.

British & Foreign Medical Review; or, Quarterly Journal of Practical Medicine and Surgery. 24 vols. London, 1836–1847.

Brooke, A. E. *A Critical and Exegetical Commentary on the Johannine Epistles*. New York, C. Scribner's Sons, 1912.

Brooks, Charles W. *Japanese Wrecks Stranded & Picked Up Adrift in the North Pacific Ocean*. San Francisco, The Academy, 1874; pamphlet reprint of the original, Fairfield, Washington, Ye Galleon Press, 1964.

Broomhall, Marshall. *Robert Morrison: A Master Builder*. London, Church Missionary Society, 1924.

Bryan, Leon S., Jr., "Bloodletting in American Medicine, 1830–1892," *Bulletin of the History of Medicine* 38:516–529 (1964).

Bryan, Wilhelmus B. *A History of the National Capital*. 2 vols. New York, The Macmillan Company, 1914–1916.

Cadbury, William W., and Mary Hoxie Jones. *At the Point of a Lancet: One Hundred Years of the Canton Hospital, 1835–1935*. Shanghai, Kelly and Walsh, 1935.

Cambridge History of India, The. 6 vols. Cambridge, The University Press, 1922–1964.

Castiglioni, Arturo. *A History of Medicine*, tr. E. B. Krumbhaar. New York, Alfred A. Knopf, 1941.

Catholic Encyclopedia, ed. Charles G. Herbermann et al. 15 vols. New York, Robert Appleton Company, 1907–1912.

Century of Protestant Missions in China (1807–1907), A: Being the Centenary Conference Historical Volume, ed. Donald MacGillivray. Shanghai, printed at the American Presbyterian Mission Press, 1907.

Chamfrault, A., and Ung Kang-Sam. *Traité de médecine chinoise; d'après les textes chinois anciens et modernes.* 5 vols. Angoulême, Coquemard, 1957–1964.

Chang Hsin-pao. *Commissioner Lin and the Opium War.* Cambridge, Mass., Harvard East Asian Series, 1964.

Chater Collection, The: Pictures Relating to China, Hong Kong, Macao, 1655–1860; with Historical and Descriptive Letterpress, ed. James Orange. London, T. Butterworth, 1924.

China Mail. Hong Kong, weekly, 1845–1859.

China Medical Missionary Journal. Vols. I and II. Shanghai, 1887 and 1888.

Chinese Repository, ed. E. C. Bridgman and S. Wells Williams. Macao or Canton, monthly, 1832–1851.

Chinese World Order, The, ed. John K. Fairbank. Cambridge, Mass., Harvard East Asian Series, 1968.

(Chinnery, George). "George Chinnery: 1774–1852," catalogue of an exhibition at City Hall Art Gallery, Hong Kong, March–April, 1965.

Chu, Clayton H. *American Missionaries in China: Books, Articles, and Pamphlets Extracted from the Subject Catalogues of the Missionary Research Library.* Cambridge, Mass., Harvard University Press, 1960.

Clendening, Logan. *Source Book of Medical History.* New York, Dover Publications, 1960.

Cochran, Joseph Wilson. *Friendly Adventurers: A Chronicle of the American Church of Paris (1857–1931)* . . . Paris, Brentano, 1931.

Colledge, Thomas R. "Suggestions with Regard to Employing Medical Practitioners as Missionaries to China," *Chinese Repository* 4:386–389 (1835).

―――― *The Medical Missionary Society in China.* Philadelphia, 1838, pamphlet.

Collis, Maurice. *Foreign Mud.* London, Faber and Faber, 1947.

Coltman, Robert, Jr. *The Chinese: Their Present and Future, Medical, Political, and Social.* Philadelphia, F. A. Davis Company, 1902.

Comrie, J. D. *History of Scottish Medicine,* 2nd ed. London, Baillière, Tindall and Cox, 1932.

Crawford, D. G. *A History of the Indian Medical Service, 1600–1913.* 2 vols. London, W. Thacker and Co., 1914.

―――― *Roll of the Indian Medical Service, 1615–1930.* London, W. Thacker and Co., 1930.

Creegan, Charles C. *Pioneer Missionaries of the Church.* New York, American Tract Society, 1903.

Croizier, Ralph C. *Traditional Medicine in Modern China: Science, Nationalism, and the Tensions of Cultural Change.* Cambridge, Mass., Harvard East Asian Series, 1968.

Cronin, Vincent. *The Wise Man from the West.* New York, Dutton, 1955.

Currier, John J. *"Ould Newbury": Historical and Biographical Sketches.* Boston, 1896.

Cushing, Caleb. Papers. Manuscript Division, Library of Congress, Washington, D.C., Boxes 42–47, 164.

(Cushing, Caleb). Cushing Correspondence. 28th Congress, 2nd Session, Senate Exec. Docs., No. 58 and No. 67 (1844–45), 2 vols., Ser. 450.

Cutter, William Richard. *New England Families, Genealogical and Memorial.* 4 vols. New York, Lewis Historical Publishing Company, 1914.

Cutting, George R. *Student Life at Amherst College.* Amherst, Mass., 1871.

Danton, George H. *The Culture Contacts of the United States and China: The Earliest Sino-American Culture Contacts, 1784–1844.* New York, Columbia University Press, 1931.

(David, Père). *Abbé David's Diary,* tr. and ed. Helen M. Fox. Cambridge, Mass., Harvard University Press, 1949.

Delano, Edward. Diaries for 1841, 1842, 1843–44, 1844–45, 1846. Franklin Delano Roosevelt Library, Hyde Park, N.Y.

Dennett, Tyler. *Americans in Eastern Asia.* New York, The Macmillan Company, 1922.

Dictionary of American Biography, ed. Allen Johnson. 22 vols. New York, C. Scribner's Sons, 1928–1958.

Dictionary of National Biography, ed. Leslie Stephen and Sidney Lee. 22 vols. London, Smith, Elder and Co., 1908–09.

Dorland's Illustrated Medical Dictionary. 23rd ed. Philadelphia, W. B. Saunders, 1957.

Dorsey, John Syng. *Elements of Surgery.* 2 vols. Philadelphia, 1818.

Downing, C. Toogood. *The Stranger in China: Or, the Fan-Qui's Visit to the Celestial Empire, in 1836–7.* 2 vols. in 1. Philadelphia, 1838.

Dulles, Foster Rhea. *The Old China Trade.* Boston, Houghton Mifflin, 1930.

Dunne, George Harold. *Generation of Giants: The Story of the Jesuits in the Last Decade of the Ming Dynasty.* Notre Dame, Ind., University of Notre Dame Press, 1962.

Dwight, Timothy. *Memories of Yale Life and Men, 1854–1899.* New York, Dodd, Mead and Company, 1903.

Eames, James Bromley. *The English in China.* London, Sir I. Pitman and Sons, 1909.

Eddy, George Sherwood. *Pathfinders of the World Missionary Crusade.* New York, Abingdon-Cokesbury Press, 1945.

Elsbree, O. W. *The Rise of the Missionary Spirit in America, 1790–1815.* Williamsport, Pa., The Williamsport Printing and Binding Co., 1928.

Embassy to China, An; Being the Journal Kept by Lord Macartney during his Embassy to the Emperor Ch'ien-lung, 1793–94, ed. J. L. Cranmer-Byng. London, Longmans, 1962.

Encyclopedia of Missions. 2 vols. New York, Funk and Wagnalls, 1891.

Encyclopedia Sinica, ed. Samuel Couling. Shanghai, Kelly and Walsh, 1917.

Erikson, Erik H. *Young Man Luther: A Study in Psychoanalysis and History.* New York, Norton, 1958.

Everett, Edward. Letterbook. Massachusetts Historical Society.

Fairbank, John K. "The Creation of the Foreign Inspectorate of Customs at Shanghai," *Chinese Social and Political Science Review* (Peking) 20:42–100 (1936).

———— *Trade and Diplomacy on the China Coast: The Opening of the Treaty Ports, 1842–1854.* 2 vols. Cambridge, Mass., Harvard University Press, 1953.

Faling, Mable Fern. *Genealogy of the Webster Family to Which Daniel Webster Belonged.* Boston, New England Historic Genealogical Society, 1927. Typescript.

Farley, David L. "Nathaniel Chapman and His Lectures on the Practice of Physic, Philadelphia, 1818," *Annals of Medical History* 10:480–485 (1928).

Forbes, J. M. Letters of J. M. Forbes, 1843–1867. Manuscript Division, Baker Library, Harvard University.

Forbes, Robert Bennet. Ms. "Journal of Return from China on the *Niantic*: sailed from Macao July 5, arrived New York Dec. 10, 1840." Collection of R. Forbes Perkins, Manchester, Mass.

———— *Personal Reminiscences.* 3rd ed., rev. Boston, 1892.

Franklin, James H. *Ministers of Mercy.* New York, Missionary Education Movement of the United States and Canada, 1919.

Fuess, Claude M. *The Life of Caleb Cushing.* 2 vols. New York, Harcourt, Brace and Company, 1923.

Garrison, Fielding H. "The History of Bloodletting," *New York Medical Journal* 97:498–501 (March 1913).

Garwood, G. "The Leech: Past, Present and Future," *University of Western Ontario Medical Journal* 22:168–170 (1952).

Gaustad, Edwin Scott. *A Religious History of America.* New York, Harper and Row, 1966.

Goodman, Louis S., and Alfred Gilman. *The Pharmacological Basis of Therapeutics: A Textbook of Pharmacology, Toxicology, and Therapeutics for Physicians and Medical Students.* 3rd ed. New York, Macmillan, 1965.

Goodsell, Fred F. *You Shall Be My Witnesses.* Boston, American Board of Commissioners for Foreign Missions, 1959.

Grant, Asahel. *Life in Koordistan.* 2 vols. 1841.

———— *The Nestorians; or the Lost Tribes.* New York, 1841.

Greenberg, Michael. *British Trade and the Opening of China, 1800–42.* Cambridge, The University Press, 1951.

Griffin, Eldon. *Clippers and Consuls: American Consular and Commercial Relations with Eastern Asia, 1845–1860.* Ann Arbor, Mich., Edwards Bros., 1938.

Gross, S. D. *Lives of Eminent American Physicians and Surgeons of the Nineteenth Century.* Philadelphia, 1861.

Guide to Archives and Manuscripts in the United States, ed. Philip M. Hamer. New Haven, Yale University Press, 1961.

Guthrie, Douglas. *A History of Medicine.* Philadelphia, Lippincott, 1946.

Gutzlaff, Karl F. A. *Journal of Three Voyages along the Coast of China in 1831, 1832, and 1833, with Notices of Siam, Korea, and the Loo-Choo Islands.* 2nd ed. London, 1834.

Haagensen, C. D., and W. E. B. Lloyd. *A Hundred Years of Medicine.* New York, Sheridan House, 1943.

Haggard, Howard W. *Devils, Drugs, and Doctors.* New York, Harper and Brothers, 1929.

Hall, Gordon, and Samuel Newell. *The Conversion of the World or the Claims of Six Hundred Million and the Ability and Duty of the Churches Respecting Them.* Andover, Mass., 1818, pamphlet.

Hall, Marshall. *Researches Principally Relative to the Morbid and Curative Effects of Loss of Blood.* London, 1830.

Harvey, Samuel C. "Peter Parker: Initiator of Modern Medicine in China," *Yale Journal of Biology and Medicine* 8:225–241 (1936).

Hasse, Adelaide R. *Index to United States Documents Relating to Foreign Affairs, 1828–1861.* 3 vols. Washington, D.C., Carnegie Institution of Washington, 1914–1921.

Higgins, Charles C., and Ralph A. Straffon. "Urolithiasis," in *Urology,* ed. Meredith F. Campbell. Vol. I of 3 vols. Philadelphia, 1963.

Ho Ping-ti. *Studies on the Population of China, 1368–1953.* Cambridge, Harvard East Asian Series, 1959.

Hobson, Benjamin. *Reports of Chinese Hospital at Shanghai, 1847–48 to 1857.* Pamphlets, Shanghai, 1849–1858; bound in Medical Missionary Society Reports, vol. IV, pamphet-volume no. 37, LMS.

Hsü, Immanuel C. Y. *China's Entrance into the Family of Nations: The Diplomatic Phase, 1858–1880.* Cambridge, Mass., Harvard East Asian Series, 1960.

Huard, P. A., and M. Wong. *La Médecine chinoise au cours des siècles.* Paris, Editions R. Dacosta, 1959.

Huc, Evariste R. *Christianity in China, Tartary and Thibet.* 3 vols. London, 1857–1858.

Hume, Edward H. *The Chinese Way in Medicine.* Baltimore, The Johns Hopkins Press, 1940.

—— *Doctor's East, Doctors West: An American Physician's Life in China.* New York, W. W. Norton and Company, 1946.

———— "Peter Parker and the Introduction of Anesthesia into China," *Journal of the History of Medicine and Allied Sciences*, Anesthesia Centennial number, New York. 1:670–674 (1946).

Hummel, Arthur W. *Eminent Chinese of the Ch'ing Period, 1644–1912.* 2 vols. Washington, D.C, Government Printing Office, 1943–1944.

Hunter, William C. *The "Fan Kwae" at Canton before Treaty Days, 1825–1844.* London, Kegan Paul, 1882.

In Memoriam, Rev. Arthur Tidman, D.D. London, n.d.

India Office. China and Japan Factory Records, Abstracts of Factory Consultations; Court Minutes; Miscellaneous Bonds; Miscellaneous Letters Received; and Miscellanies, 1831.

Irick, Robert L. "The Chinese Emigrant in Sino-American Diplomacy," draft of dissertation, Harvard University.

IWSM-TK,-HF: *Ch'ing-tai ch'ou-pan i-wu shih-mo:* 清代籌辦夷務始末 (The complete account of our management of barbarian affairs). Photolithograph of the original ed. Peiping, 1930. Later Tao-kuang period, 1836–1850, 80 chüan; Hsien-feng period, 1851–1861, 80 chüan.

Jardine, William. Private Letter Books. Correspondence Section, Jardine Matheson Archive, Cambridge University Library.

(Kearny, Lawrence) Kearny Correspondence. 29th Congress, 1st Session, Senate Docs., No. 139 (1845–1846), ser. 473.

Keys, Thomas E. *The History of Surgical Anesthesia.* New York, Dover Publications, 1963.

King, Charles W., and G. Tradescant Lay. *The Claims of Japan and Malaysia upon Christendom Exhibited in Notes of Voyages Made in 1837, from Canton, in the Ship Morrison and Brig Himmaleh.* 2 vols. New York, 1839; I: C. W. King, *Notes of the Voyage of the Morrison from Canton to Japan*; II: G. T. Lay, *Notes Made during the Voyage of the Himmaleh in the Malayan Archipelago.*

Kuo Ping Chia. "Caleb Cushing and the Treaty of Wanghsia, 1844," *Journal of Modern History* 5:34–54 (1933).

Lamb's Biographical Dictionary of the United States, ed. J. H. Brown. 7 vols. Boston, James H. Lamb Company, 1900–1903.

Langley, Harold D. "Gideon Nye and the Formosa Annexation Scheme," *Pacific Historical Review* 34:397–420 (1965).

Latourette, Kenneth Scott. *A History of Christian Missions in China.* New York, The Macmillan Company, 1929.

———— "Peter Parker: Missionary and Diplomat," *Yale Journal of Biology and Medicine* 8:243–248 (1936).

Laws of the Medical Institution. New Haven, 1813.

Lectures on Medical Missions, Delivered at the Instance of the Edinburgh Medical Missionary Society. Edinburgh, 1849.

Le Duc, Thomas. *Piety and Intellect at Amherst College, 1865–1912.* New York, Columbia University Press, 1946.

Lennox, William. "Medical Missions," in Orville Pelty, ed., *Layman's Foreign Missions Inquiry, Fact-finders Reports: China,* V, Supp. Ser., Pt. II (New York, 1933).

Lin Ch'ung-yung 林崇墉. *Lin Tse-hsü chüan* 林則徐傳. (Biography of Lin Tse-hsü). Taipei, Chung-hua ta-tien pien yin hui, 1967.

Lin Tse-hsü 林則徐. *Lin Tse-hsü jih-chi* 林則徐日記 (The Diary of Lin Tse-hsü, 1839–1841), in *Ya-p'ien chan-cheng* 鴉片戰爭 (The Opium War), ed. Ch'i Ssu-ho 齊思和, et al. 6 vols. Shanghai, 1954.

Liu Kwang-ching. *Americans and Chinese: A Historical Essay and a Bibliography.* Cambridge, Mass., Harvard University Press, 1963.

Ljungstedt, Anders. *A Brief Account of an Ophthalmic Institution during the Years 1827, 1828, 1829, 1830, 1831, and 1832 at Macao by a Philanthropist.* Canton, 1834, pamphlet.

Lockhart, William. *The Medical Missionary in China: A Narrative of Twenty Years' Experience.* London, 1861.

London Missionary Society. Archives, South China.

Lovett, Richard. *A History of the London Missionary Society, 1795–1895.* 2 vols. London, 1899.

(Low, Harriet). *My Mother's Journal: A Young Lady's Diary of Five Years Spent in Manila, Macao, and the Cape of Good Hope from 1829–1834,* ed. Katherine Hillard. Boston, G. H. Ellis, 1900.

Lubbock, Basil. *The Opium Clippers.* Boston, Lauriat Co., 1933.

Lutz, Jessie G. *Christian Missions in China: Evangelists of What?* Boston, D. C. Heath, 1965.

Mabbs, Goodeve. *Catalogue of Books contained in the Lockhart Library and in the General Library of the London Missionary Society.* London, 1899.

(McLane, Robert M.) McLane Correspondence. 35th Congress, 2nd Session, Senate Exec. Docs., No. 22 (1859), 2 vols., Ser. 982–983, pp. 1–495.

(Marshall, Humphrey). Marshall Correspondence. 33rd Congress, 1st Session, House Exec. Docs., No. 123 (1854), Ser. 734.

Maurer, Oscar Edward. *A Puritan Church and Its Relation to Community, State, and Nation.* New Haven, Yale University Press, 1938.

Medhurst, W. H. *China: Its State and Prospects, with Especial Reference to the Spread of the Gospel* . . . London, 1840.

———— *The Foreigner in Far Cathay.* New York, 1873.

Medical Missionary Society in China. Reports (1838–1880). The MMS Reports, found at irregular intervals in the *Chinese Repository* from 1838 through the 1840's and as individual pamphlets both then and later, contain minutes of meetings and accounts of the activities of the society's members. Dr. Parker's hospital reports are sometimes included, as are those of other MMS physicians.

Medical Society of the State of Pennsylvania. *Transactions of the Medical Society of the State of Pennsylvania.* Vol. 5. Philadelphia, 1860.

Miller, David Hunter. *Treaties and Other International Acts of the United States of America.* 8 vols. Washington, D.C., Government Printing Office, 1931–1948. Vol. VII used.

Milne, William C. *Life in China.* London, 1858.

Morison, Samuel Eliot. *Maritime History of Massachusetts, 1783–1860.* Boston, Houghton Mifflin, 1921.

—— *Builders of the Bay Colony.* Boston, Houghton Mifflin, 1930.

Morrison, J. R. *A Chinese Commercial Guide.* Macao, S. Wells Williams, 1844.

Morse, Hosea Ballou. *The International Relations of the Chinese Empire.* 3 vols. I: *The Period of Conflict, 1834–1860.* London, Longmans, Green, and Company, 1910.

—— *The Chronicles of the East India Company, Trading to China, 1635–1834.* 4 vols. Oxford, The Clarendon Press, 1926.

Morse, William R. *Chinese Medicine.* New York, P. B. Hoeber, 1934.

Myers, John B. *William Carey, the Shoemaker Who Became "the Father and Founder of Modern Missions."* New York, 6th ed., pref., 1887.

National Cyclopaedia of American Biography. 51 vols. New York, James T. White and Company, 1892–1969.

The Nation's Capitol, Washington City, D.C.: Bird's Eye View. Baltimore, A. Sachse & Co., 1883 (?), map.

Needham, Joseph. "The Roles of Europe and China in the Evolution of Oecumenical Science," *Journal of Asian History* 1:3–32 (1967).

Nelson, M. Frederick. *Korea and the Old Orders in Eastern Asia.* Baton Rouge, Louisiana State University Press, 1945.

New York Evangelist, New York, weekly, 1830–1902.

New York Observer. New York, weekly, 1823–1912.

North China Herald. Shanghai, weekly, 1850–1867.

(Olyphant, David). Selections from Letters of Mr. D. W. C. Olyphant, 1827–1851. Missionary Research Library, New York, typescript.

Osterweis, Rollin. *Three Centuries of New Haven, 1638–1938.* New Haven, Yale University Press, 1953.

Owen, David Edward. *English Philanthropy, 1660–1960.* Cambridge, Mass., Harvard University Press, 1964.

Pálos, Stephan. *Chinesische Heilkunst; Rückbesinnung auf eine grosse Tradition,* trans. from the Hungarian by W. Kronfuss. Munich, Delp, 1966.

Parker, Theodore. *Genealogy and Biographical Notes of John Parker of Lexington and His Descendants . . .* Worcester, 1893.

Pearson, Alexander. "Vaccination," *Chinese Repository* 2:36–39 (1833).

Peking, Academy of Traditional Chinese Medicine. Research Institute of Acupuncture and Moxibustion. *Chinese Therapeutical Methods of Acupuncture and Moxibustion.* 3rd ed. Peking, Foreign Languages Press, 1964.

Pfister, Aloys. *Notices biographiques et bibliographiques sur les Jésuites de l'ancienne mission de Chine, 1552–1773.* 2 vols. Shanghai, Imprimerie de la Mission Catholique, 1932–1934.

Phillips, Clifton Jackson. *Protestant America and the Pagan World: The First Half Century of the American Board of Commissioners for Foreign Missions, 1810–1860.* Cambridge, Mass., Harvard East Asian Series, 1969.

Plymouth Church, Framingham. *Revised Manual . . . Present Church By-Laws: Historical notes . . . Compiled by Deacon John H. Temple.* Framingham, 1930.

(Reed, Andrew). *Memoirs of the Life and Philanthropic Labours of Andrew Reed, D.D., with Selections from His Journals,* edited by his sons, Andrew Reed, B.A., and Charles Reed, F.S.A., 1863. 3rd ed., 1867.

(Reed, William B.) Reed Correspondence. 36th Congress, 1st Session, Senate Exec. Docs., No. 30 (1859–60), Ser. 1032, pp. 1–569 (Reed).

Re-thinking Missions: A Layman's Inquiry after 100 Years, ed. William Ernest Hocking. New York, Harper and Brothers, 1932.

Ripa, Matteo. *Memoirs of Father Ripa, during Thirteen Years' Residence at the Court of Peking in the Service of the Emperor of China . . . ,* trans. F. Prandi. London, 1855.

Rowbotham, Arnold H. *Missionary and Mandarin: The Jesuits at the Court of China.* Berkeley, University of California Press, 1942; re-issued, New York, 1966.

San Kuo, or Romance of the Three Kingdoms, trans. C. H. Brewitt-Taylor, 2 vols. Shanghai, Kelly and Walsh, 1929.

Savage, James. *A Genealogical Dictionary of the First Settlers of New England.* 4 vols. Boston, 1861.

Scholz, Roy O., *SIGHT: A Handbook for Laymen.* Garden City, New York, Doubleday, 1960.

Seventy-Five years of Medical Progress, 1878–1953, ed. Louis H. Bauer. Philadelphia, Lea and Febiger, 1954.

Shelley, Harry S. "Cutting for the Stone," *Journal of the History of Medicine and Allied Sciences* 13:50–67 (1958).

Simpson, J. Y. *Account of a New Anaesthetic Agent as a Substitute for Sulphuric Ether.* Edinburgh, 1847.

Smith, Rev. A. H. "The Life and Work of Peter Parker," *Chinese Recorder* 44:499–503 (1913).

Smith, George. *The Life of William Carey, D.D.* London, 1887.

Smith, Sidney. Review of a book by John Styles, *Edinburgh Review* 14:40 (1809).

Smithsonian Contributions to Knowledge. Vol. XVI. Washington, D.C., 1870.

Snow, Edgar. *The Other Side of the River.* New York, Random House, 1962.

Snyder, Charles. "7 Green Pea Street, the Canton Ophthalmic Hospital and Its Founder," *Archives of Ophthalmology* 75:887–891 (1966).

So Kwan-wai and Eugene P. Boardman. "Hung Jen-kan, Taiping Prime Minister, 1859–1864," *Harvard Journal of Asiatic Studies* 20:262–294 (1957).

Soothill, William E. *Timothy Richard of China: Seer, Statesman, Missionary and the Most Disinterested Advisor the Chinese Ever Had.* London, Seeley, 1924.

Spence, Jonathan. *To Change China: Western Advisors in China, 1620–1960.* Boston, Little Brown, 1969.

Stevens, George B., and W. Fisher Markwick. *The Life, Letters, and Journals of the Rev. & Hon. Peter Parker, M.D., Missionary, Physician, and Diplomatist, the Father of Medical Missions and Founder of the Ophthalmic Hospital in Canton.* Boston, 1896.

Stokes, Anson Phelps. *Memorials of Eminent Yale Men.* 2 vols. New Haven, Yale University Press, 1914.

Swisher, Earl. *China's Management of the American Barbarians: A Study of Sino-American Relations, 1841–61, with Documents.* New Haven, Far Eastern Publications, Yale University, 1953.

Taylor, Fitch W. *A Voyage around the World in the United States Frigate Columbia, . . .* 2 vols. New Haven and New York, 1847.

Taylor, H. F. *A Century of Service (1841–1941): A Sketch of the Contribution Made by the Edinburgh Medical Missionary Society to the Extension of the Kingdom of God at Home and Abroad.* Edinburgh, 1941, pamphlet.

Taylor, Louise M. *Catalogue of Books on China in the Essex Institute.* Salem, Mass., The Essex Institute, 1926.

Temple, J. H. *History of Framingham, Early Known as Danforth's Farms, 1640–1880, with a Genealogical Register.* Framingham, Mass., 1887.

Thompson, Augustus Charles. *Protestant Missions, Their Rise and Early Progress.* New York, 1894.

Thomson, E. H. "Physician-Missionary-Diplomat," Yale University School of Medicine, *Alumni Bulletin* 1:6 (1954).

Thomson, Joseph C. "Medical Missionaries to the Chinese," *China Medical Missionary Journal* 1:45–59 (1887).

———— "Historical Landmarks of Macao," *Chinese Recorder and Missionary Journal* 18:392–393 (1887).

———— "Semi-Centennial of the Medical Missionary Society," *China Medical Missionary Journal* 2:101–113 (1888).

———— "Rev. Peter Parker, M.D. First Medical Missionary to China and Dr. Kwan A-to First Chinese Surgeon," *China Medical Missionary Journal* 2:169–172 (1888).

Tong Te-kong. *United States Diplomacy in China, 1844–60.* Seattle, University of Washington Press, 1964.

Transactions of the China Medico-Chirurgical Society for the Year 1845–46. Hong Kong, 1846.

Trumbull, Henry C. *Old Time Student Volunteers: My Memories of Missionaries.* New York, Fleming H. Revell Company, 1902.

Tyler, Alice Felt. *Freedom's Ferment: Phases of American Social History to 1860.* Minneapolis, University of Minnesota Press, 1944.

Tyler, W. S. *History of Amherst College during Its First Half Century, 1821–1871.* Springfield, Mass., 1873.

United States. National Archives, Consular Despatches: Canton, vol. IV; Amoy, vol. II; and Hong Kong, vols. III and IV.

—— National Archives, Records of the Department of State, Diplomatic Instructions: China, vol. I.

—— 28th Congress, 2nd Session, Senate Documents, No. 138 (1845), Ser. 457.

United States Congressional Documents. (See under Cushing, Kearny, McLane, Marshall, Parker, Reed.)

Vattel, Emerich de. *Le Droit des gens; ou, principes de la loi naturelle appliqués à la conduite et aux affaires des nations et des souverains.* 3 vols. Washington, D.C., Carnegie Institution of Washington, 1916.

Wakeman, Frederic E., Jr. *Strangers at the Gate: Social Disorder in South China, 1839–61.* Berkeley, University of California Press, 1966.

Waley, Arthur. *The Opium War through Chinese Eyes.* London, Macmillan, 1958.

Washington, City and Capitol. Washington, D.C., American Guide Series, 1937.

(Webster, Daniel). *The Writings and Speeches of Daniel Webster,* ed. J. W. McIntyre. 18 vols. Boston, 1903.

Wei, Tsing-sing Louis. *La Politique Missionnaire de la France en Chine, 1842–1856.* Paris, Nouvelles Editions latines, 1960.

Wei Yüan 魏源. *Hai-kuo t'u-chih* 海國圖志 (An illustrated gazetteer of the maritime countries), 100 chüan. 1852.

Werner, Georges H., Bachisio Latte, and Andrea Contini. "Trachoma," *Scientific American* 210:79–84 (1964).

Whitmore, Clara Belle. "An History of the Development of Western Medicine in China." Unpub. diss., University of California at Los Angeles, 1934.

Williams, Frederick Wells. *The Life & Letters of Samuel Wells Williams, LLD, Missionary, Diplomatist, Sinologue.* New York, 1889.

Williams, S. Wells. Letters to Dr. Peter Parker. Historical Manuscripts Department, Yale University Library.

—— "Narrative of a Voyage of the Ship Morrison, Captain D. Ingersoll, to Lewchew and Japan, in the Months of July and August, 1837," *Chinese Repository* 6:209–229, 353–380 (1837).

—— *The Middle Kingdom.* 2 vols. New York, 1848.

Wong, K. C. (Wang Chi-min). *Lancet & Cross.* Shanghai, 1950.

Wong, K. C. (Wang Chi-min), and Wu Lien-teh. *History of Chinese Medicine; Being a Chronicle of Medical Happenings in China from Ancient Times to the Present Period,* 2nd ed. Shanghai, National Quarantine Service, 1936.

Bibliography for Maps

Hunter, William C. "Journal of Occurrances at Canton, during the Cessation of Trade at Canton 1839," in E. W. Ellsworth, ed., with added notes by Sir Lindsay T. Ride and J. L. Cranmer-Byng, *Journal of the Hong Kong Branch of the Royal Asiatic Society,* 4:9-41 (1964 [printed April 1965]). (Map of the Foreign Factories on the Canton Waterfront, 1840.)

Narrative of the Voyages and Services of the Nemesis from 1840 to 1843, and of the Combined Naval and Military Operations in China: Comprising a Complete Account of the Colony of Hong Kong, and Remarks on the Character and Habits of the Chinese. From Notes of Commander W. H. Hall, R.N., with Personal Observations, by W. D. Bernard, Esq. A.M. Oxon. 2nd ed. London, H. Colburn, 1844. (Map of the Approach to Canton from the Sea.)

◆ Index

◆ Harvard Studies in American– East Asian Relations